Promise to the Land

PROMISE
TO THE
LAND

ESSAYS ◆ ON ◆
RURAL ◆ WOMEN

Joan M. Jensen

UNIVERSITY OF NEW MEXICO PRESS
Albuquerque

Library of Congress Cataloging-in-Publication Data

Jensen, Joan M.
    Promise to the land : essays on rural women / Joan M. Jensen.
        p.   cm.
    Includes bibliographical references and index.
    ISBN 0–8263–1247–0
    1. Rural women—United States.   I. Title.
HQ1410.J46   1991
305.42′0973—dc20   90–49165
                                                    CIP

Design by Susan Gutnik.

*For all my rural grandmother Matilda was
and could never be*

Contents

Preface

PROMISE TO THE LAND IS THE HARVEST OF MORE
than a decade of writing on rural women. Half of the essays have
been previously published, but half are unpublished and move in
new directions, to biography and autobiography, to iconography,
and a linking of professional work to the more personal, emotional
context that gave rise to them.

In 1977 when the first article here was published, rural American
women were seldom written about by the new historians of women.
Urban women held center stage and were the focus of the most
exciting new research generated by the feminist movement of the
1970s. Rural women, the historical majority, had almost completely
disappeared from professional and academic history though they
lived on robustly in oral tradition and local history. Neither a part of
the new women's history nor of older agricultural history, rural
women were part of living memory but not of that literary historical
tradition that winnows the past for the present.

Today, while much remains to be written about rural women,
they have achieved a new place in history. Older scholars now recognize
their importance and younger writers, both within and outside
the academy, write about their lives. There is little doubt now that
their lives will continue to receive increasing attention, in books, at

conferences, and in the historical consciousness by which a people remember its past. Rural women now have a past.

Because so many writers and scholars now look to my writings as forming a foundation for the study of rural women, the time seems right to reprint them together here. In addition, I have added as many new essays, some delivered as talks or at conferences, and others the result of more recent research. Two essays are family history and one is a memoir of my own experiences on a farm commune in the 1970s. Together they form what I have had to say about farm women over the last fifteen years, since I became a farm woman, briefly, in 1970.

It is more than fifteen years since I left the farm. And it is still referred to as "the farm" by those of us who shared that tempestuous time. We were, I think, fairly typical of those new farmers who hastily bought and settled. We had a fever to get on the land in those days. There seemed nothing else more important to do. The Vietnam war was not over but the passion of our opposition was subsiding as the painfully slow deescalation began. The war had disrupted our lives, making our old lives seem somehow not too satisfactory. The war also left many of us with a political critique that, typically Californian, involved a critique of life styles as well. We knew vaguely that Easterners or Europeans would never react quite this way. Politics was one thing; how you lived quite another. When we said the personal was political it also meant the political was personal and as the children of migrants who had headed west, we began to mill about, eager to resume the transient lives that many of us had known as children. Back to the land was a lure that will probably never know that freshness again. We did not care that it was utterly improbable, impossible of any longterm success.

I left my tenured teaching position without a qualm, shared the few possessions I had accumulated in the less than ten years since I had finished graduate school, and headed out to the land. Two years later I was back in San Diego, not utterly defeated by the failure of our experiment but surprisingly energized. I remember the departure that early January in 1972, heading over the Cumbres pass from Colorado into New Mexico and then on to Arizona just ahead of a blizzard and ready for anything. We had fifty dollars, a few clothes, an old spinning wheel that I had promised to an urban friend, and the tools that would allow us to keep our Volkswagen van running. The tools were stolen the first week back in the city. I had wanted to stay in Colorado. I loved the farm, even its terrifying conflicts as I attempted to achieve physical and psychic strength. I felt stronger when I left than I had ever felt in my life, but I had no idea how I would use that energy. A month later, on one of those damp days that Southern Californians suffer because they think they should not need heat, I sat in the kitchen trying to get warm by the stove and trying to envision my future. In my journal I scrawled that I wanted to write about farm women.

These essays are the fruit of that scrawled commitment. The voyage out and back was over. I had returned a feminist, an ex-farmer, and somehow, despite the years when I had written very little, I still had a compulsion to write. History was my urban skill and because I had to do something in my born-again urban life, I returned there, not to the old place where I had been but to a new place where feminism and the farm had taken me, to a decision to write about women on the land.

Over the past fifteen years, between projects and teaching, I have written these essays and tried to define a field that did not exist. Rural women are now an essential part of women's history, not because of my work but because a number of people, for totally different reasons, were coming to a similar conclusion: that the lives of rural women were central to American history as they were, and are, central to the histories of other countries.

The first summer after I left the farm—I was to be out of the academic world for four years it turned out—I drove north to Santa Rosa, California. There I planned to do farm labor for a month, trying to make up my mind, finally, what I would do for a living. I wanted to do migrant farm work—a dream that also helped carry me through that first year off the farm. My partner and I would follow the crops, living out of our van—it was the only way we could think of to keep working on the land. We worked in every spare moment rebuilding the engine of our VW van and outfitting the inside to be a camper that we thought we could live in on the road. The van was now done and I was to take it north on a trial run while my partner worked in the south to save money for our departure. I worked picking apples and prunes, when work was unavailable in an apple-sauce cannery, and when the cannery closed down for a day as it periodically did, I sat in my van and wrote in my journal. One day, I sat there watching women hoe and wrote self-consciously about sitting there writing about farm women working. There was a communion that day. Though I wrote while they toiled, I felt that I was close to them and would be able to translate that hard work into a place in history. Soon after, I ended my cannery work, and soon after that the dream of migrant farm work died too. The oil embargo drove gas prices up and we no longer believed we could support ourselves, even at a subsistence level, doing migratory labor. I began to think of returning to academic work, the only kind of work I knew that would support me and give me time to write about farm women. The next September I returned to teaching.

These essays do not quite form the pattern that I would want of them. They tend to reflect my background and its lower middle-class preoccupation with how farm women survive, why they do the kind of work they do, how the people who came to assist viewed them and how farm women used this assistance, how work changes and persists. I have ranged from iconography to demography, material objects to oral history. There is a coauthored article here because I have always felt good about sharing labor. The articles follow, as well, a range of styles, from staunchly academic to memoirs about living on that farm commune in the 1970s, and to family history of my grandmother Matilda, and of Rozalija, a Lithuanian farm woman. Rozalija came to the United States as a refugee after World War II, from a farm that seemed to me to be eighteenth century in its operation, and her memories helped me understand how farm people worked and felt about their work when it was still subsistence and simple commodity production. She showed me the energy and strength, the flexibility that had allowed farm women to survive in earlier times. And she treated me as one of her small refugee family though I refused to marry her son while continuing to live with him.

Those images of farms, and farm women, of my life and theirs, are amazingly vivid to me yet. They nourished the emotional side of my life as my professional life as a historian has never done. It is here that the personal and political met for me and transformed my life.

Introduction: Rural Women in American History

THE STUDY OF WOMEN IN AGRICULTURAL DEVELOP-
ment begins with the inescapable reality that women have seldom had
control over the land they have labored on. Land owning, one means
of control over farm work, was not generally available to women for
much of American history. During the period before 1850, American
common law deprived married women in the United States of direct
ownership of land. Most rural women married and, once married,
they lost their civil rights, including the right to own land in their own
name. There were exceptions allowed by law, but, in practice, few
women except widows held land directly. They worked on land
legally owned by their fathers, husbands, or sons and participated in a
patriarchal system where land was passed down from father to son.

In the twentieth century, long after legal disabilities were removed in most states, social custom continued to restrict ownership
and control by women. Even when women held land as joint tenants
with their husbands, federal tax laws discriminated against them.
In common law states, if the husband was the first to die, the entire value of the estate belonged to him and was subject to federal
estate tax but if the wife died first, the husband had to pay no federal
tax. The wife had to prove her contributions to the farm through

canceled checks or mortgage releases. After a petition campaign in which women's farm organizations and farm journals collected over 230,000 signatures and testified before congressional committees, the law was finally changed in 1982. After that year no tax had to be paid on the estate of the first spouse of either sex to die, and spouses could give each other property without paying federal gift taxes. During the 1980s the campaign to establish legal equality for farm women continued. Both wives and daughters were claiming legal rights denied to women for centuries and raising issues about their right to participate in decisions regarding incorporation and inter-generational transfer of farm land. This questioning is not new but the culmination of over a century of debate about the relationship of land ownership and family law.[1]

In a system where property was the main source of economic and political power, the American common law played a significant role in depriving women of their property rights. Under common law all women who married lost their right to hold property and their testamentary rights as well, unless special pre- or postnuptual contracts specifically retained family property in their name. In southern states, eighteenth-century married women could sometimes retain family property through the use of equity courts. During the nineteenth century women organized to regain their right to own property in their own name after marriage. Throughout American history, however, land was normally controlled by men unless there were no male heirs, in which case widows or daughters might inherit land and dispose of it. Most land, therefore, remained under the control of fathers and sons, giving a solid patriarchal base to agriculture in most regions for most of American history.[2]

The exceptions to this generalization are worth emphasizing. The first exception is an ethnic group. In most American Indian tribes women had access to land, were able to exercise management and control, and to share to some extent vested rights in community ownership of land. Native American women did not acquiesce to the catastrophic loss of their land. Women fought openly and in guerrilla warfare. They urged their men to violent resistance, eluded their captors time and time again to return to their homelands, and when other forms of active resistance were crushed, women turned to passive resistance. Indian women remained the most rural of all women for all of American history. When large numbers of Indian

Siwash Indians digging potatoes in Washington, 1907. Native American Women adapted traditional food production to new crops and methods. Source: J. A. Blosser, 1907, Library of Congress.

women migrated to urban areas in the 1960s, they translated their old relationship with the land into a literature expressing rich awareness of the natural environment and the human place in it. Their identification with the land and their reluctance to give up control has made them the great exception.[3]

The second great exception is regional and ethnic in origin. In the west, Spanish and French community property laws created a distinct pattern to women's land holding and use. These women never had complete individual management and control over land but they did share ownership with men to a greater extent than women in the East. Under community property concepts married women had a right to an equal share of the property; land therefore was commonly owned outright by widows and often inherited equally by daughters as well as sons. After eastern Americans asserted control over the eight western states that shared this common legal heritage, the extension of Anglo-American common law principles eroded women's tenuous land rights.[4]

Nevertheless, the history of women in these western states is different. In 1844, for example, at a time when eastern women were battling to obtain married women's and widows' property rights and when most land normally went to sons by law and by custom, French widows in Louisiana owned and managed large numbers of sugar plantations. Widows, alone, in partnership with sons (Mrs. Charles Perret and "fils" produced 535,000 pounds of sugar), and in partnership with other men produced almost ten percent of all the sugar on plantations in 1844. In the Southwest, Hispanic widows also inherited large ranches that they continued to operate in their own names. In California, Doña Vicenta Sepulveda, twice widowed and the mother of twelve, ran Rancho Sepulveda for over thirty years. One sea captain remembered negotiating to buy brandy from Doña Sepulveda. "There was no haggling over price," he later wrote, "she quietly named it." California was dotted with women who held large ranches in their own name, managed large cattle raising and processing enterprises, and sold their products. In the Southwest, divorce was also much more common in the late nineteenth century than in the East or South, and courts were generally very scrupulous in dividing estates equally. In New Mexico, for example, in one case where a wife admitted to adultery, a court held that she was entitled to one-half of a one hundred thousand dollar ranch rather than the four thousand dollars that the husband had attempted to force her to take in settlement.[5]

It is hard to tell just how many women elsewhere actually owned their land. In the West, however, where land was cheap and more readily available, women may have more frequently owned land and increasing amounts of land in the late nineteenth century. A comparative study of Bucks County, Pennsylvania, and Los Angeles County, California, in 1880 indicates that women in Los Angeles received more land than women in Bucks County. But even in Bucks County, increasing numbers of men left property to their wives outright in their wills demonstrating a dissatisfaction with Pennsylvania laws. In the East as well as in the West, widows were more likely to own land outright in the second half of the nineteenth century and

Winnowing in Chimayo, ca. 1920. Hispanic Women increased their role in agriculture as many men left villages for seasonal work. Source: Prudence Clark Collection, Menaul Historical Library, Albuquerque, New Mexico.

to farm the land themselves, usually with the help of kin. It may be that women simply had more influence in the West because it remained more rural than the East, that community property gave women a greater ownership right, and that a higher proportion of employed women owned land than in the East.[6]

This land ownership should not be overemphasized. Single women were seldom able to hold substantial acreage. Widows still found it necessary to have male kin—brothers, uncles, or sons—actually manage their large estates. The larger the estate, the less control women had in the East and Midwest. Yet as Sonya Solomon and Anna Mackey Keim have shown in their study of German women in the twentieth century, land ownership can make a difference. It is likely that the experience of owning land and bringing land or capital from the sale of land into a marriage gave women a sense of greater control over the land they farmed with husband and family. A small number of women also derived power from their role within this patriarchal system because their families held high status and wealth in a society divided by class. Women in poorer classes might have more access to their families' limited wealth.[7]

Yet another exception to patriarchal control came as the result of changes in homesteading laws. By the 1840s single women and widows were bringing suits to gain access to the public domain, and some courts were deciding they had a right to homestead. As Lee Chambers-Schiller points out in *Liberty Is a Better Husband,* women's overall land ownership had increased by 1840. That modest increase and the demands for married women's property laws in the states were followed by a federal Homestead Act in 1862, the first major legislation to open land in the federal domain to women with its explicit use of "he or she" in the legislation. Only widows and single women could homestead but after proving up women could sell out, join their lands to those of a male through marriage, or as a few did, choose to retain it. By 1880 increasing numbers of women had access to land ownership. This was, however, no guarantee that they either wished or were able to farm themselves. Large numbers of single women sold their land, using the capital to reinvest in joint ventures as married women. For homesteading women, the main problem was surviving in partnership with their husbands, under severe economic stress. In western New Mexico in the early twentieth century, most homesteaders, unable to survive, sold out to ranchers.[8]

Farm land was the primary capital held by most Americans before 1920, when the rural population became a declining minority. During this long period of history, Americans lived on and from the land. Women had access to capital but little control of it. Exceptional women had little else in common except their direct control of the land. For most women control came not through ownership or even through management of land but through the labor they invested in the land. If women were almost universally deprived of land ownership, they also almost universally provided the labor that allowed investment in land to bring both subsistence and profit to landowners. By providing goods and services for use and sale, by providing labor as indentured servant or tenant, and through the forced use of labor against their will, women provided a major component of agricultural development in America.

Forced labor provided the most extreme case of the expropriation of women's labor in agricultural development. Slavery had become embedded in family law by the early eighteenth century in many colonies. Slave laws provided that women and their children, as well as men, could be inherited or sold in the same way as personal property. As slave law was grafted onto family law, white plantation women brought enslaved black women with them into marriages, sometimes keeping legal title as personal property and willing them to their descendants, sometimes allowing their husbands to take title, but almost always allowing husbands to control the labor of these enslaved women and the products of their labor. Like land ownership, ownership of slaves could give white women power within the family despite male control over the labor of slaves.

The work of these enslaved black women is not yet well studied. Scholars estimate that between 70 and 90 percent of black women worked in the fields. The rest of the women produced goods and services for the market as well as for the black and white members of the plantation. In Virginia, where slavery had become widespread by the 1720s, the productivity of plantations began to increase markedly. A century later, far more women were involved in producing commodities—perhaps as many as one-fourth by 1800. By the early nineteenth century black women were producing large quantities of textiles on Virginia plantations as spinners, weavers, and seamstresses. As Carole Shammas has concluded, most women were in the fields or in the plantation "manufactory," not working as household servants.[9]

Black women deprived of their own labor power resorted to other strategies. A few attempted alliances with white women. There is some evidence that white women manumitted their slaves more frequently than men and more frequently provided training in skills such as literacy. Most often, however, alliances with other kin similarly enslaved provided the most successful strategies for black women. One of the main strategies was to free some member of the family who would then attempt to liberate other family members by assisting in escape, by purchase, or by offering psychic support. Deborah White has offered an important analysis of these strategies in her study of black women. The valuing of a woman's labor by whites might provide status in the black community but more often a woman had to earn it. She might build this status through her own health, skill, or strength. Usually she had to add leadership skills and interpersonal skills to achieve status in black rural communities. These could best be obtained through experience; thus, an older woman might achieve greater status over a period of years.[10]

Two patterns of discontent had emerged among black females by mid-nineteenth century. The first was caused by the controlled location of the homes of enslaved families, usually near to the plantation family. The second was caused by the use of forced work gangs under the supervision of white men. This discontent was manifest by the end of the Civil War as black families began to move away from plantation owners. While the period of reconstruction after the Civil War did not drastically change ownership patterns in the south, black families did change their labor patterns. Jacqueline Jones has argued persuasively in *Labor of Love, Labor of Sorrow* that black married women preferred to work on their own family farms rather than for wage labor, or as Jones says, to practice "household determination." By refusing to exchange bond labor for wage labor, black women maintained considerable control over their lives and the lives of their families.[11]

Black women continued to labor in the fields, but they combined that labor with caring for their families. They preferred kin labor groups to groups organized by white landowners. The compromise was the sharecropping system with the black husband usually maintaining major contact with white owners and supervisors while women decreased contact with them. Many black women combined household work with other types of work, such as laundering, selling chickens, farm produce or processed food, and doing seasonal field work. This diversification helped give the black rural family some flexibility in devising survival strategies in a hostile South that seemed only to want to exploit their labor. Meanwhile, black men performed wage labor as well as family labor and attempted, while they were able, to develop a political structure receptive to issues of land reform and debt relief for their families. This struggle kept most black people in rural areas of the South where they made up 40 percent of the farmers and farm laborers. Women usually lived in nuclear families with kin close by, with whom they shared windfall and disaster, dissatisfied with their poverty and oppression but determined to make life better for their children.[12]

Enslaved labor was a crucial part of agricultural development in the South and the lower Mid-Atlantic states. Before the Civil War black women provided the same type of labor as other farm women: birthing and caring for children, field work, manufacturing and processing, and domestic work or service work for other farm members. But even before the war, two distinct patterns seem to have emerged in the South. In the Upper South, black women may have been moving from manufacturing of textiles to household service, while in the deep South, especially in states like Mississippi, women remained in the fields.[13]

Another kind of female bond labor, indenture, also existed in colonial America. Never widespread, indenture meant that a woman contracted her labor for a certain period of time, usually in return for her travel costs from Europe to America. At one time indentured servitude provided an avenue to participation in family farm ownership. After being bound a certain period, a woman might receive land or marry a man who owned land. Indentured women were fairly common in seventeenth-century Maryland, and some women perhaps did end up happy freeholder wives. Recent research shows that indenture in the South was soon replaced by the more profitable slave labor of women. Mortality was very high among single white servants, and black families probably were better able to survive through cooperative care, especially on larger plantations where many of the black people were related. Indentured servants also disappeared in the Mid-Atlantic by the end of the eighteenth century. It was cheaper to install tenants or to hire wage labor seasonally and to allow the family to care for the worker's welfare.[14]

Tenancy was very common by the late eighteenth century. Through tenant contracts, men often bound their families to provide certain labor to the landlord. Contracts might include the work of the woman in the fields at harvest time, spinning of wool from the owner's flocks, providing dairying services, care of small livestock, or even personal services if the landlord maintained a house for his own use on the same land. Tenant contracts varied with different regions but continued into the twentieth century to bind women's as well as men's labor. Where a tenant paid in shares, the work of women in the family was normally included. The exclusion of certain of women's products, such as chickens and eggs, also became a tradition in some areas.[15]

Regardless of the form of contract that controlled women's la-

bor—marriage, purchase, tenancy, short or long-term wage labor—
most women labored in certain fairly predictable ways. Many women
worked in the fields at harvest time. Until the late eighteenth century
when scythes and cradles became common for harvesting grains,
women probably worked with their sickles. Black women plowed,
hoed, and performed other field work, but so too did white women
during most of the eighteenth century. This practice continued into
the nineteenth century on tenant farms. When the farm household
could afford the equipment for processing and manufacturing, field
work became less necessary for women. Then the woman, regardless
of her legal status as wife, slave, or hired servant, could spend her
time in the production of textiles and food. By the end of the
eighteenth century the colonies produced a sizable surplus of both
food and textiles so that an increasing number of women, particularly
in the North, were engaged in such labor. Sales of cheese, butter, and
poultry, as well as cloth, brought in needed cash to farms where
prices for field crops and livestock were volatile and unpredictable.
Women supplied commodities for the use of the household and a
salable surplus. In addition, they provided services for the farm
household, which in wealthier families included management and
care of increasing amounts of material goods. And, certainly not least
important, they reproduced the farm family. This included large
amounts of time devoted to the care of dependents, whether too
young, too old, or too ill to care for themselves. Women, in other
words, provided an immense range of work that combined family
work of caring for other workers and maintaining households with
farm work of manufacturing, processing, and field work.

Tasks performed within the household consumed most of the
time and energy of men as well as women. The labor of women,
however, allowed men to spend a greater portion of their time
outside the household. For most preindustrial and precommercial
farm families, the public and private was blurred and indistinct.
Probably both women and men influenced communities through kin
and social groups. As labor became better organized males began to
spend a part of their time away from farms in distinctly public areas.
This might simply involve more frequent trips to town to sell and
purchase, but it might also include more time spent talking and
engaging in political or church activities. During the eighteenth
century politics replaced religion as the major public interest of most

white males, and they spent increasing amounts of time on it. Women, on the other hand, probably devoted increasing amounts of their time to religion and to public aspects of that religion, whether as preachers, organizers of charity, or organizers of prayer groups. Eventually, of course, women began to be more actively involved in political change relating to the conditions of women and blacks. By the late nineteenth century they had organized in thousands of clubs that provided welfare for others and a political focus for their own gender-specific concerns.

Despite the fact that most women remained within the household, they did exercise some power in society. Middle-class women during the nineteenth century began to interpret the domestic sphere as more important, extending that sphere and their influence in society. These exponents of domestic power claimed to have extraordinary influence over both the home, and in the late nineteenth century, over municipal welfare as well. Working-class women had a long tradition of family-based change. This provided a continuation of the tradition of egalitarianism that emphasized participation of men and women in decisions that affected the family. Both these traditions that emphasized women's greater power within the home had special rural models. Rural women seldom adopted full-blown theories of domestic power that emphasized the home as an exclusive sphere for women, for both women and men were present on the farm, and women worked in the barnyard and the field as well as in the home. Although rural men less often crossed the boundaries of gender labor than rural women, they had more flexibility in their work than most city men, at least during part of the season. Wealthier rural women adopted the ideology of domesticity in almost identical form to that of urban women, but less wealthy women retained a strong orientation to production for the market just as did urban working-class women.[16]

Rural male management concepts were also important. If the male owned the land, he might subscribe to an ideology of family management and consider himself representative of the interests of family members as expressed by them. If he did not, he might consider himself as sole proprietor who looked after his own interests, the interests of male or males who would inherit the land, or the presumed interests of wife and daughters. We know far too little about how these attitudes differed by class and ethnicity.

While some rural women and men resisted or modified the ideals of domesticity and women's sphere, others seem to have embraced it. John Mack Faragher has argued that rural women heading west in the nineteenth century resisted doing "men's work." This may have been because women were still expected to perform male work when necessary, but the same flexibility was not normally expected of males. Once on the frontier, the uncertainty of household, kin, neighbor, or hired labor meant women often had to perform a wide variety of tasks. Families fragmented on the rural frontier; nowhere did more than a small percentage of the population achieve the ideal of the nuclear family working together on the family farm.[17]

Mormon communities openly opposed the nuclear family ideal with their practice of plural marriage. Scholars are still debating the effect of Mormon polygamy on the lives of western rural women. Because the rearrangement of sex roles may have encouraged women's independence and resourcefulness, some scholars have therefore concluded that Mormon women in the West escaped the idealization of genteel domesticity that seemed to pervade eastern middle-class urban Victorian America. But Jessie Embrey has argued that while Mormon women might have stepped out of traditional roles occasionally, they returned to the narrow Victorian ideal as quickly as possible. Their work was gender segregated and although women may have performed outdoor jobs, such as gardening, milking, and poultry raising, all women shared household tasks and most strongly believed in the Victorian prescription that women's place was in the home. The contradictory evidence may be due to change over time. In a detailed study of women in Ogden, Utah, Justina Bernstein concluded that there was considerable change during the late nineteenth century in work and attitudes. During early settlement days women were equal partners in creating an inhabitable community, but after the railroad reached Utah women's "proper places" were increasingly defined for them. From varied agricultural tasks acknowledged by the community as crucial, women moved into industrial tasks and into virtual invisibility as workers. An ideology of "Mormon womanhood" increasingly defined the women who worked to lay the basis for Mormon prosperity.[18]

Studies of rural women elsewhere have shown variations of this adaptation to rural domesticity. Farmhouse plans at mid nineteenth century still emphasized productivity rather than domesticity, according to Sally McMurry. The farm kitchen was the center of a complex productive enterprise in which house care and farm task intermingled on middling and even prosperous farms. During the next half-century progressive farm families reorganized their farmhouses. Women became more servicers of families in these homes and they designed private and smaller kitchens separated from dining rooms, separate housing for hired hands, sitting rooms instead of parlors, rooms for daughters, and indoor plumbing. These progressive farm families created a unique rural context different from both their urban counterparts and the poorer families that still predominated in the countryside. Large numbers of American families in the Midwest, the West, and the South still shared cramped multipurpose rooms where farm women produced and served their families. They made do with inadequate houses as they did with other conditions.[19]

Regardless of what women wanted, or what the dominant ideology dictated, the marketplace profoundly affected farm women during the late nineteenth and early twentieth centuries. The external market forces that led to concentration of capital in agriculture combined with male control of farm policy, property, and family labor increasingly confined women to consumer and subsistence roles in the farm household. Capital intensive farming also intensified the cycles of boom and bust, alternating periods of expansion and recession. Policy makers and farmers increasingly devalued women's farm work as irrelevant to these larger patterns. One consequence of this commitment to market values was the reinforcement of gender differences. Nancy Grey Osterud probed these relationships in her analysis of Nanticoke, New York, where dairy families produced butter for the market. She asked how women and men valued their own and each other's labor. Her conclusion—that women modeled their cooperative labor on kinship while men modeled theirs on the market—showed a deep division in the way women and men looked at work. Women's work was valued by both men and women on its own terms rather than in terms of market value, but such attitudes, in fact, reinforced gender differences. These attitudes persisted for a half-century in Nanticoke Valley.[20]

What Osterud explained as a pattern of the late nineteenth century, Corlann Bush and Sue Armitage explored further in their research on Pacific Northwest farm women. These scholars traced the full cycle, from early pioneer women still providing subsistence for farm households—including work in dairy families and on large wheat farms where women cooked for immense crews—to fruit-growing areas where Native American and Anglo women worked at picking and packing. Then, in the last stage, as farms mechanized after 1945, women's productive labor was increasingly marginalized on farms. Women became consumers and involved in off-farm work. Ironically, home food processing, once a necessity for survival, now became the prerogative of wealthy farm women. The devaluing of women's traditional work went hand in hand with capital intensive single-crop production.[21]

These overall trends in American agriculture were punctuated by crises during which women performed on a national scale the tasks they had performed in individual families or during economic transitions. During World War I and the Great Depression, women performed these tasks as part of government policy. Margo McBane has shown in her work on the California Women's Land Army how the government attempted to develop a female farm labor force that would undercut the attempts of male laborers—particularly Japanese males—to maintain high wages. Women had frequently performed such harvest labor in the past, but government policy insured that this declining source of labor would be maintained through the crisis of the war years. Following the war, the government encouraged the immigration of Mexican families who provided a large labor pool at wages California growers felt they could afford. The depression that California farmers and farm laborers faced in the 1920s became nationwide in the 1930s. The government encouraged expansion of women's home production during these decades through the Agricultural Extension Service. This work was calculated to help keep farm families on the farm and self-sufficient even during economic downturns.[22]

As Deborah Fink and Dorothy Schweider showed in a case study of Iowa, women turned their efforts to producing additional farm income and to decreasing expenditures. In Iowa women concentrated on poultry-raising and, the authors argued, this money kept the farm family in food, clothing, and other household items, and often provided money to enable the farm enterprise to survive. Federal policies of rural development held out hope for the urban amenities that farm women wanted—especially electricity and improved roads.[23]

Despite a few government policies to support women's farm activities throughout World War II and the early post-war period, the government primarily saw the small family farm on which both husband and wife produced as archaic and outmoded even before World War I. The government shifted its policy to support increased mechanization and capitalization—with ever increasing debts—that emphasized specializing in traditional male crops or in transforming traditional women's work into highly capitalized and specialized enterprises. Such a policy inevitably devalued women's farm roles.

On family farms, a woman's work was less capable of making the difference in survival after World War II. Not surprisingly, women of the poorer farm families now joined landless farm laborers in creating a new wage-labor force. As the number of farms declined and mechanization proceeded, the labor force became increasingly poorly paid and feminized. In some areas, such as the San Luis Valley in Colorado, women became the workers who drove large fleets of trucks from the potato fields. But they were not allowed to drive the smaller number of trucks in the fields, a higher paying job reserved for males. Similarly, as Adela de la Torre has shown, in the tomato harvest women were relegated to the lowest paying jobs on the new harvester while men occupied the higher paid, more permanent jobs. Women made their way to the bottom of the new job hierarchy and stayed there as a new low-paid, seasonal work force. The story was the same elsewhere. At this point both women farmers and farm laborers increased their political organizing.[24]

Women had been publicly organizing around farm issues since the late nineteenth century. Women first became visible as members of Grange and Farmers' Alliances and then in third parties. Mary Jo Wagner analyzed the activities of women in the Populist Party, particularly their participation in defining economic issues. Women had hardly participated in earlier economic debates; thus, their emergence as economic commentators was particularly noteworthy. Through speeches, letters to editors, tracts, novels, poems, and songs, women popularized the economic discontents of the farmers. Wagner argued that because women were accepted as moral arbitrators in the late nineteenth century and because reformers saw money issues in moral terms, women were able to participate extensively in this aspect of party politics. It was, in fact, the rural counterpart of the social housekeeping that urban women were espousing because of their presumed moral superiority.[25]

The Grange Movement, 1894. The Grange was one of the first national organizations to admit white women to membership and rural women eagerly joined. Source: Leslie's Magazine, *January 31, 1894, Library of Congress.*

At the state level these rural reformers were soon branching out into many issues of concern to farm families. In her careful study of white North Carolina women, Lu Ann Jones argued that local reformers consciously attempted to attract women to their cause. Jones estimated that perhaps as many as 25 percent of Alliance members in North Carolina may have been women and that women spoke and wrote extensively. Women did not, however, speak about their own interests as women. Instead, they urged men and women to unite against their common enemies—railroads, trusts, banks, and merchants.[26]

This commonality of interest began to shift at the end of the nineteenth century. With the disintegration of the Populist Party and hope of political success through third party movements, women seem to have turned their attention inward to the farm family and to questioning the distribution of power in it. Seen through the prism of the North Carolina *Progressive Farmer,* this shift began to support a separate domestic sphere for women and, consequently, separate interests. Like other newspapers of the time, the *Progressive Farmer* created an older wise woman who could advise farm women. In this case, "Aunt Jennie" reflected tensions between men and women on the farm over gender-specific complaints. Here then was the emergence of the same changing reality documented elsewhere—cash crops, mechanization, commercialization of their traditional work, and the consciousness by women that their needs were not always the same as their husbands'. For reformers, at least, there seemed a need to glorify housekeeping, or to "professionalize" it as compensation for the loss of the general farm and women's important productive work on it. Farmer's Institutes provided a mechanism for preaching "scientific housework" to rural women.[27]

By 1914 when the federal government joined the task of retraining farm women, the North Carolina State Department of Agriculture had already reached thousands of women. Its message was to make the home more efficient and scientific; its assumption, that the home was not as central a part of family farm production as it had been previously. The home now had the primary function of servicing the farm family. The goal seemed to be to increase the living standards of the rural family through intensifying the domestic labor of women. Direct income production was to be left more strictly to male farmers. The Institutes did, however, give some emphasis to what they considered traditional female enterprises on the farm— producing and selling butter and eggs, vegetables and fruits. Thus, although male agricultural agents assumed control over the major commercial products, they still recognized women's productive role. The overall message was to produce more through their services and industry and to consume more. Indeed, it seemed at times that reformers responded to increased mechanization and commercialization of agriculture with criticism not of the individuals responsible for profiting from the new agriculture but of husbands who would not or could not provide the consumer items offered to rural people in compensation for their intensified labor.[28]

It is not surprising then that the Agricultural Extension Service, which built on the growing state institute traditions, such as that developed in North Carolina, emphasized a similar gender division of labor. Although the federal government had subsidized education among the Indians from the early nineteenth century, it had done little more than provide funds for land grant colleges for the rest of the population. After an initial reluctance to admit women on the part of some, and several legal challenges, land grant colleges admitted white women. Colleges channeled women away from agriculture courses and into teaching. Toward the end of the nineteenth century, after a bitter struggle women economists became segregated in home economics departments. Males controlled schools of agriculture; females either went elsewhere or into departments of home economics made subservient to the male-dominated schools of agriculture.[29]

When the federal government expanded its adult agricultural education program in the early twentieth century, it built on a system of state education already deeply segregated by ethnicity and gender. While many of the early Institutes and Agricultural Extension Service programs recognized women's work in dairying and poultry raising, along with their domestic work, gradually the programs shifted to focus almost entirely on "domestic science." Aimed increasingly at keeping middle-class farm families on the farm and happy, these programs routinely ignored the very poor and ethnic minorities. For the middle class, the programs did indeed help make farm life more attractive. Programs offered assistance to women in performing their domestic roles more efficiently, but failed to help women effectively integrate their farm and house work. Because they failed in this task, the less affluent farm family remained increasingly vulnerable to the economic development that threatened their ability to remain on the land.[30]

The experience of black women in the rural South was different but parallel to that of other women. To be eligible for federal funds, sixteen southern states established segregated black land grant colleges under the second Morrill Act of 1890. Twelve black colleges, four new black land grant colleges, and Tuskegee eventually obtained land grant status. These seventeen black colleges in sixteen states provided education for rural black women in agriculture and teaching. They did so with very little financial help from the federal government or states, as most public funding went to white land grant colleges. These historically black land grant colleges were separate and unequal.[31]

Tuskegee always occupied a special place in the education of black rural women. Between its opening in 1881 and 1910, it trained hundreds of rural women to teach. These women went out from Tuskegee, often with only the promise of meager salaries, to teach a rural black population eager for education. Accounts sent back to the school and published in *The Southern Letter* show that time after time these young teachers found their first job was to raise money to build a school. Ella Thomas Flake, for example, on reaching Notasulga, Alabama, in 1907, reported that she found there had been no school in the community for five or six years and some children had never been to school before. Parents had to buy land to get any public aid at all. Most teachers also cultivated land at rural schools to provide training and income to buy supplies. These ranged from Hattie Womack's acre of potatoes at Dollington School to Susee Mitchell's twenty-eight acres at Big Swamp School. Teachers organized Mothers' Clubs that raised money for pictures, maps, and ground maintenance. As in other parts of the country, rural teaching at the primary levels became the responsibility of rural women.[32]

For these new teachers the ideology of the "true woman" was not one of simple "domesticity" but one of responsibility to the black family and community. Rosa Mason of Tuskegee preached a rigorous discipline for young black women: "a true woman does not need jewelry, ribbons and lace to make her attractive, and beside these things, it is selfish for them to rob their little brothers and sisters of the necessary things of life." She recognized that mothers who could not read could not very well provide guidance for book-reading daughters. While Mason subscribed to the idea that the "home is woman's sphere" the teachers knew that their job was to teach the "dignity of labor" and for most rural women that included a large portion of time outside the home in fields and farmyard. As the daughters of ex-masters entered the work force in the late nineteenth century, black women had to be able to compete with them in a gender-segregated marketplace. "An idle girl with nothing to do cannot develop a high, noble truthful womanhood. Every girl should have a trade, a profession, some honorable way of making a living," preached Anna Duncan who addressed the black Alabama State Teachers' Association in 1888. Thus the ideology of true womanhood for black rural women always had a strong work component. While black women may have seen purely household work as desirable, they all expected to participate in work outside the home, either for wages or in volunteer work for the community. Margaret Washington, wife of Booker T. Washington, president of Tuskegee, seemed to embody the ideal of true womanhood in her elaborately formal home life in Tuskegee, but she also organized an evening extension school for mothers and a women's club that sponsored projects to help rural women. And she always worked at Tuskegee Institute and directed the mechanical trades for young women there.[33]

Because of this ideology, Tuskegee offered rural women training in a wide range of trades. Margaret Washington supervised the teaching of upholstery, mattress-making, cooking, sewing, dressmaking, millinery, laundrying—all occupations meant to allow rural women to compete in the marketplace, not primarily as domestics, but as specialized wage workers and small entrepreneurs. They did learn housekeeping, but it was primarily for their own homes. Women also participated in tailoring, type-setting, health care, market gardening, poultry raising, bee keeping, horticulture, floriculture, and dairying courses with male students. While always mixed with the rhetoric of "womanhood," the training provided by the school met the needs of rural women.[34]

When Tuskegee began institutes for farmers, mechanics, school teachers, and ministers, women argued that men and women be encouraged to work together on farms they owned. Women did not want to work in "white folks' kitchens" but on black owned and cultivated land where they could raise their own food supplies and a surplus for the market. They wanted better homes and schools. Poultry-raising, they had learned, could be more profitable than field work, and women formed groups to encourage selling hogs, chickens, and eggs, as well as to pool money to buy commodities together at cheaper prices. The Tuskegee emphasis on landowning, responsibility to a black community, and agricultural skills helped implement the desire of most blacks to own land. Between 1870 and 1910 the percentage of black rural families in Alabama that owned land rose from 1 percent to 15 percent, gains painfully wrested from a white population determined to resist the increase of black land ownership. The training of Tuskegee women in community and family survival skills always emphasized self-sufficiency and community support. It enabled the survival of black southerners during a time when political action was increasingly difficult for the men and gave them the basis for community organizing skills that would allow black women to become leaders in their local communities.[35]

South Carolina rice raft, 1895. Black women continued to be a crucial part of the Southern agricultural labor force. Source: Strohmeyer & Wyman, 1895, Library of Congress.

The participation of Tuskegee women in agricultural education dwindled after 1910. In that year Booker T. Washington began to exclude women from the annual Tuskegee Negro Conference. The school's agricultural curriculum for women also narrowed considerably. After 1914, however, Tuskegee became the headquarters for the Extension Service for a seven state area, and Smith-Lever funds enabled the hiring of black home demonstration agents to train rural women in gardening, poultry, and housekeeping. The program even hired a rural nurse. Between 1914 and 1920 the program flourished, only to be cut back when federal funding decreased.[36]

Despite real gains, the ability of rural women—black or white— to affect larger agricultural policy remained minimal. And black farm women were not the only ones unable to change what they perceived to be the injustice of the American agricultural system. Few rural people could. One of the few political groups to have a potential for change was the Nonpartisan League. Moving toward an agrarian socialism, the league called for a larger role for the state in regulating the agricultural economy. More of a platform than a party, the league sought out candidates of major parties to endorse its farm policies. As Karen Starr has shown in her research, the league continued the older tradition of populism, emphasizing the unity of the farm family and involving women in active political roles. The Nonpartisan League strongly supported suffrage, a place for women in reform politics, and a reaffirmation of traditional family values. The league's support for greater state control of agriculture made it vulnerable to attacks from the right, however. In the anti-radicalism of the post–World War I period, the league was attacked for being a threat to the family, ironic since there seems to be little evidence that the Nonpartisan League ever advocated any major change in family or gender relations. Starr concluded that the league provided farm women in North Dakota and Minnesota with a fund of political skills used later in other Midwest farm movements.[37]

Despite the involvement of women in some political organizations and the attempts of the government to organize white women, they became increasingly marginal both politically and economically as the American agricultural system industrialized. Farm families in many parts of the country weathered the depression of the 1930s well compared to urban groups. During this depression thousands of farm worker women struck for higher wages and organized into agricultural unions for field and cannery work. Women were particularly conspicuous in the California harvest fields where corporate farming had already expanded. Hispanic women emerged as militant organizers. In a berry strike in El Monte in 1931 and in an orange pickers' strike at Santa Ana in 1936, women played leading roles in winning concessions. In the San Joaquin Valley, Dolores Hernandez and Delfino Davila lost their lives in bitter strikes. Elsewhere unionization was less successful. In the South, despite the organization of groups such as the Southern Tenant Farmers Union, thousands of already marginalized sharecroppers were forced off the land as the mechanization of agriculture continued.[38]

Farm Security Administration photographers left moving portraits of the rural women who came to symbolize the misery of the depression, the human cost. While the images certainly reflected the misery of these white sharecroppers as they moved west in search of migratory labor, the women were victims not so much of the depression or even the drought, but of a political system that insured the survival of larger, capital intensive farms at the expense of the poorer, labor intensive family farms. Such dislocation had been continuous since the late nineteenth century. Poorer families had usually become farm laborers or tenants or had migrated west to take up the remaining parcels of the public domain. Such farm families remained vulnerable to market changes, government agricultural policies that favored more wealthy farmers, and an inability to organize politically. Before the 1940s many of these families had been able to shift to other rural places. Some black families had migrated north, but the depression of the 1930s made urban areas less attractive to rural people. Thus the 1940s, with the abundant war work, quickening economy, and military mobilization proved to be a major turning point for farm families. Agricultural policy following the war consciously promoted fewer and bigger farms, more mechanized, more highly capitalized, requiring fewer farm laborers. During the 1950s, an increasing number of farm daughters and wives found their traditional work not only devalued but also discarded. A woman's work no longer provided the margin for survival, much less success.[39]

Modern farm women can be studied from a variety of perspectives. Some sociologists who have looked at a poor, tobacco-growing area of North Carolina have tapped traditional views of male patriarchy—males dominant, females subordinant in decision making. On the other hand, when Rachel Rosenfeld asked farm women about their lives, she found they performed a wide range of roles in agricultural production. Almost 10 percent of farmers and farm managers were women by 1980, and women remained part of almost all the family farms that constituted 3 percent of the population. The work of farm women still remains varied and impressive. In addition to household tasks and child care, over 80 percent in Rosenfeld's study raised some food, the majority did bookkeeping and general farmkeeping, most helped care for animals and helped in harvest, and some did field work as well. Half participated in farm expenditure decisions with husbands and 40 percent on production decisions. Almost two thirds participated in voluntary community organizations and half in farm organizations and extension activities. Over 20 percent worked at additional home businesses. Twenty percent also had off-farm jobs, most in low paid clerical work. At least 55 percent considered themselves a main farm operator, and 60 percent of the married women felt they could run the farm alone. Another researcher, Judith Kalbacher, concluded that in the future farm women would receive greater recognition, that more would become farm operators, and more would operate large units.[40]

Farm women will experience more stress as well. Gould Colman and Sarah Elbert, who have done extensive oral interviews with contemporary farm women, think that sociological decision-making studies and other single snapshot studies mask some harsh realities of family-farm labor. Farm women often cope remarkably well with farm tasks, housework, and child care, and increasingly with off-farm jobs as well, but there is frequent confusion between labor coordination and labor control in farm families. Male farmers remained husband/father/boss of the operations, and family workers, who thought they were laboring for "our" farm, found greater emphasis on making it "his farm." The hidden work of women and children on family farms had enabled these farm family enterprises to occupy a precarious "niche" in the larger industrial capitalist system. As family operations increased in scale they tended to adapt the bureaucratic or corporate pattern of labor control that was a hallmark of urban industry.[41]

After World War II extension agents and the farm press had encouraged families to consider farms multi-generational firms. From 1920 to 1941, farming was often a one generation business because families were large and income was small. Now the experts encouraged farm men to pay attention to passing on the farm to a son, not to manage the farm for the welfare of the family. Inflation of land prices in the 1960s had already closed land ownership to most newcomers. Heavily in debt to modernize, weakened by growing inequality within, the family farm was at risk should another downturn come. Farm programs gave stability in farm prices and incomes for two decades. It was, in a sense, the linking of the "yankee" tradition of short-term economic profit to the immigrant tradition of generational stability. Mark Friedberger calls this the triumph of the ethic of corporate ideology.[42]

The farm crisis of the 1980s hit farm families selectively. A majority experienced financial concerns, but a large minority continued to do well. Like other economic downturns, this one skimmed off those who failed to make the transition to a new system, sending them into the small towns or at least into off-farm jobs. Again farm policies seemed to have directly influenced farm failure. Only those with help from kin already owning land could hope to remain on the land. Estate taxes hit farm widows particularly hard in the 1960s. Many widows still received only a life interest in their husband's estates, thus giving them little flexibility in managing family farms. What seemed new was that for the first time the government saw the family farm as destined to become extinct. The Office of Technology Assessment predicted in 1986 that the middling farm, so long a successful survivor, would die in the 1990s. All the government programs seemed geared to helping the large, more corporate farm survive at the expense of the middling farm. Only small part-time "hobby" farms and large manager-run farms could survive, the experts predicted.[43]

But farm families had survived before, primarily by assessing the market and by utilizing flexibility of labor. In fact, the farm families that survive may be those that do not adopt the corporate strategy. With the development of the women's movement in the seventies, many farm women gained confidence to reach for greater control. They began to question the insistence that the family farm insure succession to the males rather than the welfare of the entire family. Now women—wives and daughters—asked that the family business benefit them all. The crisis galvanized women into protest, for the family farm but also for their place in it.[44]

Contemporary farm women are fighting on many fronts to maintain their place on the land. They are sometimes fighting each other. Women who organize within the United Farm Workers seem to have little in common with the middle-class landowners in W.I.F.E., who see the unionization of farm workers as a threat to their survival. Farm workers and large farm owners seem to be able to accept the growth of agribusiness, while middle farm owners see largeness as a threat. In the early twentieth century, owners of middle-sized farms often fought to retain their farms at the cost of small land owners; the descendants of these middling family farms now see the landless laborers as a threat. At the same time, government policies seem to favor the large-scale landowners who can survive mortgage debt, huge capitalization, and higher labor costs. The middling farm family, which has absorbed so many of the costs of farming through its own labor, will need to find a solution to mounting debts, uncertain markets, and unsympathetic urban consumers.[45]

Nor is the answer to growing conflicts within the farm family and community an easy one. Farm daughters are demanding a greater role in the inter-generational transfer of land. Like their brothers or spouses, they too can attend agricultural colleges and obtain technical training to equip them to manage mechanized and complex farms. More young urban women are also training to join the farm economy as experts. Some agricultural colleges are already one-third female. Where once women accepted the dominance of males as the trained experts, they are now challenging that dominance. At times, they are challenging agricultural training itself, demanding more attention to environmental factors—for both the land and its workers.[46]

Wives, too, are demanding a larger role in private as well as public decision making. Farm women risked community approbrium by speaking out in favor of the Equal Rights Amendment, by demanding expanded legal rights for farm women, and by seeking attention to the health and well-being of farm families by public policymakers. Some wives are reluctant to give up power to husbands or sons, wishing to retain or attain decision-making roles in successful farm ventures, as well as in unsuccessful ones. The crisis on farms thus comes from within as well as without. In this atmosphere of crisis, farm women are calling for a reevaluation of their place in American rural development, both in their historical and in their contemporary roles. Women, on and off the farm, are seeking a usable past, a more viable present, and a central role in rural development of the family farms.

PART I

Autobiography &
Biography

COMING OF AGE AS A HISTORIAN IN THE 1960S I ONCE
promised never to write biography. Groups seemed all important and
I saw the focus on an individual as too narrow to help explain history.

My students taught me differently. When I began teaching wom-
en's history, I never gave an individual woman space in my syllabus.
My concept of biography was "great women," and I thought we had
gone beyond that to find out what women as a whole did. Students
protested. They wanted individual women and "great women" as
well. And so by the second year of my teaching, a few "great women"
came sneaking back into my teaching. But not into my writing. I held
the line until I encountered Esther Lewis.

Esther Lewis was a Quaker farm woman who lived from 1782 to
1848 in the Philadelphia hinterland. I found her quite by accident
while doing research for a book on Mid-Atlantic farm women. I had
been busy with my groups, but they still seemed distant to me. I was
unsure if my generalizations were quite right, almost as if my historical picture was out of focus. Then someone suggested that I contact
Margaret Bacon who was writing a biography of Quaker reformer
Lucretia Mott. I met Bacon at the Cherry Street office of the Quakers
in Philadelphia. That was a magic meeting. For years, most academic
historians had been rather amused at my project, skeptical that rural
women were worth all the hours of labor I had put in on their lives.
The few who were supportive did not know how to help me. Bacon

knew. She immediately agreed about the importance of rural women, saying that the backcountry Quaker women were much more active in the women's rights movement than Philadelphia women. Mott's correspondence showed that. Had I heard of Esther Lewis and did I know that her papers were still in the hands of a kinswoman who lived in Media, Pennsylvania? Bacon asked. Would I like her address?

Within a week I was settled at a card table in the study-bedroom of Saize Macauley, a descendant of Esther Lewis, pouring over diaries and letters. A week later I was walking with Saize through the houses where Esther had lived. My visual image of farm women was clear now. I knew at least one of them. And I realized that Esther would have a chapter of my book to herself, a mini-biography.

Since encountering Esther Lewis, I have been interested in biographies and what they can tell us about the lives of farm women. The family is the primary social institution within which human energy is produced and socialized. Biographies can help us see how that basic energy takes form in society. It is true that written records still limit us to literate middle-class women but having models of rural women expands the range of knowledge of women's lives and how they arranged them. And if, for the more recent period, we combine research with reminiscence and oral history then we can again expand that range of models. There may not be enough material available for book-length biographies of rural women, unless like Susan B. Anthony they entered public life or like Grace Milhous happened to have a daughter, Jessamyn West, to hear stories of growing up on a farm in southern Indiana. Biographical experiences told by mothers and grandmothers have often ended up as novels or short stories, but they deserve also to be preserved as non-fiction biographies, told with grace but with absolute attention to the details that help people understand the texture of these lives.

These three essays attempt to use memoirs in various ways. The first is autobiographical, set down as other women have set down their experiences on the land. The second moves farther back to approach biography through reminiscence and family history. The third was done with a living farm woman who shared her experiences with me in such great detail that I could almost taste the rye bread that came from her large farm oven and hear the clack of the loom as she wove the linen into exquisite toweling. I have learned much from looking at farm women through this closeup lens of autobiography and biography.

1 *Memoirs of a Rural Communist*

SOME PEOPLE CALLED US HIPPIES. WE PREFERRED TO think of ourselves as communists, with a small *c*. After all, we had put everything we had into our small rural communal enterprise, each according to his or her ability, we made all decisions by consensus, and we divided the work up equally between men and women. That was our concept of communism, at least at the beginning, although we were probably much closer to anarchist in our philosophy than to any brand of communists we knew. Our political philosophy, to the extent that there was one at the beginning, was non-violent anarchism, but we thought of ourselves as communists in our living arrangements.

As I look back on it now, there was also a strong strain of Christian Socialism in our thinking, although most of us professed agnosticism or atheism. We thought, for example, that we should help our neighbors. And we did. We found the "oldtimers," those families who had lived in "the valley" a long time and who still lived simply, most receptive to our help. As strong young people who were available to help out older rural folk, we were well paid in exchange— with food, equipment, and advice. We were always well-treated by all our neighbors, who did not ask too closely about our beliefs or the activities that went on inside our farm household. We worked hard at home, hired out our labor at the low wage rates prevalent, and tried to help out our neighbors. That seemed to be enough.

It was not our neighbors in that beautiful, but desperately diffi-cult to farm, San Luis Valley of Southern Colorado but ourselves who caused the most difficulties. The environment, it is true, was harsh. "Why be so masochistic?" a visiting friend inquired on my telling him the growing season was ninety days, the temperature reached minus twenty degrees on some winter nights, and that we had less than twelve inches of rain in our semiarid land. We loved the valley with all its harshness because of the flaming sunsets, the clear dry air, the cool summers. The problem was we had to make our living there, where it would have been quite pleasant to just live. Not only did we have little capital and few skills for either building or maintaining a farm; we also were dedicated to this crazy experiment in gender equality.

The idea was that we would share work inside and outside equally. We knew that a strong gender division of labor existed both on the other farms and on the other communes that were scattered around the southwest. In fact, communes seemed to have the most rigid gender lines, usually with women performing household and child care duties while men built and plowed and worked off the farms in similarly gender-segregated jobs. Once a few of our group took a trip over the mountain to the nearest commune and reported back that these people, who called themselves "The Red Rockers," were trying similar experiments in gender equality. It was hard, everyone agreed.

Our small group underwent constant change during its two brief years of life. Most of that time, we had no children in the group. When we did, we simply included child care in our rotation of jobs. Many of us had never had to care for children. At thirty-six, I had not done child care for twenty years. I babysat for twenty-five cents an hour during World War II and occasionally before I began working part-time at other wage work in 1950. Since that time I had hardly been near children. Child care duties certainly increased our skills, but I doubt that we really gave quality child care. There were, however, plenty of animals and the outdoors to hold the attention of our small charges. I remember mainly following them around to see that they did not dismember themselves or the animals.

Hardest to equalize was the housework. Here the women had the edge in experience. We women were not particularly well-trained in household skills, but over the years we had practiced them more than any of the men. Both men and women agreed that cooking was the hardest physically. We alternated indoor and outdoor tasks rigidly with a schedule. At its most stable period, our commune had five members, three men and two women. We simply rotated the job of cooking daily, but this included also clean up and keeping the kitchen/ living room area swept and clean. Each person was responsible for his or her own living space—we each were able to have a small room of our own. Cooking was thus our principal communal household chore.

The cook began work an hour earlier than anyone else because even cooking simple breakfasts required an hour of constant labor. A fire had to be built, water heated, and cereal cooked. We had plenty of goat's milk, local honey, and carob which we brought back from Denver on periodic shopping trips. Hot carob milk with a cooked mixed grain cereal was a favorite in winter. We liked eight- or ten-grain cereals with cracked wheat and corn, buckwheat, oats, millet, and rye. I do not remember what the other kinds of grain were but I do remember the large barrels as they stood in the storeroom and the pleasure I had in mixing them for breakfast cereals. We often had eggs, too, but seldom meat. For almost half of one year we all joined one of the women in her vegetarianism, but she gave it up at the end of that time because of the enormous work it became to prepare and eat enough vegetable protein to do the heavy work we had assigned ourselves.

Even more than preparing, I remember eating our way through enormous mounds of beans, rice, and grains at the evening meals. When we added rabbit to our evening fare, cooking and eating time went down. I remember the pleasure of eating small quantities of meat. Raising and slaughtering the rabbits was one of my assigned tasks, and I gladly performed it to be able to add it to our diet. Rabbit turned out to be cheap and delicious. I miss the rabbit stews.

Once breakfast was over, the dishes had to be quickly washed (carrying water in and out) and dinner (our noon meal) begun. We tried to bake pies and cobblers, muffins, and quick breads. One of the men got quite good at baking bread, but I never did very well. I loved the *Tassajara Bread Book* and with it could always produce near perfect scones, three-layered cornbread, and inscrutable muffins (named because of all the different grains and spices). Along with the breads and desserts, there was a main course to prepare, usually a vegetarian soybean or rice casserole. Soybeans had to cook interminably, and without proper timing the cook might have to serve slightly hard beans. Despite our array of herbs, it was hard to make the vegetarian dishes taste good and to get enough variety, especially when we lacked fresh vegetables much of the year. But the praise or condolences were lavish. Everyone knew the labor that went into a bad dinner, and deprived of the satisfaction of a good dinner, we had to expend extra energy on making the cook feel good.

For supper we could sometimes get by with leftovers, made over, recombined, and added to. But there was never enough for an entire meal and so, after the midday meal and clean up, the cook seldom got much of a rest. After breakfast, the cook usually rested by sweeping the floor and tidying up. In the afternoon, one might actually get to sit down for a few minutes, although I do not remember having as much as an hour. Usually, it was fifteen to twenty minutes, enough for a few minutes outdoors or, in the winter, a short time spent before the living room stove, gathering energy for the last third of the day. I do not even remember spending this time reading; usually, I just sat and thought about what I still had to do. I remember coming in one day when one of the men was cook. He was a technician with a fine mind who had real trouble organizing his material life. I remember his utterly hopeless look as he sat there exhausted, the dishes still undone, the remnants of the last meal preparation scattered about. But gradually even he improved, although we constantly worried that he might break under the strain of the need to be organized in this work. His best meals were a real triumph for us all.

Cutting into any possibility of a mid-morning break or afternoon rest was also a break for the outdoor workers. I should add that in winter, several people usually went off to the city so that our outdoor work lasted about six months of the year. The break often consisted of carob-honey milk with eggs whipped into it and cookies. To see the cook bearing these treats after two or three hours of hard physical labor was one of our greatest pleasures. Knowing the pleasure, we cooks did our best to make the break food as good as mealtime food. When the supper dishes were over, the cook usually simply collapsed in a chair, gathering enough energy to crawl to bed, looking forward to the next day outside.

The outdoor work was glorious, hard but exhilarating. We eventually divided up the animal chores—one looking after the chickens, another the rabbits, another the cattle, one the goats. I do not remember how we handled these chores when we cooked. I suppose we must have had someone else do them. I also remember rotating the milking of goats because we all loved that job so much. Tired as we were in the evening, cold as it often was in the morning, leaning against the side of Juana or Ashanti and pulling was like meditation. We all became expert milkers and expert with our own animals. Even the chickens became individuals to the person who cared for them daily.

The other homework was divided between building, repairing machinery, and gardening. We had no power tools and few building skills but gradually we all learned carpentry. In remodeling the house, building an insulated chicken house, and repairing the barn, we all used carpentry skills. I do not remember any particular problems about this rough carpentry except how hard it was to use hand tools. Much of the work was crude but adequate. We all learned to chop wood and, like milking, this turned out to be a favorite job. Splitting a log perfectly was like what some people call centering and others call being "Zen." Filling the wood box by the stove and piling wood outside the door was satisfying work.

So too was gardening, although this was one of our shortest jobs because of the seasons. We never grew what was produced commercially in the Valley—potatoes, carrots, onions, lettuce. We could glean or buy these cheaply when we worked out. I remember one person lavished much time on a tomato bed, well-protected with bales of hay, however, and we were repaid with the best tomatoes I have ever eaten. Men and women shared this work without too much problem as I remember.

Fixing machinery was another matter. Here some of the men had brought expertise and women had none. The problem was not so much that the men refused to share their skills but that they did not know how. There seemed to be a real gender difference in how one taught and learned. Women wanted a lot of encouragement, hands on, and the freedom to do an inadequate job. Men did not know how to encourage, intervened constantly, and expected high quality work. Sometimes this problem spilled over into building and farming skills, such as plowing, as well. The women had never done many things and hungered to learn by doing. The men wanted to perfect their skills. Anger, resentment, discussion, community meetings usually followed. We seldom felt good about this process, but gradually the women learned and the men became more supportive teachers. This was one of our greatest difficulties—transferring technological skills. Both learning and teaching traditions seemed to cause the difficulty here. Eventually, we divided up some of these tasks as well. I took mechanics and began to learn from J. This was an all year job, and since our trucks and cars were old, they broke down constantly. Summertime repairs were pleasant, but I remember lying on the frozen ground on my back one February replacing a kingpin in a truck and wondering why this seemed so important for me to learn. I could not remember.

Difficult as it was to change the gender division of labor at home where we all wanted to, it seemed almost impossible when we did wage work on other valley farms. Most outdoor wage work was done by men. Women may have done the same work on their own farms but seldom for other farms. Women were most likely to do more work on the farm while the men worked out. If a woman worked full time, it was usually as teacher, nurse, waitress, or clerk in the nearby town. Women's jobs were hard to get. There was a shortage of male labor for the outdoor jobs, however, because the wages were low. Lettuce workers were unionized at the time we were in the valley, and we avoided competing with the Hispanic people for the limited jobs in the lettuce fields. Potato harvesting was not unionized, however, and available close by, as was irrigation and other types of work, such as disking. Irrigating and plowing were usually done by men, although we were sometimes able to hire on as a crew and alternate irrigation jobs. The potato harvest was more complex.

The gender division of labor then current in the potato harvest (and the cellars where potatoes were processed) was this: men employed year-round usually drove the harvester, temporary male help drove the truck under the boom, men and women sorted on the harvester, women drove trucks from the cellar to the field empty and then back to the cellar full. There was a fifty cents an hour differential for driving under the boom, the rest of the temporary workers made the same wages. I later read a farm journal article that encouraged farmers to hire women for driving to and from the fields because they were "gentler" with the huge trucks. The article also mentioned the shortage of male labor at the wages generally paid. The women who drove in the valley were skilled drivers and eager to get the jobs. I liked truck driving because of the sense of power it gave me. Our main complaint was that the owners did not maintain the trucks. Women constantly complained about poor brakes and lights. Once working after dark we convoyed the trucks without adequate lights between us. Another night, we refused to take the trucks out after dark even though the owner wanted us to. We simply stopped work; he did not insist.

My most memorable encounter with the potato harvest system occurred one morning when we showed up as a crew to work a potato field. One of our men had hired us out as a group. "I can have five people here tomorrow morning," he said and the grateful owner said fine. The problem was that two of the "people" were women; the grower had expected all men. After accusing A. of promising five men, the grower reluctantly agreed to let me drive under the boom. I was an experienced driver by this time and was confident that I could do well. It simply involved watching the boom so that the potatoes distributed themselves evenly in the truck rather than on the ground or in one heap, then getting out and into the empty truck that a woman had driven out into the field when she judged the other truck to be full. She then drove out of the field with the loaded truck and I filled the empty truck. Not very challenging work (actually driving to the cellar was more fun), but it took constant attention and paid better than the other driving job. I thought I was doing quite well when I noticed a young man running alongside the truck motioning me to stop. I did so. "The boss says I should drive," he yelled, "you drive to the cellar." Feeling the power of my new skills, I protested and refused to get out. The boss came over. I asked him if I was not doing the work well. He said I was doing well, but I was a woman and he wanted a man doing that work. But why? I protested. The argument continued after I finally relinquished the truck to my replacement, and the harvester and truck moved in tandem slowly down the rows. I stood in the harvested field arguing with the boss. "God did not mean for women to drive trucks," he finally said. The harvester often broke down and the driver usually had to crawl under to help fix the machine, and God did not want women crawling under his machines. "Where in the Bible does it say women should not be drivers or mechanics?" I insisted. When I reached the end of the row where the women waited in their trucks, they clustered around me wanting to know what happened. They were very upset.

They had been pleased to have me driving. Furthermore, they volunteered to debate the boss on what the Bible said about women. Chapter and verse. Some women were quite skilled at biblical exegesis, although I had to admit to general rather than specific knowledge of the Bible. I was quite confident it said nothing about women mechanics and drivers. Not knowing how a born-again feminist should handle this situation, I decided to complain loudly.

At the potato cellar where we waited for our loads to be weighed (women did this too) and emptied, I continued to complain. "Well," said one of the older women, "I remember before he got religion *and* money, he didn't mind having women down on the ground under the harvester helping fix it. I remember one fall years ago, I was down on my back in the snow. Didn't seem to bother him then." Vindication helped. We did no more than share a righteous anger. I felt a sense of female solidarity. They had shared my indignation, proved him a hypocrite, and showed their personal disdain. We all needed our jobs and could not do more.

That experience probably had something to do with my decision to go to diesel mechanic school. There was a federal training program at the local college. People could compete by taking a test, and the four highest scorers were to be given tuition and a stipend to attend. I expected the test would be gender neutral—it tested only general knowledge and motor skills. With a college education and a quick hand, I expected to do well. I realized that here too I would be competing with locals who needed the training. But I did too. As diesel mechanic, I thought, there was so much demand that the male farmers would have to ignore the customs and hire me. I planned to be the "best damned mechanic" in the valley and to grow old, acquiring a reputation somewhat like the legendary country doctor. I would be the savior, getting there in the nick of time to save the harvest by fixing the trucks and harvesters. I could imagine the farmers saying, "She's a woman but the 'best damned mechanic' around." At last I would be appreciated for my skills.

I passed the exam as one of the top four. But they did not rank us, and the final decision was up to the officer who administered the grant. Three slots suddenly disappeared, and the fourth went to a man, how deserving or able I had no way of knowing. I could still enroll tuition free, the official assured me, but there would be no stipend. Without the stipend, I could not get the support of my own community. We had mastered the gender division of labor at home only to fail at translating our new power structure into political philosophy. The old anarchist-communist split was emerging and a mini-cultural revolution was going on at home. Release time to get training as a mechanic was considered by some to be a form of elitism that would give me a skill that the others did not share. I seemed to be showing signs of intellectualism that were cutting me off from the masses. I must share the work of the others.

They were probably right. After the decision had been made, I lost a lot of my energy. The personal dynamics at home were degenerating. How can five people split into groups based on differing political philosophies? By three to two, that is how. Two felt very lonely on our isolated farm; I am sure three did too. And so I ended my first attempt at farming and dealing with the rural gender division of labor. I did not want to leave the farm. But I had accumulated and took with me back to the city such physical and emotional strength that now, fifteen years later, I am still drawing on that reserve.

2 "Tillie": German Farm Woman

TILLIE. I NEVER CALLED HER THAT, OF COURSE. OR
even her given name Matilda. Children always referred to her by her
more formal kin term, Grandma Schopp. Grandma Schopp lived in
our family during my teenage years. She came to us in 1947, after we
had returned to California from a brief stay in New Mexico and I was
thirteen. She left in 1956, after my mother was diagnosed as having
incurable cancer. I had moved away to college two years earlier.[1]

Many years passed before I realized that a decade of living with
my grandmother changed my life. And years more passed before I
was curious enough about her life to use my professional skills as a
historian to reconstruct that life. I have tried to write here as honestly
about Tillie's life as I can—first of what I learned from others and
from the historical records, then of my own memories. By knowing
her hardships and her great survival skills we can perhaps understand
her legacy to us. Tillie always remained religious, frequently reading from her German Bible, and attending church each Sunday.
She saw to it that each child received religious instruction, First
Holy Communion, and confirmation. Her life was hard but she
survived. She was humble about her physical and moral stamina. She
never boasted. "Self-praise stinks," was a German saying her children
learned and remembered. Tillie was a strong woman who survived

the settling of the frontier through endurance, self-sufficiency, and tenacity. The land upon which Tillie farmed and survived is no longer in our family, but we have the story of her life to pass on to the generations ahead.

Neither Mother nor Grandma shared their past with me or their feelings about it. They did not keep diaries, Grandma wrote few letters, and her daughters did not write much about their early farm days. But there are still memories that Grandma's other children are willing to share and documents that tell the outline of Tillie's early life. This is as much as I have been able to learn so far.

Matilda Rauscher was born in 1870 in the village of Christian-berg in Bohemia, then a part of the Austro-Hungarian Empire. The village is now called Křišťanov and is in Czechoslovakia. She was one of seven children of Peter Rauscher and Cresencia Misbauer. We know very little about Tillie's first years in Austria except that in 1884 at the age of fourteen, as required by law, she obtained a work permit before taking her first job. The permit, which I still have, states that Matilda Rauscher completed her work well.[2]

Four of the children and the father were to emigrate to the United States. Cresentia died in Austria in 1891; the two twin daughters died in infancy, and a third daughter Aloisie also died there. Theresa arrived in 1890, Matilda and brother Ignatz in 1892, brother Frank sometime between 1890 and 1896, and father Peter in 1896. We know little about Frank except that he fought in the Spanish-American war, never married, settled in San Francisco, and died there in December 1938. The other Rauschers all settled in Marathon County, Wisconsin.

Theresa was the first to emigrate. She had married Joseph Kuss in 1890, probably before leaving Austria, and they settled on a farm near Dorchester. Ignatz married Kamila Youngworth in 1882 in Austria, and they brought their ten year old son Edward with them to the United States. Tillie, Ignatz, Kamila, and Edward probably first traveled north to Hamburg, the port from which most German emigrants left, through Ellis Island in New York, and then by train to Dorchester, Wisconsin. Tillie, then twenty-two years old, went to work immediately in a boarding house for lumberjacks in Phillips, forty-seven miles north of Dorchester. The first picture we have of Tillie is a group picture with the other young women who worked at the boarding house, all looking carefully dressed.

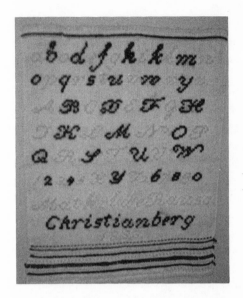

One of the few possessions that Matilda brought with her from Christianberg, Bohemia in 1891. The town is now part of Czechoslovakia. Source: Family photograph.

Tillie did not work there long. On September 10, 1893, she married Karl Schopper, a thirty-year-old immigrant from Austria. She moved with him to a log house that he had built with his brother and father on forty acres near Dorchester. Bridal pregnancy was an old German tradition that Matilda carried on in the New World. Mary, her first daughter was born on March 13, 1894, six months after her marriage.

The Schopper family had only been in the United States a few years more than the Rauschers. Karl's parents and his younger brother Frank came to Milwaukee from Schwartzenburg in Upper Austria in 1883. Karl followed in 1887, as soon as he completed military service, and the brothers bought two forty-acre parcels for farms. They built the first log house in 1887 and the second in 1893 when Tillie and Karl married. The land was part of a "cut over" area owned by the railroads, cleared of timber, then sold for low prices to immigrants. The land was still covered with stumps and debris from the lumbering operations. The first task, after hauling logs to construct small log houses, was to clear the land of stumps, a difficult task even for skilled lumber workers. The forty-acre plots of the two brothers were separated by another eighty-acre plot, but that was only a distance of one-quarter mile. Theresa Rauscher and Joseph Kuss had forty acres another one-half mile north, and Ignatz Rauscher and Kamila Youngworth had eighty acres three-quarters of a mile north. Most of the neighbors were German-speaking and had emigrated recently from the German or Austro-Hungarian empires. The Jantsches, Tanzers, Dreschers, Kuenzels, and Gridels, together with other families formed a community based on the German language, the Catholic religion, and similar folkways. Most came from small villages where the economies had been disrupted by increasing industrialization that offered few jobs and displaced many from their farmlands.

These families came to one of the last Midwestern frontiers. Within a few decades trappers had hunted out most of the fur-bearing animals. The Winnebago and Menominee Indians had then ceded their lands to an impatient American government and moved north. Railroads were laid out to the edge of the dense forests, and lumber companies cleared wide swathes, first along the Wisconsin River and then farther West. Now only a few Indians remained, most of them married to a few last descendants of the French trappers. The early Yankee and Irish frontiersmen had moved on, and the Germans had moved in to clear the land and farm. Tillie and Karl were part of that first group of German settlers on Wisconsin's last frontier.

By 1900, when Tillie first shows up on the American census, she was well settled on the small farm. Her father Peter had joined them in the 18 × 24-foot log house, together with a son Francis Joseph, a second daughter Anna, and a third daughter Rose. The log house must already have been crowded with three adults and four young children. None of the children were yet in school, not even Mary who was six. The census-taker noted that Karl and Peter could speak English, but Tillie, after eight years in the United States, could still speak only German. They could all read and write German. The farm had no mortgage.

We know from family tradition that both Tillie and Karl, who later went by the name Charles, were hard workers and good farmers. Karl worked at the nearby Rietbrock Land & Lumber Company in the winter to bring in cash. In the summer Tillie helped in the fields and with the animals, as well as preserving food, organizing the small household, caring for the children and for her father who was now seventy-seven.

Despite the hard work, these were probably the happiest times in Tillie's life. She loved her husband, they were building a farm and family together, she was robust despite her four pregnancies, and was expecting a fifth child, Bertha, who was born in December 1900. There was plenty of nourishing food for her children—potatoes, cabbage that she made into sauerkraut, pork that she fried and packed in crocks, then covered with lard to preserve, milk, butter, cheese, and summer vegetables from the garden. Both young parents liked working with animals. Five miles away in Dorchester, there was a Catholic mission church, where a priest came on weekends to say mass, and a general store that carried the items needed for the household. German peddlermen stopped by the farm with their wares. Tillie had a sister nearby from whom she could receive support, a mother-in-law not far away, and a good neighbor just across the road, Maria Mueller Jantsch. At forty-three, Maria had already birthed nine healthy children, the youngest just three years before. Like Tillie, Maria and the children ran the farm while her husband worked out in the winter. Johann was a carpenter and was able to make more than the men who lumbered in the winter. He and Maria had been farming longer so their farm was built up a bit more, but Maria was not much wealthier than Tillie. The older Jantsch daughters did housework in nearby Chippewa Falls during the winter, then returned to help with the haying and raking in the summer. Maria was a midwife and helped Tillie birth her first children.[3]

On Friday, August 1, 1901, around four o'clock as the local newspaper later noted, Karl was leading a mare and her colt through the yard. Karl loved horses and that day, feeling playful, he grabbed the two back legs of the colt. Startled, the young colt kicked Karl in the stomach. In great pain, Karl staggered to the house where Tillie put him to bed and cared for him. The next morning he died.

The swift kick by the colt had left Tillie a widow at thirty-two, with five young children, the oldest eight years, the youngest eight months old. That must have been a difficult harvest. Sometime that fall Tillie met Leo Schopp. He was a thirty-two-year-old Bavarian immigrant who had come to the United States with three half-brothers in 1893. Leo's mother was Anna Ziegersperger, and he listed his father as George Schopp. The family never knew the name of his real father, however. He had refused to marry his mother because she was too low-born. On their marriage certificate, Leo listed his occupation as a farmer in nearby Athens. Tillie and Leo probably met through Tillie's twenty-year-old nephew, Ed Rauscher, who was a cook at the same lumbercamp where Leo worked in winter. Ed apparently brought Leo over to meet his widowed aunt, perhaps in the fall harvest when Tillie needed help. Leo returned to visit that winter and by January Tillie was pregnant. Tillie and Leo were married in Dorchester by the same priest who had buried Charles eight months earlier, on April 1, 1902, with Ed Rauscher and Olga Kulas as witnesses. During the next eight years Tillie bore three more children, Theresa in 1902, Edward in 1904, and Emma in 1908.

Those eight years were the most difficult Tillie ever knew. Her father died two weeks after her marriage. Her brother-in-law died soon after, and her sister Theresa remarried in 1904 and moved to a farm sixteen miles away in Medford. Brother Ignatz died in 1906, leaving his widow with a mortgaged farm. Leo did not turn out to be a good partner. He did not like farm work, and he brought little money home from the woods after a winter of work. He liked to sit on the porch of the log house, to play his accordion, and entertain the children. Tillie and her son Frank worked the farm. When the census taker visited the Schopp farm in 1910, he listed Frank, then fourteen as "farm laborer" on the home farm. Fifteen-year-old Mary had already left home to work elsewhere. The other five children were in school, but sometimes they had little to take to school in their lunch pails. According to one daughter, at times Tillie was afraid they might starve. Her sister Theresa sometimes brought food from her Medford farm. Maria Jantsch loaned her money against the milk check that their six dairy cows brought in each month. They sold eggs in town.

Hardship had soured this marriage of convenience. When Leo returned each spring there were alternate bouts of fighting and sullen silence. Once Maria Jantsch asked the priest to come out to counsel the feuding couple, but his visit seemed to do little good. Edward left to work off the farm in 1918, when he was only thirteen. One by one the daughters left the farm to look for work in the city. Rose and Betty left for Milwaukee, Anna and Theresa went to St. Paul. Emma, the youngest, left for New York in 1927.

Times were better between 1919 and 1927. Some of the daughters sent money back from the city and brought things for the house—a table, a chest, a clock. Prohibition brought a chance to supplement the farm income with a little rural bootlegging. A brass

In 1910, children and friends of Matilda Rauscher Schopp gathered in front of their log home for this picture. Matilda's second husband, Leo Schopp, is at the far right. My mother, Theresa Schopp, is fourth from the right. Matilda could not afford to buy shoes for the children in the summer so Theresa treasured the cap bought for her by Leo. Source: Family photograph.

cooker ordered from the catalog provided the necessary equipment, and Frank delivered liquor to customers in nearby villages. In 1919 the family mortgaged the farm to build a new frame house and moved to it from the old log cabin. In 1923 Frank took over the operation of the farm, and four years later he married Lucille Wagner. Tillie stayed on the farm off and on for another twenty years, helping Frank farm while he and Lucille raised their four daughters.

During these years, Tillie began her migratory life style. She stayed with her sister Theresa in Medford and with her niece Katherine Liberty. Then in 1947 she joined us in California. She stayed with her daughter Betty in Milwaukee from 1956 until her death in 1958.

Teenage granddaughters are likely to remember grandmothers

with whom they live in a very special way. I remember Grandmother Schopp as a quiet woman who did not want people to make a fuss over her. I suppose our home was selected as the place for her to live because we were a relatively stable family, though we did have a tendency to move around. I remember Grandma Schopp in at least four houses over those years. My mother and father got along relatively well together, my mother did not work outside the home, and both my parents treated Grandma Schopp well. At least I do not ever remember her being treated badly, and I do remember mother and dad fussing over her. That is how I know that she did not want to be fussed over.

Food was one thing my parents fussed about because Grandma Schopp had no teeth. She could not eat what we did. We cut up food or put it through the blender. And I remember my father coaxing her to eat an avocado. No, she said stubbornly, she did not want to try that strange green fruit. But when at last she had consented, she grinned toothlessly and said, "Soft, just like butter." Thereafter, avocados were a special treat, and there was always this sense of pleasure that we had found something new that Grandma truly liked to eat.

The problem for us was that in a Southern California world where we, like everyone else, seemed to be scrambling for something better—a larger house, a newer car, clothes—Grandma Schopp always seemed satisfied with what she had. Ours was not an affluent family by Southern California standards, but my mother, father, and I were fairly greedy accumulators. I did not always get what I wanted, but I always knew what I wanted. Even with food. Father was traditional enough and his Italian immigrant family had been poor enough that we always had to eat what was put on our plates. But if we did not like some food, it was not put on our plates. I let it be known that I did not like beets and never had to eat them. I was encouraged constantly to choose what I did and did not like— especially in clothes. My father seemed to make most of the decisions for the entire family, except those peaceful three years when he was overseas in World War II. But I always had an opinion about the smaller decisions in life and often tried new things. We urged Grandma Schopp to do the same but she usually refused. "I ain't so baticular," she often replied stubbornly, refusing to make a decision and forcing us to decide for her.

Grandma Schopp did not want or need fancy clothes. My mother, on the other hand, craved them so much growing up as a poor farm girl, that she taught me to want them also as a teenager. My mother occasionally got Grandma Schopp to exercise a mild veto over fabric selected for her. Grandma preferred a dark flower print for Sunday and plaid for weekdays but always insisted on the same style. Each of her dresses had long sleeves, an inset waistband, a high neck, and a round collar. If mother was lucky, she might get Grandma to select two fabrics at once, to be put away in her trunk until needed, and a seamstress could be found to fashion the simple dresses for Grandma who was by then quite short and stocky.

That trunk seemed to be Grandma's one major possession. On a few occasions, I got to see its contents. I was impressed with its abundance. There were always extra pairs of the beige cotton stockings that Grandma insisted on wearing and several new aprons that the last dressmaker had made up. There were dishtowels and some linens and extra elastic garters, the kind that looked like bracelets and fastened the rolled stockings right up under the knee. I wish now I had an inventory of each item in that trunk. My reaction I do remember. The trunk symbolized contradictory things for me. It conveyed a sense of plenty that I did not have because I had to go to the store to buy each item I wanted. At the same time, I knew Grandma kept these things because she had learned she might not be able to get what she needed because of the insecurity of her life. I often buy two of some articles of clothing, and I wonder if that feeling of satisfaction is not the same I felt when I saw her stockpile of identical clothes, differing in color but not in style.

Grandma's utilitarian sense of propriety extended to her hair. She always wore it pulled back in a knot at the nape of her neck. I have seen her wedding picture. There her dark hair was pulled back but it framed her face attractively and she had curly bangs. By the time she lived with us, however, she always pulled it back tightly. My mother never thought her hair stylish enough and often coaxed Grandma to let her fix it. Before holidays, such as Christmas and Easter, Grandma would usually consent to have her hair washed and set, and on Sunday morning mother arranged a pretty halo of soft fluffy white hair in a chignon high on her head. Even Grandma agreed that it looked "swell." The halo of white hair was still visible around her head after she had clamped her black hat down firmly and jabbed it with a big shiny hat pin. We could never get Grandma to change her hat styles either, although we once convinced her to get a new summer straw. I think we may even have succeeded in decorating it with a discreet flower. I know we never encroached on her headgear prerogatives very far. By Easter Monday or the day after Christmas, her hair was firmly pulled back in place at the nape of her neck.

There was a quiet dignity in her determination to keep her life simple and close to what it had been during all those hard years on the farm. She would accept a small surplus for the sake of security, and an occasional deviation to please us and stop our pestering, but she had owned very few possessions in her life and she seemed to wish little more now. Her poverty had not left her with the need to accumulate but to keep her life simple and adequate, always insisting "I ain't so baticular."

Grandma never taught me any particular household skills. She did not know how to sew clothing although she darned socks with a beautiful straight weave. I do not remember her cooking though she supervised my mother's occasional celebratory holiday *kuchen*. She did not crochet those fancy chair doilies with the pineapple designs that my Italian grandmother turned out endlessly. When asked to produce a pair of stockings, however, she could do so in a day. Her thin metal needles flashed along, and I marveled that she never needed directions. To this day I enjoy knitting but have never mastered the intricacies of crochet. Grandma never took me aside like some grandmas do their granddaughters to instruct me on how to live my life in accordance with her ideals. But I wonder now at the number of attitudes I share with her. There is a sense in which I too am "not so baticular," a sense of comfort with what I am given, and a reluctance to have too much complexity in my life.

Most of Grandma's conversation with my mother was in German. They spoke "Plattedeutsche" not "Hochdeutsche," my mother explained to me one day when their mention of the term somehow caught my attention. My mother replied it was the language of the common people, not so fancy. Later, when I asked a German teacher, she explained rather that Low German was spoken in one region of Germany, High German in another. It had nothing to do with class or status. My grandmother was convinced it labeled her as coming from a lower social class, however, an indication that she had suffered discrimination for it. I thought she did not feel proud of her language.

Nonetheless, she always spoke German to her children, and she never learned English well. One Sunday, our family drove south across the border into Mexico, something we did often. This time we decided to take Grandma along for a ride, and she consented. We had a new Chrysler with a plush back seat and she did like to ride. As we approached the border to return, my father suddenly realized that we had not brought any identification papers for Grandma proving her resident status. Grandma had never become a citizen. Neither of her two husbands became citizens before 1922, when she would automatically have become a citizen by being married to one. After that time, she never learned enough English to pass the examination on her own. I remember my father saw to it that she registered as an alien when the law required, but we never thought much about Grandma not being a citizen, even though she had lived in the country over fifty years.

Crossing the border necessitated only identifying oneself as a United States citizen and my father quickly instructed Grandma to do so and if asked where she was born to say Medford, Wisconsin. We chirped our citizenship answers to the immigration official. When he got to Grandma and she identified herself in broken English, the immigration official looked skeptical and began to ask her more questions. She lapsed into guilty silence and the official turned to my father for an explanation of his attempt to bring this alien into the country illegally. My father then nervously identified himself further as a naturalized citizen but also as a retired Air Force colonel, and after a stern reprimand, the official allowed us to take Grandma back across the border. Grandma would never cross the border again, and we did not encourage her.

Grandma's inability to speak English and my mother's determination never to teach German kept me from learning about our family past. I never asked. Grandma never offered. Nor did my mother offer to tell me about that history. Mother said little at any time. We knew they had been poor because my mother's feet were crippled and when asked why, she would always explain that she had to wear whatever size shoes were brought home from town. My mother had a horror of my appearing at the front door of our comfortably middle-class home barefooted because, she said, someone might think I had no shoes. Mother never mentioned her father—my grandfather—and I grew up never noticing his absence. The only time I saw my mother cry was in 1947 when she received a letter telling of his death. Mother once mentioned that his mother was unwed, a condition she seemed to attribute to his father being well above his mother in the German social scale. Mother liked the story of the "Princess and the Pea," where the Princess is discovered because she becomes bruised even after sleeping on a stack of feather-beds with a pea placed underneath. Mother hinted that her own nobility would also always be evident to others. But she never talked about family history. In fact, mother seldom told us how she felt about anything. She must not have told my father much about her feelings either. One day, a few weeks after she died, I found him looking deeply depressed. He had spent the entire day looking for a letter from mother. "You know she did not talk much about how she felt," he said, "and I was sure she must have left a letter, but I could not find it."

This is that letter, written to be passed down in our family so that something of the experiences of our immigrant family may be known. Tillie was our founding mother in a real sense. Despite her diffidence and reluctance to praise herself, she left with us a strong heritage that has grounded us deeply in this new land.

3 Rozalija: Lithuanian Farm Woman

ROZALIJA GUSTINIS ARRIVED IN UPSTATE NEW YORK
in 1949, after five years in a displaced persons camp in Western
Germany. She was born in 1910 in northern Lithuania into a peasant
household, later married the landowner for whom she worked, then
fled with him from the danger of reprisals from Communist officials
whom her husband had criticized as corrupt. On her Lithuanian
farm, Rozalija had supervised a subsistence household that manufactured almost all the items used—including shoes and textiles; Rozalija herself was an accomplished weaver of linen.

As an immigrant woman, Rozalija became part of the American
working class, using her weaving skills to repair oriental carpets for a
large carpet and furniture store in Rochester, New York. She raised
her two sons in a black and immigrant neighborhood and saw them
through college before she died in 1985.

This biography is based on a series of oral histories conducted by
the author and Rozalija's son over a period of several years with
Rozalija and her husband Voldemar. They were conducted primarily
in Lithuanian and translated into English. In the interviews Rozalija
describes growing up in a peasant household, developing skills in
household manufacturing and processing, going out to work on the
neighboring farm, becoming the landlord's wife, leaving Lithuania,
and adapting to the American way of life.

Rozalija was acutely conscious of the differences between her life in Lithuania and the United States. She lived her early life on a subsistence and small commodity production farm of a type that was common before the early nineteenth century in Europe and the United States. Then she made the transition to a working class, ethnic community in an industrial society. In Lithuania she had worked hard, but there were dances, celebrations, and a community of workers whose culture she shared and enjoyed. In the United States, she worked less hard, made what she considered a good cash income, and received a pension and social security benefits when she retired. Here it was financially and physically easier; there it had been a better life culturally. This chapter shows how oral history with women, such as Rozalija, can illustrate the lives of large numbers of women who at one time lived and worked on farms similar to that of Rozalija, those women whom we can no longer ask about how they lived and what they did to manage their farm household.

In January 1931 Rozalija arrived at the Gustinis farm in Valakai, Lithuania. She came, probably by sleigh, from the nearby village of Šakyna where she had worked the previous year. Although Rozalija was only twenty years old when she arrived in Valakai, she had already worked as a farm servant for eleven years. She was an experienced and skilled worker.[1]

The farm stood back from the road, at the end of a long drive bordered by two rows of linden trees. The trees were bare now, black tracery above the snow covered fields. Beyond the trees stood the farm buildings all of wood except a large barn that had thick clay walls and a stone and cement foundation. To the right was a 60-by-30-foot granary and beyond that an apple and pear orchard and a huge 120-by-40-foot barn for storing oats, rye, and barley. Farther on the right was another building for the pigs and for farm wagons. Across the main path was the large barn, 180-by-35-feet, where there were cows and horses and storage for beets and for hay. Beside it stood a coop for chickens. South of the farm yard was a small blacksmith shop and a wood pile, and in the center of the yard was a well with a well sweep. Beyond the yard, in the distance, were woods.

In the center of the farm yard, stood a large wooden farm house, 35-by-70-feet. The farm house had a large entrance hall on the north and a porch, but almost no one entered there. Instead Rozalija entered on the west, like everyone else, into an entryway that opened to the kitchen and the rooms of the servants—one for the two men,

Map of Lithuania with location of farm and nearby towns.

and one that she would be sharing with the other woman servant. Between the two rooms was a large fireplace. There was a baking oven and a large storage room. These were the working spaces of the farm house where Rozalija would spend many hours when she was not working in the farm yard, the barns, or fields. Beyond the working areas were rooms for the family, a separate room for each parent and one for their only son Voldemar, now twenty-eight and sharing the running of the farm with his fifty-seven-year-old father Peteris.

The Gustinis Farm was larger than any in the neighborhood, 55 hectares (about 137 acres). All of the other farms in the village of Valakai were small by comparison, usually no more than 6 hectares (about 15 acres). Of the fifteen to twenty farms in the village, the Gustinis farm was clearly the most impressive one. It seemed like a model farm with all the substantial buildings and the huge farm house dominating the farm yard. The Gustinis family had a reputation for managing their farm carefully and for paying their workers well. Rozalija was glad to be coming to work for them. She was a good worker and wanted to work for someone who appreciated her abilities.

Rozalija came from the Bernotas family. As a young unmarried woman, Rozalija went by the name Bernotaitė because the Lithuanian language changed surnames depending on the sex and marital status. The Bernotas family had no land but they had a reputation for being good workers. Everyone wanted them. When the Gustinis family heard in December that Rozalija was not pleased with the working conditions on the farm where she was working, Peteris Gustinis immediately went to Šakyna to meet her and to ask her to work on their farm. Everyone said she was a good worker.

Two generations back the Gustinis family had been as poor as the Bernotas family. Janis Gustinis was a serf in Latvia in 1863 when the Czar decreed that the serfs should get land. Janis was a good worker and already managed one of the estates. He received a small homestead when the estate was divided. Janis had many children, five sons and four daughters, but they all worked and pooled their earnings to buy land for the sons. In 1900, when Peteris had saved five hundred roubles, he asked his sister and her husband to buy a farm with him, twenty kilometers south of the Latvian border in Lithuania. After a few years, Peteris bought out his sister and brother-in-law and became sole owner of the land. Gradually, he purchased more land. The farm prospered. In 1910 Peteris put in an orchard, and after the barn burned that year he put up a new one. In 1927 he added a second large barn.

By the time Rozalija arrived in 1931, Voldemar, the only child of Peteris and his wife Mile, was working the land with his parents. Voldemar grew up speaking Latvian, the language of his parents, but at eight he learned Lithuanian. The Russians controlled Lithuania at this time, and Voldemar's first school was a Russian-language grade school with a teacher so mean that he kicked and hit the students. When World War I started and the teacher was drafted, the school closed, but in 1919 Voldemar was able to attend a two week agricultural course in Šiauliai, thirty-five kilometers from the farm. Later he attended a four-year agricultural college, specialized in animal husbandry, and after graduating in 1924 concentrated on improving the farm. Voldemar developed a herd of thirty dairy cows and was active in the cooperative dairy, two kilometers away in Šakyna. Selling milk provided the main cash income for the family, but they also sold grain and pigs.

The Gustinis farm had been one of the first in the area to introduce agricultural machinery. In 1914 the family purchased a McCormick reaper, which reduced and speeded the work of the men in cutting grain. The reaper did little to lessen the work of women who continued to tie the bundles of grain, but it did leave the grain in tidier piles for them to bundle. Other machines followed in the 1920s: a hay cutter, a seeding machine, a potato digging machine. The establishment of creameries in 1925 significantly changed the labor of women because the cooperative creamery took the whole milk for buttermaking. Women still milked cows but discontinued making butter. Then Peteris took the whole milk to the creamery in Šakyna and picked up skim milk to feed to the animals.

Because the Gustinis farm was so large and so oriented to the market, Rozalija did not have to perform some tasks that Lithuanian women had done traditionally. At the Gustinis farm, Rozalija would not have to make butter. She was used to this task but was relieved to know that the Gustinises got their butter from the cooperative creamery. Rozalija remembered buttermaking from the old days when the women just skimmed cream from the milk with a spoon. Later they had a glass container with a spiggot to let out the skim milk at the bottom. In 1910, about the time Rozalija was born, a few people began to buy cream separators. The first people to buy the separators, Rozalija remembered, let their neighbors bring their milk to separate. "Did they pay?" I asked. "No," she replied, "some people work for pleasure. Somehow, there was more friendliness." The women then churned the cream in simple wooden dasher churns, with a stick and cross sticks as a dasher. Her parents then took the butter to the market to sell along with poultry, eggs, pigs, and baskets that her father made. The market sold everything, and her family sold as much as they could. Her father's fodder and potato baskets were much in demand, and Rozalija remembered people patched and made them last as long as possible before returning to buy new ones.

At the Gustinis farm Rozalija also had to do less weaving and processing of textiles. The Gustinis family purchased some cloth from the local mills and wool cloth from England for suits for the men. Tailors did this task, not frequently to be sure, for the men still expected to wear the same suit for most of their adult lives. Servant women had one dress for good and simple blouses and skirts for farm work. Women prepared flax and spun and wove linen for shirts, blouses, and underwear. Women spun wool for stockings and mittens. Most of the time they still wore *naginès,* mocassin-like footwear made from hides of farm animals, fashioned to fit each foot by simply folding the leather around the bottom of the foot and lacing it on top. They had shoes but wore them only to church and for special occasions.

Of the outside tasks, animals remained the major daily responsibility for Rozalija. Women took care of all of the animals except the horses. "Women don't work with horses, usually," Rozalija explained. Women fed the pigs and chickens. They also fed and milked the cows twice a day. This was a year-round task and on Sundays when the women took turns milking, the task was particularly hard. "Men were more free than women on Sunday," Rozalija said.

The major year-round indoor tasks were processing and cooking food, washing and cleaning, and making large quantities of bread. Rozalija remembered making bread the most vividly. She learned to make bread at ten for her family because her mother had to work out. Rye bread was the staple bread, but they made all kinds, usually every two weeks. The dough was mixed in a large three-foot diameter barrel, one and one-half feet deep. Rozalija said she mixed it like pancakes, just flour and water, then left it overnight. The next morning she began the hard work of kneading. The more kneading, the better the bread. The women usually baked six loaves at a time, each over five pounds. The women loaded the six-foot-long baking oven with wood that they burned, then cleaned the oven with a birch switch and moved the coals to the front with a shovel-like tool. The loaves came out crusty with a slight ash flavor. They stored the loaves in a side room and brought them out as needed over the next two weeks.

Of women's winter tasks, textile production was the most important. Families usually had three or four spinning wheels, one for each woman in the family and a loom. January and February the women spent spinning, both linen and wool. Then in March they wove and made linen and wool cloth.

Weaving was done in two ways. For weaving with a pattern, both white and gray linen yarn was prepared and then complex patterns woven on overhead looms. For plain linen cloth, the women wove the cloth from dark yarn, then boiled the cloth with ashes and spread it on the grass to bleach. Women sewed linen clothes by hand—blouses, sheets, pillow cases—and itinerant tailors came to the farms to make the men's woolen pants and coats. Before World War I some people began to buy Singer sewing machines with hand cranks. That made work for some women a lot easier, although they still knit stockings and mittens and did a great deal of hand sewing and mending.

Most of the women's outdoor tasks were also seasonal. Once a year, usually in spring, the men cleaned the barns and dumped the manure on the fields. Then the women spread it with small forks. It was not a hard task for young, healthy women and could be arranged when the weather was not too unpleasant. In spring women sheared sheep. They caught the sheep and tied them up, put a foot on the neck, and with large shears started cutting at the neck. The sheep were of different breeds, but most were grey. The women left most of the processing of wool for evenings and for winter when they prepared it for spinning and spun and wove it.

In the summer women were busy with the harvest. During haying women usually worked atop the wagons, stamping the hay down and loading the hay into the barns. After haying it was time to cut the rye. When the men cut the rye with scythes, they could work much faster than the women who had no tools. "Fast, fast, some of the women could not keep up," Rozalija remembered. With a reaper the women had an even more difficult time keeping up and some of the men usually helped them with the tying.

During spring and summer women also took care of the gardens. Men prepared gardens and carried water at transplanting time. Women planted the beets, sowing in the seeds close together, then thinning the seedlings and planting them farther apart. Beets were always women's work and an important part of the Lithuanian diet. Women also took much of the responsibility for planting and harvesting potatoes, another mainstay.

In winter women prepared the flax. The women pulled the flax up by hand when the seeds were formed and stood it in piles to dry. They threshed out the seeds to use for oil and fed the leftovers to the cattle. Then they laid the stems outside for four weeks, spread thinly so the sun, rain, and wind could rot them. They rubbed the stems occasionally with their hands to test them. Too long and the linen would rot and weaken; too short and the stems would still be tough. Just in time, the tough stalk would separate easily from the flax strands within. Some women trampled the flax; on other farms they rented a big wheel to run over the stalks. Men went from farm to farm with the wheel.

Threshing was the major fall task, usually done in September and October. Rozalija never learned to thresh. By the time she began farm work in the 1920s, threshing machines were already in use. But she remembered that her mother would get up at 3 A.M. to go to thresh with flails and after putting in long hours in the dark threshing, would go to the fields to work during the day. The grain was usually dried in a special barn room before threshing, a room with a special stove and thick walls. Rozalija remembered that her father constructed these special stoves out of clay bricks that he made himself. He dug the clay, put water in it, mixed it with his feet, made a dough, and then put it in forms. When dried these bricks would form a hollow wall that conducted the heat from the fireplace to wherever heat was needed. Houses might also have these "warm walls."

Once threshed, the rye was stored and taken to the mill for grinding as needed. Farmers with large farms often paid the seasonal workers from neighboring farms in rye. Mills were close by, usually within a few kilometers, for ordinary coarse milling. In the 1930s the Gustinis family still took the rye to a wind powered mill as needed during the year.

In the fall of Rozalija's first year in Valakai, the Gustinis farm added one other seasonal task. In 1931 the Lithuanian Ministry of Agriculture began to subsidize an agricultural school for farm children at Valakai. Students, both boys and girls, could apply for admission. The school took 40 students each year and some years as many as 120 applied. For the first two years, the school took both young men and women, but applications came predominantly from young women because young men had other educational opportunities. For young women the agricultural school was an important way to get an education. By the third year the school was entirely female.

Each woman student at Valakai school had three parts to her education. The first part, taught by a male teacher, consisted of a general education in Lithuanian language, "farmer's writings and correspondence," and arithmetic. Voldemar taught the second part himself with another male teacher. This was agricultural training in dairying, beekeeping, supervision of domestic animals, poultry, horticulture and gardening, book-keeping for the farm household, and agricultural cooperative societies. In the third part, a woman trained in home economics taught specialized household tasks, such as cooking, baking, conserving, food storage, washing, needlework, weaving, and sewing. The teachers were recent graduates of the Agricultural College and earned money as they gained practical experience. The farm itself was the laboratory and training ground for the young women. Classes began in early November and lasted until early April, five months.

For the first few years Rozalija looked on while the school took place amid the slower farm activities in the winter. Finally, in 1934 Voldemar asked if she would like to attend the school. He had noticed what a good worker Rozalija was and how orderly she was. He thought she might help keep the kitchen organized for the teachers. Rozalija already knew most of the farm skills, but she would now be able to learn arithmetic. She later said she loved doing arithmetic in her head and could do it very fast. Upon completion of the school in spring 1935, she received Certificate 109, with a special seal signed by school master Voldemar Gustinis and the three other teachers certifying that she had completed the "Winter's Agricultural School for Girls at Valakai."

For a young peasant girl such a degree was a great accomplishment. Young women had difficulty in getting any kind of education. Lithuanian schools were free, but there was no rule that parents had to send their children. They also had to buy books and proper clothes (including shoes) to send their daughters to school. Mothers usually taught their children to read at six or seven years of age, frequently while they spun. If the children started school at seven they might learn how to write. But many people still argued that girls did not need school, they needed only to know how to cook and make clothes. A woman could come in to teach needlework in the home. Boys were different. They would go into the army. They had to know how to write letters home. Boys needed to go to school. Rozalija did learn how to write but not in school. Her brother went to school and then taught her.

Like Rozalija, young girls began working at home and by nine were working as servants on the farms of others. Their money always went back to the family as long as they remained single, which for women was usually until twenty and possibly until thirty. Although Rozalija earned money for fifteen years before she attended school, she did not keep that money. It went back to the family to help buy land for her older brother and to provide the dowry of her older sister. Being able to get an education was one of the few things that she had been able to obtain for herself. She was now one of a small group of young farm women who had specialized training in agriculture. Once Rozalija completed her training, she took charge of the kitchen.

The school seemed to be a great success, so much so that the government decided to establish its own schools and stop giving subsidies. The agricultural school for girls closed down in spring 1937. For Rozalija, who enjoyed the interaction with the students and teachers, the prospect of the routine farm work in the next winter must have seemed a bit dull.

During the two years of involvement in the school something else happened, however. Rozalija had spent a great deal of time with the young agronomist who was head master of the school as well as manager of the farm. By 1938 Rozalija and Voldemar Gustinis had decided to marry.

The marriage of Rozalija and Voldemar was not traditional in any sense. Rozalija and Voldemar had fallen in love and agreed together to marry. While couples occasionally chose their partners, it was still customary for the family and for matchmakers to be very involved. Matchmakers were generally people in the community who enjoyed socializing and who acted as informal marriage brokers. The matchmaker knew which families had eligible sons and daughters, how much the families planned to give to sons, how much to daughters as a dowry. The matchmakers, as Rozalija recalled later, always promised, "I bring the best." They negotiated for pigs, cows, wagons. The family had to know the matchmaker well, and the matchmaker had to know the families well. Sometimes, Rozalija laughingly recalled, the families would borrow animals and clothes to appear prosperous and had to be watched carefully. If all went well, however, the girl would put a silk scarf on the boy and the boy would give the girl a token of money, and they would be engaged. Girls were expected to remain celibate, at least until the engagement. To have a baby while unmarried was bad. But since marriage normally soon followed the engagement, bridal pregnancy was not a problem. To celebrate the marriage, families feasted for five days, three at the girl's home and two at the boy's.

Although Rozalija and Voldemar avoided the complicated marriage arrangements, they did make a visit to her widowed mother to ask if they could be married. Rozalija's mother lived only ten kilometers from the farm, but she had never met Voldemar. Rozalija did not want a dowry, nor did Voldemar. Instead he said he wanted to hire Rozalija forever. Rozalija's mother gave her permission, and the couple went to the local church to arrange the marriage. In Lithuania marriages could only be performed in a church.

At the local Catholic church the couple encountered difficulty. Rozalija's mother, as a widow, did not pay taxes to the church. Rozalija had not paid either because she had been away from the parish for eleven years and had not been an active church member. The churches were not close to the farm, and on Sunday morning Rozalija had to share milking chores. Voldemar was also reluctant to agree to raise the children Catholic. In addition, there was a jurisdictional squabble between the priest at Šakyna, the nearest church, and the priest at Rozalija's parent's parish. This was too much.

The young couple found that they could marry in the Lutheran church with less difficulty. After three weeks of announcing the bans, the Lutheran minister married them in a simple ceremony with her brother and sister-in-law as witnesses. Instead of an elaborate five day feast, as was the custom, the young couple had a dinner at a hotel, spent the night there, and returned to the farm on Monday morning.

Did marriage change her life? I asked Rozalija years later. "It changed my life lots," she responded, "I was more free." No longer did she have to milk cows and cook meals. She did just what she wanted. She might go to market with Voldemar if she chose or go with him when he went to town and stayed for a day or two. For Rozalija, the hard working farm servant, marriage with a farm owner provided the freedom to choose her work. She still worked in the fields and in the house, but she now had other women to help her and to take the responsibility for routine chores. When her first son Jonas was born, ten months after her marriage, she had hospital care, and after she returned to the farm a young girl took care of him. When

Rozalija and Voldemar at their marriage, 1938. Source: Family photograph.

Rozalija chose to work in the fields, she did not have to worry about her son. Voldemar's mother was an invalid and could not help, but there were many adults to share child care. Rozalija breast fed her first child for nine months, then weaned him but did not bear her second child, Algirdas, for another nineteen months. The first years of marriage and motherhood were the easiest time of her life.

Despite World War I and the depression, Rozalija and Voldemar had experienced relatively secure lives before 1941. Rozalija was only four when World War I began in Europe. Of that war, she remembered mainly the difficulty of getting things—kerosene for lamps, matches, needles, sugar, salt. Her father used to wait in line in the city

Rozalija, Voldemar, and son Jonas, 1942. Source: Family photograph.

for salt. The Germans did attempt to control grain and milling, but Rozalija remembered that her parents dug a space under the floor with a trap door, hidden by her father's carpentry tools. There they ground grain with a hand mill all night. With a little subterfuge her family experienced only a slight disruption of their lives. The German occupation lasted one year and was not too hard.

Voldemar remembered the war as more difficult, for battles occurred near the Gustinis farm. One side would occupy the area one day, the other the next. During battles the family loaded things in a wagon and went off into the forest. After the battle they came back, often to damaged buildings and fields but not to a looted house. The Germans in the First World War had a reputation for cruelty, but the Gustinis family did not suffer and they found that neither army looted their farmhouse. Battles not armies caused damage. One tragedy occurred as a by-product of the war. Voldemar's mother, Mile, took the wagon to market one day, and while there the Germans commandeered her wagon, loaded it with dead bodies, and ordered her to drive it. The horror of that experience left her broken. She spent more and more time in her room, seldom left it, and was an invalid by the time Rozalija arrived at the farm.

After World War I, during the 1920s and 1930s, the rural people had not suffered. Rozalija's father died in 1928, at eighty-three years old. He worked hard all his life but took great satisfaction in his many skills and continued to work until he died. Her mother also died before World War II, but her death came at the end of a long productive life. The depression that so devastated Germany and other parts of Europe had little effect on Lithuanians. Because Lithuania was primarily an agricultural land with relatively little market orientation, most Lithuanians did not suffer unemployment. They continued to produce their own food and clothing as they always had, and for some, like the Gustinises, the 1930s were a time of prosperity. While Lithuanian farms began to mechanize in the 1920s, and rural people began to buy some ready-made clothing—primarily underwear and shirts—Lithuanian families remained relatively self-sufficient. Families like the Gustinises and the Bernotases, though unequal in wealth, had both gained from the long peaceful period of economic development. The absence of rural impoverishment combined with widespread ownership of small farms and a fair amount of fraternization between middling and small farmers and laborers promoted a fairly homogeneous population in the countryside.

The European war that began in 1939 had immediate repercussions on Lithuania. Although Lithuania was not a war zone, Polish refugees began pouring across the Lithuanian border, seeking asylum from the German invasion of Poland. During 1939 Russia and Germany secretly agreed to give part of Poland to Lithuania and part of Lithuania to Germany and to establish a mutual assistance treaty between Russia and Lithuania. Under threat of invasion Lithuania signed the pact and allowed fifty thousand to seventy-five thousand Russian troops to be stationed on Lithuanian soil.

The first Russian troops who arrived were well disciplined and avoided conflict with the Lithuanian people. By May 1940, however, relations between the two nations were strained. Russia had fifteen divisions poised along the Lithuanian border when it delivered an ultimatum to the Lithuanian government to form a new government whose task was to assure the fulfillment of the Mutual Assistance Treaty and to allow additional army units to be stationed there to ensure enforcement of the treaty. Soon after, the Lithuanian President resigned and left the country. Soviet troops occupied Lithuania. One of the strategic cities occupied by the Russians was Šiauliai, thirty-five kilometers from the Gustinis farm.[2]

The occupation of Šiauliai in June 1940 did not immediately disrupt the daily routine of the farm. The Russians made no move to nationalize or collectivize the farms, but by July 1940 the Russians had engineered an election in which Communist Party officials were essentially put in control of the country. Arrests silenced dissenters and the newly elected People's Diet, dominated by the Communist Party, voted for incorporation of Lithuania into the Soviet Union in July 1940. Collectivation soon followed. Five Russian families arrived at the farm. The Communist Party gave the Gustinis family a choice to stay and farm or move to a smaller adjacent farm they owned. They were allowed to continue farming alone, but it was clear that eventually the farm would become a state farm.

The military presence increased around the Gustinis farm. Thirteen kilometers away the Russians built an airfield and filled it with Russian planes. Voldemar managed to maintain good relations with local Communist Party officials through the next year. As the regional agronomist, Voldemar's job was the difficult one of explaining the new land policies to his neighbors. Voldemar remembered that the Russians arrested the local teacher, the post master, and the local police and sent them off to Siberia, but no one else was disturbed.

When the Germans attacked in June 1941, however, the Lithuanians welcomed them. The Russians put up very little resistance. An estimated one hundred thousand partisans organized an insurrection to coincide with the German attack. The insurgent government lasted six weeks, then the Germans began a three year occupation. In Valakai the occupation occurred quickly. The Germans sent one plane over the nearby airport and destroyed every plane on the ground. Within two days of the attack Germans occupied the countryside. The Russian soldiers left, but the Russian farm families remained to work in the area. The Germans allowed the Gustinis family to return to the Valakai farm, though they maintained that the farms now belonged to the German state. For the non-Jewish Lithuanians, ninety-five percent of the entire population and almost all rural people, the German occupation was not difficult or particularly repressive. The Germans were kind to most Lithuanians. The Gustinis children remembered the German soldiers always gave them candy. Following the repression of the Russians, the Germans did not seem such fierce occupiers.

When the Russians reinvaded Lithuania in summer 1944, the prospects for remaining on the farm quickly dimmed. Between July 14 and July 31, the Russians occupied the main cities of Vilnius and Kaunas. The army also headed for Šiauliai. Voldemar was convinced that if he stayed, he would be deported to Siberia and the farm reoccupied by Russians. On the night of July 27, three days before the Russians occupied Šiauliai, Voldemar and Rozalija gathered together their cash savings, a few belongings, food, and loaded their five- and two-year-old sons into a wagon. They made their way north for twenty kilometers to the Latvian border and sought refuge with relatives.

After two months in Latvia, in convoy, the family headed southwest toward the German border following the retreat of the German armies. The countryside was everywhere marked by the war. Burning tanks littered the roadside. When the family stopped one night, they encountered a German soldier who was Lithuanian. He told them that roadblocks would be set up that night and Lithuanian refugees sent to labor camps. He warned them to keep moving. The weary family kept moving south and west through the war-gutted land of Elblag. There Germans confiscated the wagon, and they continued west by rail to Prebereda, in Mecklenburg, where they worked in a German labor camp. Voldemar harvested beets, wheat, and potatoes.

Then, as the Russians began their sweep through Germany in April 1945, the family left on bicycles for Lübeck, a hospital town where refugees believed they would be safe from the relentless bombing of the Allies. The war ended within days, and from Lübeck the family went to Spackenburg, a displaced person camp set up by the British for Baltic refugees on the Elbe River. The family spent the next four years at this camp, part of an estimated sixty thousand Lithuanians who fled before the advancing Russians and scattered across Western Germany in DP camps.[3]

The German camps were not hard but food was short. Voldemar had contracted TB and needed constant care. A picture of Rozalija taken at the camp shows her thin. It was also crowded, fifteen to twenty to a room, bed to bed, young and old. Americans sent food, though not always what the Lithuanians found palatable, corn for example, something Lithuanians had never eaten and could not quickly acquire a taste for. Refugee organizations, such as CARE and the Red Cross sent supplies. Lithuanians in America collected clothes and sent them to refugees. Eventually, more cabins were built, and each family had a small room of its own with an iron stove and a good supply of coal. Lithuanians opened schools where the boys could study, and there was plenty of room where they could roam around, poking into old ruins of war, feuding with Latvian boys from the neighboring Latvian camp. They were secure but not settled.

Gradually the camps began to empty out. France and England, then Canada and Australia began to take young single Lithuanians who could easily be absorbed into the work force. About thirty thousand, almost half of the World War II Lithuanian DPs, eventually came to the United States. In one case, a church in Rochester, New York, arranged to settle almost thirty families. The Gustinis family was not so lucky. For some time, they searched for an American relative who might sponsor them. The Lithuanian Consul in New York finally located a relative through an advertisement in a Lithuanian language newspaper. They were among the last families to leave, late in August 1949. Through the sponsorship of a relative—the daughter of Voldemar's aunt—the family received passage and the promise of a new, stable life.

Passage to that new life was terrifying in its own way. The United States government arranged passage from Germany and saw the family safely delivered to their hosts, but they now had to build an entirely new life, one for which all the accumulated agricultural skills of a lifetime counted for little. Language was the most difficult. The boys quickly settled into schools and were soon fluently bilingual, speaking English in public and Lithuanian at home. For Rozalija the transition was much more difficult, however. Only their relative, a second generation Lithuanian, spoke Lithuanian. To help support her family, Rozalija immediately took a job in a canning factory. She would go to work—canning tomatoes or cherries, or whatever was to be canned—and return home at night, all without speaking to anyone. The isolation was terrible.

Voldemar also found English a problem. After one year the family moved to Rochester, and there they attended citizenship school and began to learn English. But the process of adding yet another language was a strain. Voldemar had learned Latvian and Lithuanian at home, Russian in school, then German in order to survive occupation. Learning another language at forty-seven was not easy. At one point he took a civil service examination to become an agronomist but his English was just not good enough. While the examiner urged him to continue his studies and return, Voldemar was too discouraged to try again. In Rochester, he found a job as a janitor. He turned inward to nurture his family.

Rozalija, now calling herself Rose, did find a job in which she could use some of her farm skills. On the farm she had been an excellent weaver; now she found a job with a carpet store mending oriental carpets. It did not pay very well and involved long hours of painstaking detail work, but the work was steady and the benefits good. The family bought an old house in the Rochester ghetto and began to remodel it. They got along with black and Polish neighbors who shared their ambitions to own a house, educate their children, and live quiet lives. On November 29, 1955 Rose and Voldemar became citizens of the United States. In the small photograph attached to her citizenship paper, Rose looks well and happy.

The transition from being a Lithuanian farm woman to an American working-class woman was almost complete by 1955. Rose worked hard during the day and helped Voldemar on the weekends to remodel the house. They shared household tasks. Both her sons finished high school and graduated from college.

Which was better, I asked Rose, the farm or the city? The farm was hard work, she replied, but there had been a community. They

Rozalija at work in the United States. Source: Family photograph.

had dances and celebrations and were happy. Here the work was easier but they had no community, only a family.

The loss—what generations of immigrant farm women had lost in their coming to the urban United States—was that sense of belonging to a community. Like Rozalija most of them felt they could not go back, even if they did not flee foreign domination. Far fewer women than men ever went back to their native lands. They gave up community, worked hard at whatever jobs they could find to support their families, and raised their children to be hard-working Americans.

Rose had a strong sense of herself and her skills. She also had a strong sense of the equality of women and men. Russian women, she once said, had much less freedom than Lithuanian women. Still, she always considered the man the "boss." What she meant was that men had the role of supervising property for the family, of being the family manager. It was a patriarchal family but one within which Lithuanian women exercised considerable influence. Rose felt they had a real partnership.

Freedom for Lithuanian women, like Lithuania itself, was always relative. Better than the Russians, but not quite equal with other Lithuanians. What gave her confidence was less a sense of abstract equality than a sense that she was a good worker with important skills. Those skills and the willingness to work gave her a central place on the farm and allowed her to move with confidence into a new urban world. Where she could work freely, she could feel free.

PART II

Oral History, Iconography, and Material Culture

WHEN RURAL WOMEN CAN SPEAK THROUGH A REMEM-bered past, whether written or oral, the record is complex, intriguing, and satisfying. When historians move beyond the remembered past, when the oral tradition dies in the memories of rural women and their voices are stilled, the record is more difficult to reconstruct. Rural women have left relatively fewer records than urban women. Their silences are sometimes eloquent testimony to the hard work, the poverty, and the lack of formal institutions they endured. Still, an intransigent historian determined to make the record speak to the lives of rural women, can not only find immense amounts of written material but also pillage other disciplines to find methodologies adaptable to the study of the rural majority. In this section, I use oral history, iconography, and material culture to expand the history of rural women, combining traditional historical records with strategies developed by scholars in other disciplines.

The first essay in this section is an invitation to join in the collection of women's rural past through the use of family and oral history. Originally a talk based on a few of the hundreds of oral histories gathered by the Extension Homemakers, this essay shows what can be learned from moving from individual family history to collective oral history.

As the second essay shows, oral history can also be valuable in other ways, especially joined to demographic data and public policy history. Combining highly personal accounts and impersonal aggregate numbers can show the relationship between the individual rural woman who survived and made her voice heard and the others who did not. Careful work with census material—both manuscript and published aggregate data—can ground oral histories of survivors in the public records of those who did not. Here these women speak not just for themselves but for their neighbors as well, women who have left their mark only in the public records but who still clamor to be heard.

The hops article uses a different technique—iconography—the analysis of visual images left from the past. Iconography includes the traditional arts of painting and sculpture, as well as items of mass culture, such as etchings and photographs. Many of these art forms are highly stylized to represent an abstract version of the past, but less highly stylized images show groupings of women and men caught in both family and community ritual. They are informal and revealing in what they say about how rural people were perceived by themselves and others. The record expands with the addition of iconography as a methodological tool. It can move us backward in time, not just to nineteenth- and twentieth-century photography and etchings, but beyond to earlier representations of female deities to whom rural people turned in their quest for control over the seasonal variations and environment so necessary for survival on the land.

The Salinas essay looks at the material culture left by women, as well as historical records, to reimage the lives of Pueblo women during the first century of Spanish contact. Much archeological work describing prehistoric cultures and sites does not describe the lives of women. Nor does much of the early history of Spanish contact. Combining these two disciplines allows a sharper picture of these women as social agents to emerge. We know more than we thought, even about women on the seventeenth-century frontier between European and Native Americans.

4 Recovering Her Story: Learning the History of Farm Women

IN 1892 MY GRANDMOTHER, MATILDA RAUSCHER, then twenty-two, left a small village in the Austro-Hungarian Empire and traveled more than three thousand miles to North Central Wisconsin. There she worked as a servant in a small town for a year before marrying another young German immigrant from Austria. She was already three months pregnant when they married, an old German custom. In the next six years she bore four more children in a small log cabin but was, according to all reports, very happy. Then one summer afternoon a colt with which her husband was playing kicked him in the stomach. The young wife put him to bed, nursing him as best she could. The next day he was dead. She remarried quickly, hoping to provide a stable family for her young children.

My mother was born six months after that marriage, into a family where her father and mother shared more poverty than love. My mother sometimes walked to the rural schoolhouse carrying only an apple for lunch. She often went barefooted because she had no shoes. At the end of the seventh grade, she began working as a servant on a neighboring farm. At sixteen, desperate to escape rural poverty, she ran away from the farm to the city. That was in 1918. She married in 1925 a man who wanted someday to grow things. After working to purchase a nursery farm and operating it one year, his National Guard unit was called up. My mother canned one hundred quarts of tomatoes that year and vowed never again to live on a farm. She never did.

Her daughter never learned to can. She always had shoes. And she was not asked to quit school. Some years later, she ran away from the city to a farm in Colorado. When she returned to the city two years later, she vowed to write about farm women.

I share this family history because I feel we must begin to study the history of farm women with our own past. Every woman has a farm woman in her family and most of us do not have to go back very far to find that woman. The best way to gather family history is to talk to women in our families. With the help of a few genealogical charts, we can begin recording birth, marriage, and death dates. Charts help in locating family farm women in time and place, and family anecdotes and stories make these farm women come alive. Were they shy? Or outgoing? What special skills did they have? What joys and sorrows did they speak about? And what did they not speak about? Asking these questions and writing down or taping memories of our lives and the lives of our foremothers is part of our task. We will find more to ask if we first search our own memories and ask ourselves questions. There are a number of guides to family history and assistance for these projects at the local library. We need to become experts on our own history. I guarantee surprises as I found in researching my family history.[1]

Learning family history is not the end but the beginning point for recovering the history of farm women. The next thing to do is to share family history with others and to compare experiences. Obviously, we need not wait until we have every detail of our foremothers' lives. This second step can begin almost as soon as one starts to collect family history. We must encourage other women, and men, to begin their family histories and then share these stories. We need to tell everything that we wish to share about our families as honestly as we can. Recapture the oral tradition by swapping stories, comparing notes on gathering them, and talking about family differences and similarities. Oral histories are like trading cards. Family histories begin to take on an additional richness by comparison with the histories of other families.

While we need to form face-to-face groups to swap histories, we also need to read some of the oral histories others have collected on farm women in the regions most relevant to our families. This can further broaden our ideas about differences and similarities. These comparisons give ideas about what kinds of questions to ask when we go back again to our family to gather more information. Someday I will return to Wisconsin to complete the history of my family farm women. In the meantime, I am finding it helpful to look at the oral histories of women in my state, oral histories collected in New Mexico by the Extension Service, by myself, and by other local historians. I would like to share some of my reflections on what these histories can tell us.

I discovered in looking at these interviews with women who grew up in the 1920s and 1930s, that, like my mother, they also knew hard times. Yet these stories gave me a much broader view of farm women, for I now had a larger context, a sort of collective oral history. Two things impressed me most: the economics of family life and the attitudes these farm women developed out of their farm experiences.

Young women did not share the same experiences while growing up, even on farms or ranches of similar wealth. Some ranch women, like Florence McDonald, for example, who grew up near Lordsburg in southern New Mexico, remembered a great deal of physical freedom. County roundups still existed when she was young. Cowboys would work their way through the country, stopping at ranches as they went. She remembered: "Of course, they had their chuckwagon and they cooked their meals out of the chuckwagon and they had a regular cook. And my sister and I would like to go out and eat with the cowboys, of course, which my dad and mother would not object to. Back in those days, cowboys had more respect for women than men do today. They had not been very well educated but they certainly had been well trained." She remembered a special cowboy friend named Black Jack, a big tall black man, who came every year and befriended her. In fact, her father, who had no hired hands, was seldom home from early spring until late fall when they shipped cattle. Florence, her sister, and her mother spent most of the time alone until they moved to town so that Florence could go to school. According to Florence, she then saw her father even less: "Mother never told him of all the things we needed punishing for. She let us enjoy him as a visitor or a friend."[2]

On the other hand, Ima Fairley of Colfax County had a much more restricted life. "Well," she remembered,

> when my mother died when I was fifteen I had to take over and my sister was only seven and I was so busy keeping house and going to school, trying to get an education so I could teach, that I always had the home to think of. . . . I had to get up at 5:00 every morning and get my dad off to work. He was a mining man and he always left by 6:00 and that meant I had to get up at a quarter of 5:00. And I was pretty well organized. Now, I'll tell you before I went to bed the night before, I usually had things pretty well lined up for breakfast and lunch and what have you. So's to get him off at 6:00.

So Ima too saw little of her father but assumed household duties at a young age.[3]

Most young women, of course, began their hardest work after they married. Florence McDonald, after a relatively easy childhood, married and homesteaded with her husband, living with him on his mother's ranch. Nine months out of the year, she recalled, they had to live on the homestead: "We had to haul every drop of water we used so we learned to be very conservative with our water. We would go in to the home ranch about once a month for washing and to have a good bath." She described a typical ranch day in this way:

> we got up in time for my husband to be out and working by 6:00 in the morning in the summer and by 7:00 in the winter. My husband and I milked range cows, just the range cows. . . . We milked twenty-four cows every morning. I enjoyed it. We were working together and we were trying to build something.[4]

Women worked at many tasks. Frances Mathews of Colfax County remembered her mother as running the post office, something many rural women have done. She also remembered her mother's production for the market. "My mother made butter and sold eggs and took them to town and traded them for what we needed," she told the Homemaker interviewer. Keeping the family going on butter and egg money was a very common experience of farm women. Nona Berry of Colfax remembered her sister teaching and her mother also marketing produce. "My mother was real good at selling the eggs and the butter and keeping things going because we were a poor family," she said. Nona's father was disabled in a mining accident, but there were numerous other families with the same experiences during hard times. The money the men could bring in on the farm, or in off-farm work simply was not enough to keep the family going. The women, by taking wage jobs, by bartering, by trading labor, or by selling their farm produce, kept many farm families going.[5]

Women also took over ranches and farms when husbands died. Mary Moore and her daughter Alice continued to operate the family ranch. "Landon taught Alice and I both very well before he died," said Mary.

> I did all the business part of it and learned that well so when he died that wasn't any problem because I had been doing it. And Alice, he taught her very well that she was able to know the different kinds of cattle and what to keep and what to do that she has been running of the ranch. The both of us. She does the outside and I do the inside. . . . We been running the ranch now for twenty-six years.

At first, Alice did not find the older cowboys willing to take orders from a woman boss. So she just hired young men, taught them the job, and had no further trouble.[6]

Most women remembered hard work and how welcome the Homemaker's clubs were in their lives. Nona Berry remarked that the Homemakers Club was particularly important to her after a nervous breakdown. Being with a group of women helped her recover and return to her regular work. Frances Mathews remembered a neighbor going to a meeting and coming by to invite her to go along. So, she said, "I just picked up my baby and went." Many other women found the clubs a place to rest from work, a support, a place to laugh, and enjoy each other's company. Clubs were an essential part of the lives of rural women.[7]

Growing up, working, and visiting with other women are important parts of women's lives we can recover from oral histories. But not everything in the past seemed good to these women. Nona Berry remembered people being "kind of chilly and distant. Maybe if we'd been raised freer everything would have been easier . . ." Frances Mathews remembered the extreme restraint about sex. "In the olden days, they kept everything so hush-hush," she said, "in fact, you wasn't allowed to say bulls and cows." Women also recalled learning values they still treasure: honesty and hard work most of all. Ruth James remembered being allowed to write checks on her father's account all the time because she was trusted to write them for what she was supposed to. Florence McDonald recalled, "the first thing that I learned in life was to be honest and deal with your fellow man as you wanted him to deal with you." Ima Farley said: "I think my folks tried to teach honesty and also you take care of yourself and then you try to help someone else."[8]

Perhaps being honest was easier because so few economic differences existed among these rural families. All seemed about equally poor. Frances Mathews said, "People had no money in those days. Nobody had money." Nona Berry replied in the same way when asked about feeling underprivileged. "No," she replied, "the people were all in the same class as far as poverty was concerned and we all, I think I was dressed just as well as any body else. . . ." Ruth James remembered the same thing:

> Everybody else was in the same boat we were. . . . we never felt deprived from a lot of these things because everybody else was that way and we just never thought about being poor. . . . You know, you didn't have to keep up with the Joneses because the Joneses didn't have any more than you did.[9]

From oral histories like these that Homemakers have been collecting we can learn the joy and pain, the pride of work, the context and variety of rural women's lives that allow us to glimpse how they felt about themselves. I like the way Nona Berry described that feeling: "Did you ever take a fine baking of bread out of the oven and felt like you had done real well?" That is what oral histories can give us.[10]

Oral histories can, and do, also give us a link to the more distant past. I have used these in my own work. When I arrived in New Mexico eight years ago, I began an oral history project to record the memoirs of rural women. I also began to have my students, mostly from rural areas, write family histories. From these family and oral histories began to emerge patterns of women's work, especially the great amount and variety of work women did on farms and ranches, the amount of food produced, processed, and sold on the market, and frequent comments about how women used that money to finance their households. I also found that these women, like Nona Berry, had a strong sense of pride in the work they had done. With these patterns, I then began a major research study in another period

Baking Bread, Ranchitos, Taos County. Source: RG83–G–4176, Bureau of Agricultural Economics, National Archives.

and place, late eighteenth-century Pennsylvania and Delaware. Because I knew so much about farm women's lives in the twentieth century, I could see the changes over time more clearly. So the work we do to recover our own family and local history can also help to understand earlier history.

The continued references to buttermaking, for example, led me to look at buttermaking more carefully than I might otherwise have done and to give it more credit for the survival of farm families. I discovered that butter was censused in federal agricultural reports beginning in 1850, allowing me to document this women's work very precisely. In the area I studied, 4760 farms produced almost four million pounds of butter in 1850. Women's skills thus provided an important source of cash income. More, it provided an important transition crop, proving that dairy products were a viable market product when grain growing, the traditional male product on the farm, was no longer able to compete with western harvests. Following the lead of these early farm women, most families in the southeastern Pennsylvania area moved into what became profitable dairy farming.[11]

I then looked more carefully for the experiences of individual farm women. Because in the early nineteenth century, men more often than women kept records, farm women usually do not emerge as vividly as they do in contemporary oral histories. At the time of the American Revolution, rural women in southeast Pennsylvania were still 75 percent illiterate. The first social revolution for farm women followed the Revolution. By 1830, a period of about fifty years, rural women achieved almost total literacy. Such an accomplishment is truly amazing. The second revolution was just as amazing. It was the entry of women into the farm economy as market producers. Spinning and the preparation of textiles, some of it for the market, was common in the seventeenth and eighteenth centuries, but late in the eighteenth and early in the nineteenth century textiles became factory products, freeing women to produce other goods for the market. With both men and women producing for sale, farms became much more commercial. A woman's work and money usually supported the household; the man's work and money brought new capital investments in land and machinery. It was an economic partnership that laid the basis for one of the strongest rural economies in history. Women's work freed capital for investments to allow the farm to grow and provide an inheritance for children. It also allowed the family to purchase consumer goods that fueled the industrial revolution.[12]

Widows provide one of the best groups to find out what women were doing in this earlier period because as they took over management of the family farm, they usually also took over records management. While men usually did not record women's work, women included it. Esther Lewis, a Pennsylvania farm widow who ran her farm during the sixteen years from 1825 to 1841, provides a good example of this kind of woman. Lewis found ore in her land several years after her husband died, established a successful mining operation, then set up a partnership with a farm tenant, and with other neighbor women produced several hundred pounds of butter for sale each year. Along with the butter, the farm sold poultry, vegetables, grain, and meat in Philadelphia. Lewis educated four girls in the best Quaker boarding schools of the period. In addition, she was active in political reform. She opened her farm to help black families fleeing from slavery, joined early antislavery organizations, circulated petitions opposing slavery and endorsing temperance, and actively supported the women's rights movement. Her farm and the farms of other Quaker women became the seedbed for women's rights. This was a movement by rural women, grounded in their needs and the needs of their families. It was based on their self-education and cooperation, and they demanded property rights, educational and occupational opportunities for daughters, and recognition of their contribution to the farm economy. The movement was rooted in families and went forward with their support. Other historians are finding similar patterns of work and politics among the rural women of the Mid-Atlantic. Such history will provide one regional base for rural women's history.[13]

Each region of the country is offering up new evidence of the importance of women for rural history. The work of enslaved black women as well as free white women was crucial for the pre-Civil War economy of the South. New England farm daughters were among the first to abandon unprofitable farming for factories and for teaching. Other farm women joined farm communities where they planned to work together for an ideal and just society.

Farms certainly have produced great women. Some of these women rejected farm life. Louisa May Alcott who grew up on farms refused the life of a married farm woman to earn her living by writing and thus left us the story of *Little Women* and her other fine writings. But most women never lost their rural roots. Susan B. Anthony also left the farm, but she returned to rural women to urge them to follow the example of their frontier foremothers in working for economic and political change. The farm woman Sojourner Truth chided men for accepting women's work and then arguing women were too fragile to have their own civil rights. Farm woman Mary Elizabeth Lease urged farmers to "raise less corn and more hell." Others swelled the ranks of Grange, populist party, and suffragist movement.[14]

All these women crowd the pages of history, and by their deeds urge us on to recover the history of the less articulate farm women—those women who sowed and reaped, planted and picked, churned and spun, stitched and baked, whose history is far more rich and complex than historians have ever imagined.

This recent research all indicates the importance of women to the economic history of America. Most farm women have always believed in their fundamental contribution to the welfare of their families and community, but we need to document that contribution. Women have not always received confirmation of their importance. Now, as historians of women begin to extend their previously narrow focus on urban women, the recognition for the work of rural women in families, community, and economy will surely grow.

Many aspects of farm women's history need further study. We know very little about some farm women's most important tasks. How did women raise children amid the heavy demands of farm and ranch work? To what extent did women participate in ownership, management, inheritance, and family property? How did women establish female networks among kith and kin in rural areas? How did cooperative extension plan and implement programs for women and girls? By expanding our family histories, first to oral histories of those closest to us, and then to farm women more distant, we can contribute to this recovery of her story, the history of farm women.

5 New Mexico Farm Women, 1900–1940

AS IN DOING A PATCHWORK QUILT, THE HISTORY OF farm women in New Mexico from 1900 to 1940 must be pieced together out of scraps of history left scattered about. Demography can form a background, public land policy a dominant motif, and the experiences of the women themselves can show us how to fit the pieces together to explain the patterns of farm life. What emerges from this work is a realization that these forty years largely represent a struggle of farm families to remain on the land. In that struggle, farm women would play a crucial role.

Demographically, New Mexico women had a different profile than other American women in 1900.[1] Living in one of the most rural states, they remained part of an agrarian way of life that American women were abandoning. Rural women were 86 percent of the New Mexico female population but only 60 percent of the entire American population. In 1900 nineteen was the median age for New Mexico females; in the United States as a whole the median age for females was twenty-four. Eighty-eight percent of New Mexico women twenty-five to twenty-nine had been married; nationally 72 percent had been married. New Mexico death rates were high in 1900 (no one has estimated precisely how high), but by 1929 the infant mortality rate was still 145 per 1,000, above what the United

States average had been in 1900. In New Mexico the birth rate was also higher than the United States as a whole. Thus, the average New Mexican woman was rural, young, married, likely to have children, and to see many of them die in infancy.

Of the seventy-eight thousand rural women, a majority were native born New Mexicans, a large majority Hispanic in culture and Spanish-speaking. This Hispanic majority was heavily concentrated in the counties to the northwest and southwest of Santa Fe. Native American women, about 7 percent of the population, remained concentrated in the northwest. Most of the Euro-Americans who migrated to New Mexico in the nineteenth century were urban and middle class, but a few had settled with their families in the southern part of the state. A few black women, less than 1 percent of the female population, lived scattered throughout the state. Over 42 percent of these rural New Mexican women were a part of an oral rather than a written cultural tradition. But whether literate or not, the Hispanic majority received and passed on a wisdom learned painfully during the nineteenth century—to hold on to any land in the family.

The typical Hispanic farm woman lived on a small subsistence farm with no mortgage. Chances were good that she would live on one of the 58 percent of the farms of less than 50 acres; even more probable was that she would live on one of the 88 percent of the farms of less than 175 acres with an average of 17 improved acres valued at just under nine hundred dollars that occupied only 12 percent of all the farm land in New Mexico. Dolores Garcia, a daughter born into a Hispanic family at Cordova in northern New Mexico about 1900, might well have been a typical woman whose life spanned these forty years. She married in 1918, bore four children, lost two of them in infancy, and worked with her husband, Domingo, to hold on to their land while raising the two remaining sons.[2] The ancestors of Dolores had long held their irrigated farm lands near villages, using more distant mesa lands for grazing. The farms were subsistence; cash came from the sale of livestock, which grazed on the dry mesa beyond the farm. Much of this land was held by common usage rather than through legal title.

The homesteading policy that brought so many Anglo women into the state between 1900 and 1940 would destroy this old Hispanic farm economy.[3] As a rural state, New Mexico's wealth depended, of course, on who could control and plan for land use.

Hispanic families had remained on the land; they combined subsistence farming on the eight hundred square miles of irrigated land in the state with livestock-raising as a source of cash. Euro-American immigrants from the East tended to cluster in cities, where the men moved into the professional and managerial positions while the women worked in the home. Low land prices and middle-class incomes, combined with a willingness to engage in large amounts of fraud, allowed this small group called Anglos to gain legal title to much of the land, which they then used for large-scale cattle enterprises. An estimated 80 percent of Hispanic land grants were lost in this first land grab begun by the "Santa Fe Ring" in the late nineteenth century.[4]

At the same time that Anglo immigrants began to monopolize the grazing lands upon which Hispanic families had depended for their livelihood, they also criticized Hispanics for their subsistence farming, urging that more modern agricultural practices be introduced to replace the older system. This new agriculture, many argued, should be geared to the market and profits and be an agriculture that could supply the needs of growing urban areas like Santa Fe and Albuquerque. Economic reformers tended to think in terms of an agricultural future based on commercial farms, and comments appeared in the English-language newspapers criticizing Hispanic subsistence agriculturalists for just "making a living" and "being content to satisfy their own needs."[5] Social reformers, on the other hand, feared land monopoly as dangerous to political liberties and, though they too seemed to consider Hispanic farming inadequate, proposed to replace it with new subsistence farms carved out of the public domain under the Homestead Act. Neither land speculators nor land reformers could agree in the nineteenth century on a plan of land use. The contending groups thus moved into the twentieth century still battling over how to divide up the landed wealth of the state.[6]

Throughout the forty years under consideration here, that battle went on with the federal government as divided as the New Mexicans on its land policy. Ultimately, the battle over land was linked to politics, for land policy was determined through state and federal politics. Congress refused in 1903 to admit New Mexico as a state, at least in part, because Hispanics were still a majority of the population and the major landowners. To achieve statehood, New Mexico needed enough Anglo settlers to assure political and cultural dominance. The only way to lure Anglos into New Mexico was with the promise of land. Large land holders realized that homesteaders, because they would have no water and could not establish the subsistence farms envisioned by social reformers, expected to be able to buy homestead land cheap. Distribution of the public land under homestead laws thus had the potential for being at once a political and an economic compromise among differing factions. The federal government did plan an irrigation project to expand the limited amount of irrigated land, but most of the land destined to be irrigated was already owned by resident Anglos. Although irrigation would become the basis of a thriving agriculture in several parts of the state, it would have almost no effect on the homesteading land that was dry-farmed.[7]

Figures for the amount of land homesteaded in New Mexico have never been estimated precisely. E. Louis Peffer says almost thirty million acres were taken from the public domain in New Mexico between 1900 and 1945, about nineteen million of them homesteads. In 1909 alone, the secretary of the Interior designated 270,000 acres of land for dry farming and each succeeding year increased acreage available for homesteading. The peak came between 1916 and 1923 when over seven million acres of land were homesteaded. Much of this land eventually fell into the hands of large ranchers who bought out homesteaders as they succumbed to drought. Ranchers also continued to buy up Mexican land grants and new land from the state as well as from failed homesteaders.[8]

The Anglo homesteaders who occupied the traditional grazing land of the Hispanics beginning in the late nineteenth century forced these older farm families into new economic patterns. At first, some families turned to herding sheep on shares as their economic situation worsened.[9] Then men began to leave the subsistence farms in the care of women who irrigated the holdings and cared for livestock while men sought day labor. Women like Dolores Garcia, in the years between 1918 and 1940, plastered their adobes each year, raised hollyhocks and put geraniums in the windows, planted melons, beans, and squash in the gardens, dried peaches, chiles, strips of meat and spirals of apples, raised chickens, sheep, and perhaps goats. During the early twentieth century this new gender division of labor allowed many Hispanics to retain their lands. During the agricultural depression of the 1920s and 1930s, however, as farmers began to mechanize and unemployed Anglos increasingly competed for the remaining jobs, most Hispanic men found little wage labor. They returned to subsistence farms only to find that without a way to make their farms more productive they could not survive the loss of their cash income. Many more sold out to ranchers, always waiting with cash as the old died and the young abandoned farms for city jobs.[10]

The farm families who homesteaded in the areas formerly used by Hispanic or Native Americans as grazing lands came in three waves between 1900 and 1940. The first wave of the 1900s settled in the high plains of northeast New Mexico in Colfax County and in the Estancia Valley east of Albuquerque. The second wave occurred about 1910 in the east central edge of the state around Clovis. And finally, in the 1920s and 1930s, a third wave homesteaded in the west central part of the state near Datil. All these areas had formerly been used by Hispanic or Native American peoples as grazing lands. [11] Eventually almost all of the Anglo men and women who rumbled over dirt roads in wagons and then in automobiles to the isolated dry-land homesteads also sold out to ranchers and moved on to buy other farms, to jobs in the city, or to become migratory workers and sharecroppers. In the memories of women who participated in the movement of people to and away from the land we can glimpse the effect land policies had on the lives of farm families.

Wealthy ranch women have recorded two different patterns of response toward the homesteaders who came into the area. Emma Muir Marble, who often visited with the homesteading women and got to know them well, was sympathetic and helpful. She wrote:

> My husband and I got on famously with homesteaders. We sent them beef when we butchered and helped them in every way possible. We really welcomed their coming, but we knew they could not make a living as farmers, no matter how much of that dry land the Government gave them. As soon as they proved up [that is, made the required improvements on the homestead] they would be willing to sell, for they did not have enough money to become cattlemen. That is the way it turned out. Because of our friendly attitude, the homesteaders always offered their property to us first.[12]

The reaction of Agnes Morley Cleaveland was far different. When homesteaders arrived in 1916 near the Morley ranch in west central New Mexico, hostility began almost immediately. According to Cleaveland's memoirs, she never got to know the homesteading women but resented their dependence on ranch families for water, beef, and tax revenue to maintain schools for the children. Homesteaders, she claimed, ran their cattle on the Morley range, cut fences, stole beef, and may even have murdered their foreman. It was, she maintained, homesteaders who in 1924 caused her brother to sell out.[13] Regardless of the response of ranch women, the larger ranchers gained by the homesteader's arrival.

The pattern of homesteading women's response to their experiences as they struggled to remain on the land is far more complex than it appeared to ranch women, as can be seen in the accounts of three homesteading women from eastern New Mexico: Florence Compary Hill, Stella Hatch, and Edna Gholson. Florence Compary Hill proved up in 1905 or 1906 near Roswell, living on the homestead with her sister, while her husband worked in town. She sold out for four mules and used them as a stake in a better farm. Stella Hatch homesteaded with her husband in 1909, while her sister homesteaded nearby. They all sold out to a large rancher, her sister returning east while Hatch moved on with her husband to another farm. Edna Gholson helped her father homestead in 1916, filed with her husband on land in the 1920s but never proved up. The stories of these three women, spanning twenty years of homesteading history, give a clear picture of the difference among the women and men who homesteaded. Yet the stories also show that the women shared typical experiences. Their farms usually consisted of a milk cow, some chickens, and a small garden plot. The women tended the farms while the men worked at day labor. All of these land-seeking women moved around, proving up, then moving on, and usually moving on again, always looking for a better way to make a living.[14]

The search for an alternative income once homesteading proved impossible is a clear pattern in the lives of all these women. Florence Compary Hill and her husband moved from farm to farm. He worked on the highways while she worked in the fields and raised chickens and hogs. For several years she even had turkeys that she shipped to Kansas City. She sold eggs and vegetables at local general stores in exchange for groceries. Stella Hatch also moved from place to place as her husband worked on railroads and in the mines. She sold chickens and eggs and ran a dairy with her husband for a time, always finding it was cheaper to live on a farm. "I made a living on the farm," she recalled, while he worked in the mines attempting to save enough to move on to something better. Hatch made butter in expectation of selling it in exchange for groceries when she first arrived in New Mexico. She found that this traditional way of paying for groceries would not work where recipes called for lard rather than butter. So she promptly went home, butchered a hog, and sold the lard. When the Hatches later moved to a small town farther north, however, she made fifteen to sixteen pounds of butter a week and sold it, along with cream and buttermilk, in the local markets. "That just kept us going through the depression," she recalled. Both Hatch and Hill resented the inability of their husbands to find permanent jobs. They would have preferred to live permanently on one farm, but they were proud of their own ability to provide for their families through farm work while their husbands moved from job to job.

The same pattern of resentment at the inability of the husband to provide a steady income was also experienced by Edna Gholson. An extraordinary woman whose mother died when she was two, Edna Gholson homesteaded with her father in 1915, driving a team and covered wagon from Texas at the age of thirteen. During the next six years, she worked in the fields with her father, growing corn, water-melons, and garden vegetables, milking the cows, and driving a wagon into the mountains to get wood to sell in town. And, she remembered, after hoeing all day, she and her father played for dances two or three times a week.

Father and daughter made a good living by hard work. But when Edna married at nineteen, she found that providing for a young family was difficult, even though her husband worked at farm day-labor while she ran the farm. During the years from 1922 to 1938, when she finally divorced her husband, Gholson worked constantly to provide for herself and her two children, working on her own farm, on the farms of others, selling things like gas irons, and even organizing dances. "I've worked, I'm not afraid to work," she re-called proudly. By 1939 she was so tired that she could no longer keep the farm. Moving into town, she began to board highway men. Rising at 3 A.M., and working until 11 P.M., she paid off nine hundred dollars in accumulated debts and bought a car. She never went back to the farm.

The homesteading and farming experiences of these women show a similar pattern and one remarked upon by other farm women: the women kept the farms while the men worked at day-labor. This was not the envisioned homesteading farm partnership where both worked on the farm, rather it was one in which the woman found herself farming alone with her children while her husband attempted to bring in cash from his off-farm work. Even in the nineteenth century homesteading had often not been the success predicted by policymakers. Many gave up and headed for the cities while others had moved west to try again. By the 1930s, however, the homesteading policy of the federal government was clearly bankrupt. Subsistence homestead farms, like smaller Hispanic farms, could no longer be expected to support a farm family.

Increasingly, then, farm tenantry and migratory labor became a way for many farm families to survive. Farm economists have noted the increase in tenantry in the West in the 1920s but shrugged it off as part of the natural development of the agricultural economy and not a flaw in the system. Indeed, even sharecropping in the 1920s could be satisfying to farm women. Ellen Grubbs Reaves remembered traveling with her husband from Alabama, to Mississippi, to Arkansas, and Oklahoma before arriving in New Mexico. "I was raised in the cotton patch," she said, explaining that she and her husband sharecropped for a Pennsylvania Dutch farmer who owned a small farm in southern New Mexico. She milked the cow, made butter, and cooked for the owner, as well as working in the fields. But times were not bad. "Eating all the good fresh milk and cream and stuff," she recalled, "got us fat."[15]

When the agricultural depression deepened, however, sharecroppers in New Mexico suffered. By the 1930s one half of the farmers in Doña Ana county, in southern New Mexico, were sharecropping and many were not making enough to feed their families. Most poorer farm families had supplemented farming with wage labor, and they found it difficult to survive. One woman recalled that her mother's family had to provide clothes and food for them because her parents made so little sharecropping.[16]

Migratory farm women faced still other trials in their struggles to live on the land. Women were half of the migratory population in southern New Mexico's Mesilla Valley as well as being half of the farm workers who picked cotton from September through December. By December it was so cold that families would go home to adobe shacks

Migratory worker families in the Southwest were the most visible poor. Dorothea Lange photographed this woman and her four children in typically inadequate housing and wrote bitterly: "Children in a democracy. A migratory family living in a trailer in an open field. No sanitation, no water. They came from Amarillo, Texas." November 1940. Source: RG83–G–44360, Bureau of Agricultural Economics, National Archives.

and climb into bed while one of the women cooked dinner. Because of wretched housing, families would usually move on to warmer areas in Arizona and California as soon as they had enough money for the road, but those who stayed found little solace. By spring most families would have disappeared west or back home.[17]

More rural families were soon forced into migratory labor. In part this was the result of an inadequate welfare structure. Rural welfare has been one of the goals of the urban-based feminist movement in New Mexico. Successful in establishing a statewide Bureau of Child Welfare in 1924, organized women continually advocated the extension of welfare throughout the state. By 1931, however, only one-fourth of New Mexico was being served by trained social workers, and welfare for indigents remained the responsibility of local officials. As in many states rural families weathered the first year of the depression by retrenchment and living off savings. By the winter of 1931 few had savings to fall back on, and social workers had begun to discuss "employment insurance" as a way to take care of needy families.[18]

Meanwhile, existing welfare agencies attempted to feed and clothe the growing number of normally self-sufficient families that could no longer care for themselves. In addition to the Bureau of Child Welfare, four types of welfare agencies existed in New Mexico in 1931: public agencies at both city and county level; private national agencies like the Red Cross; local agencies like Women's Clubs; and the federal veteran's administration. Most agencies were established to care for only certain kinds of people, thus considerable confusion existed in sorting out who was eligible for assistance. Private welfare funds were often earmarked for transient assistance. The Red Cross, for example, could pay to send back to their home states farm families who had come to New Mexico fleeing the drought in the summer of 1930. This was done in Lea County, where many had come across the border from Oklahoma. In Catron County, where six hundred homesteading families were stranded unable to make a livng, a few also were able to return home. The rest hung on while the county reported to Santa Fe that it had neither relief nor indigent funds. In Valencia, Hidalgo, Bernalillo, and Grant counties, Women's Clubs carried much of the load. Some rural counties like Sierra and Socorro were able to manage without outside assistance, while counties like Luna, McKinley, and Santa Fe combined county funds and private welfare funds and managed to feed their rural folk. Four eastern counties (DeBaca, Curry, Roosevelt, and Quay) solved their problems by sending families who applied for relief to work in the cotton fields of Doña Ana County in southern New Mexico. When cotton picking ended in January, these families would either return or become part of that county's problems.[19]

The Anglo rural population asked for and received the largest share of public assistance during the early years of the depression. Recent immigrants to the state, without settled farms or kinship networks, succumbed first to hard times. Hispanic families seemed to weather the first years of the depression through their elaborate kinship assistance system. Margaret Reeves, head of the Child Welfare Bureau, wrote in 1931 that Hispanic families in Rio Arriba County were all closely related and helped each other: "It is rare to find anyone who is destitute." By early 1932, however, even Hispanic families could no longer survive without aid. Rio Arriba families were being reported by the Child Welfare Bureau as "verging on starvation." Family histories from other Hispanic areas tell of suicides by men who saw fewer mouths to feed as one solution to the expectation of family starvation. In the spring of 1932 many children were reported as surviving by eating green melons.[20]

Not surprisingly, rural people voted heavily for Roosevelt in 1932. New Deal assistance to New Mexico families was massive and welcome; it cemented Democratic dominance in New Mexico for the next half-century. By December 1933 the Child Welfare Bureau was coordinating relief, handling almost fifty thousand dollars a month, most of it from the Federal Employment Recovery Act.[21]

Relief remained the most successful of New Deal assistance policies in New Mexico. Other, more creative solutions to the problems of farm workers, were considerably less successful. The Roosevelt administration attempted to establish resettlement programs, migrant camps, and to make loans to farm families. None of these had more than fleeting success. These policies failed, in part, because of their inability to change the basic economic structure of rural New Mexico; indeed, they failed in part because they threatened to change that structure.

The Farm Security Administration tried to help all rural people in New Mexico, but their success was minimal. They did arrange loans for Hispanic farm families while the Civilian Conservation Corps and the Youth Administration employed their sons and daughters, thus allowing children to provide the cash income that husbands had once provided to the families. The FSA resettled some families at Bosque Farms near Albuquerque, and it helped set up cooperatives, some of which, like the Taos health clinic, survived many years. Yet the overall policy remained one of increasing farm production for home consumption. The effect of this policy meant more work for farm women without introducing any basic change in the economic system, one that proved so resistant to their efforts to survive by working the land.[22] The Farm Security Administration tried for three years to establish a migratory labor camp in Las Cruces, but larger farmers and the Farm Bureau blocked it because they feared workers would organize to demand higher wages. Owners preferred males without families. Braceros and Italian prisoners eventually provided the needed workers during World War II.[23]

The consolidation of land continued. Throughout the early decades of the twentieth century and into the depression, large landowners accumulated more land. In 1900 four-fifths of the farm land was owned by less than 3 percent of the farm families in parcels of more than one thousand acres each. By 1940, after millions had been homesteaded and sold, nine-tenths of the land was held by 17 percent of the farmers in parcels of over one thousand acres each. By 1945 New Mexico had 1,566 ranches over five thousand acres, a number exceeded only by Texas and Montana.[24] In the years that followed, ranchers and large farmers would remain the dominant political power in the state, while the work of the farm women would be all but forgotten.

By 1940 the New Mexico woman was still demographically different from other American women, but the gap was closing. Sixty-seven percent of New Mexico women were still rural compared to 40 percent of all American women. Their median age was now twenty-two, but that of other American women was twenty-nine. Death rates fell dramatically to dip below the United States rates by 1938. Infant mortality rates dropped to 100 per 1000 by 1940. The average New Mexico woman still bore over three children by the mid-1930s, while other American women averaged fewer than two children. Most rural women were literate in English. Anglo women now formed a much larger percentage of the rural population. But the economic conditions of the typical farm woman had improved very little in the years since 1900; in some ways they had deteriorated. Almost half (47 percent) of the eighty-four thousand farm women would still live on farms under fifty acres and over three-fifths on farms under 175 acres worth just over $4,000 each. Over one-third (35 percent) of the farm women would live on farms which were still subsistence, producing primarily for use items that totaled less than $200 per year. Almost two-fifths (39 percent) would live on farms that produced less than $250 for use and sale each year, while almost three-fourths (73 percent) were still living on family farms that produced less than $1,000 worth of products to use or sell.[25]

It would be wrong to give the impression that all farm families suffered as did those of subsistence farmers and migrant farm workers. Anglo families able to afford small, irrigated, commercial cotton farms in the Mesilla Valley, for example, found farm life hard but still possible. Lucille Tatreault, even after becoming a widow, managed to keep her farm by hiring a man to help her year-round and four or five migrant workers to pick cotton. It was not easy but, with good irrigated land, she was able to survive, raise children, and hire a Hispanic woman to help with the housework. She belonged to the American Legion auxiliary, attended Farm Bureau meetings, bought a radio, an electric stove, and installed a telephone. With the help of her daughter she held on to the farm.[26]

Farm women showed an amazing strength and competence in their work, whether picking cotton or managing small farms. However, few were able to control their lives, even their personal lives, because their husbands usually decided if and when to move and how to dispose of the income. Occasionally, the women might use passive resistance. Stella Hatch, for example, once refused to pack because, she explained, her husband had a way of leaving to go to town every time they moved. "I said that I wouldn't do a thing until he got back and I just sat there with my hands folded and when he got back he had to move. I'd had it . . . I just got tired of moving." Edna Gholson finally divorced her husband, taking full control of her life and the lives of her children. Florence Compary Hill stayed with her husband until he died; however, when she discovered he had run up bills with another woman before his death, she refused to pay them.

These were personal protests aimed as much against an economic system that could not give them security as against the individual men who floundered in it. But there are also a few indications that farm families joined in collective protests. Small farmers in the Mesilla Valley resisted large corporate ownership of cotton gins and formed their own cooperatives. Dolores Garcia remembered that when Hispanic families threatened to march on the bank that held the mortgages on their farms, nothing more was heard of foreclosure. Most of the families simply moved off the land, glad for a chance of an easier life when wartime defense projects opened up new urban jobs.[27]

The farm worker without land had little chance to organize collectively during these years. There is almost no record of labor organizing in the fertile Mesilla Valley of southern New Mexico, for example. In late 1919 when the road between Las Cruces and El Paso was paved, seven Mexican brothers started to organize to obtain shorter hours, only to be immediately fired. To avoid any chance of organizing in the 1930s, the Farm Bureau blocked FSA plans to establish a migratory camp in Las Cruces. Not until 1943 did the Southern Tenant Farmers Union begin to organize black farmers in the valley. Without unions in which entire families could participate, farm worker women were unlikely to be politically active.[28]

In this patchwork of New Mexico history, ranchers and farmers controlled the pattern imposed on the land by being able to manipulate federal and state policies regarding the disposal of the public domain. Within this overall pattern, farm women struggled to give form to their lives; they moved across the land, living and working on it but never really possessing it. Yet somehow they changed the pattern by being there. The words of an old quilter perhaps best sum up the attitudes of these women.

> You can't always change things. Sometimes you don't have no control over the way things go. Hail ruins the crops, or fire burns you out. And then you're just given so much to work with in a life and you have to do the best you can with what you got. That's what piecing is. The materials is passed on to you or is all you can afford but . . . that's just what's given to you. Your fate. But the way you put them together is your business. You can put them in any order you like.[29]

The struggle to remain on the land, in any case, is eloquent testimony to the tenacity with which western farm women worked against an economic and political system that dictated that they, like their eastern sisters, would one day leave the land to become part of the urban working class.

6 Women in the Hop Harvest from New York to Washington
with Susan Armitage

ONE OF THE KINDS OF LABOR MOST DIFFICULT TO document is the work performed by rural women at harvest time. Since colonial times women have performed—in addition to many other types of work in field, farmyard, and farmhouse—seasonal harvest labor. Although uncensused and often unrecorded, this labor of women has often made a crucial difference in the profitability of a crop. An underpaid and available reserve army of labor ready, and often eager, to go into the fields to get in the harvest, women have performed the work, then returned to whatever other kind of labor that needed to be done: part-time or irregular wage work, non-wage work in the home, or the production in the home of goods or services for the market.

For most crops this harvest work by women has yet to be studied and reported using the resources of material culture, oral histories, and fragmentary written documents that exist. In the following chapter, we have used all these sources to explain the labor of women in the production of hops—the small but essential ingredient that gives beer its distinctive bitter taste. The history of women in the hop harvests can provide a model of how to recreate one part of women's agricultural history that can apply to other farm commodities in other areas.

Growing hops as a commercial industry in New York dates from 1808, when farmers established the first hop yards in Madison County, about one hundred miles from Albany. These first enterprising farmers hauled their crop to Albany that fall, sold the hops for twelve cents a pound, and returned prepared to plant more the following year. Early crops yielded two thousand pounds to the acre and far more income than wheat or potatoes. By 1817 some hops sold in the New York market at forty cents a pound, and crop failures in England in the mid-1820s kept the prices averaging seventeen cents a pound. Farm families found the earnings irresistible. By 1839 New York produced one-third of the entire United States crop, by 1849 five-sevenths, and by 1859 seven-eighths of the crop. The 1867 and 1872 crops brought market highs of sixty-five cents per pound. By 1879 four New York counties—Otsego, Oneida, Madison, and Schoharie—produced two-thirds of New York's twenty-one million pounds of hops and one-half of the American output.[1]

By the late 1870s, however, yields had decreased drastically to average only 559 pounds per acre in New York. Western states, while producing only a small percentage of the total crop, were averaging over one thousand pounds per acre. As long as prices remained high in the early 1880s, New York farmers continued to expand, with big growers producing a large proportion of the crop. Labor costs increased in the East, however, while yields steadily decreased. As Washington State growers discovered a skilled labor force in the Native American Indian women of the Northwest, they gradually dominated the market. A disease known as the blue mold destroyed the New York crops in the 1910s. The explanation given by the local people—that the disease had come from the West Coast crops—symbolized the destruction that the competition from Washington farms had brought to the New York growers. Farm families, most of whom already had small dairies, gradually converted to dairying as their main form of cash income. Hop-growing never recovered in New York.[2]

The labor of women was necessary because of the nature of the hop crop as well as the market demands. The hop is a flower, about two inches long with scales, resembling a pine cone. It ripens in clusters on the vine, lightening as it grows until it is very pale green or yellow when it is ready for harvest. When a broken flower reveals a yellow, fragrant, and powdery pollen within the hop is ready to pick. Usually this occurs at the end of August. Hop vines grow clockwise around poles which men, called "tenders," pull up. Then, cutting the vines, they place the poles with the vines still wound around them across wooden two-by-two-foot picking boxes. Tenders could keep teams of four women supplied with vines, and skilled teams might fill twenty boxes a day. Around this crop and the harvest process, the lives of thousands of rural New York women revolved in the nineteenth century.[3]

Women became an essential part of the labor force in the New York harvests during this century of hop-growing, as both employers and employees. Some provided lodging and food for the workers, thereby lowering cash outlays in wages by the farm owners. Others became hop pickers, usually making up most of the seasonally employed harvest crews. Preparation by the farm women for the arrival of the picking crews occupied not only the period just before and during the harvest but also much of the year. By the late nineteenth century, women had established regular work patterns in hop-growing.

Sewing was an important part of this pattern of labor. Women manufactured all the bedding needed to lodge the workers, both linens and quilts for the beds. To make sheets women sewed lengths of unbleached muslin together by hand and then hemmed them on a treadle sewing machine. They made quilts by putting cotton between two covers, then tying and stitching them by machine. They made and filled mattress ticks with straw, corn husks, or excelsior. New kiln cloths, upon which the hops dried on the kiln floor, were made up every two years from coarse cloth sewn together.

In addition to sewing, women preserved large quantities of food to serve to the workers. Because pickers chose employers by the quality of the food and their productivity depended upon it, women's ability to plan, process, and prepare food was crucial. While most of the food had to be prepared daily during the harvest, women put up beforehand large quantities of preserved fruit and baked molasses and raisin cakes that they covered with wine-soaked cloths and stored. Women also oversaw the stocking of hams, bacons, salted fish, chicken, eggs, beef, pork, coffee, tea, flour, sugar, vegetables, rice, and cornmeal, as well as other supplies needed to concoct hearty and tasty stews, pies, custards, and breads.[4]

At the end of May many women went into the hop fields with

their children to perform the tedious and exhausting work of tying the hop vines to poles with yarn or burlap strings. The vines were two to three feet high at this time. This done, the women returned to their work at the farmhouse.[5]

About mid-August women began the final phase of their preparation. This involved readying dormitory buildings and outbuildings for the male workers and part of the farmhouse for female pickers. They rolled up carpets, removed curtains and shades, disinfected, hung fly paper, and spread mosquito netting over dining tables. They made up beds, established summer kitchens in outbuildings, covered dining room floors with newspapers and hopsacking, covered tables with rolls of oilcloth. They hired other women to help cook and put in last-minute supplies.

A week before the workers arrived, the farm women began baking, preparing harvest loaves of bread (each one could feed ten pickers), making breakfast cookies, and planning menus. When the hop harvest began, the farm women switched to a nineteen-hour day. Beginning at 5 A.M. they prepared breakfasts of ham or bacon, eggs, potatoes, sometimes codfish, gravy, bread, cookies, coffee, and tea. They baked pies for dinner—lemon, chocolate, custard, and berry. They made sauces and gravies. Their excellence as a cook not only insured a happy, productive work force this year but also the return of the best workers the next. Their day usually ended at midnight.[6]

The women who came to harvest the hops were of two types, though accounts are not precise on the relative proportion of each. Workers were either local "home" pickers or of urban origin. During much of the nineteenth century "home" pickers seemed to dominate. Fetched by farmers in the morning and returned home at night, these married women might bring their own lunches and their children, and they usually picked at the smaller farms. After the 1880s both men and women came from Troy, Albany, New York, and Binghamton, many of them factory workers who picked during their vacations. Eventually big growers began to hire urban unemployed males. Local rural women, either expecting or experiencing harassment from these "foreign" workers, soon disappeared from the work force. After 1895, for example, women stopped picking in the Pierstown area because, they complained, growers hired "dissolute" pickers.[7]

Women needed no tools for these jobs, just the ability to work steadily for long hours in the hot sun. They learned to wear stout shoes and rubbers for the morning dew, old clothes, and a straw hat or sunbonnet. They cut the feet from stockings and wore them to protect their arms and wore white canvas gloves that they mended each night. They soon learned to tie kerchiefs around their necks to keep stinging caterpillars from crawling into their clothes. The four-woman teams usually picked from eight to six, six days a week, each woman picking her assigned quarter before being allowed to pick the poorer hops from her neighbor's quarter of the box. Often the hop boxes had shades to protect the workers from the sun. Sometimes farm women would bring out lemonade, tea, or switchel (vinegar, molasses, and ginger). For those boarded at the farm there was a lively social life every evening and Sunday, with singing and hop dances (square dances in the hop houses).[8]

Women workers kept watch on the boxes to see that the tender did not unnecessarily jar them and cause the hops to settle. The tender, wrote one farm advisor in the 1880s, must lay the loaded poles across the box pole "very gently or he will 'jar' down the hops already picked in the boxes and have four women in his hair at once."[9] Women considered the tenders just that, workers who must be there with the hops when they needed them, keep the vines away from their feet, and change the boxes when necessary. Every fifty pickers also had one box-emptier, who put the hops in the sack and gave the picker a ticket when she called out "Hop-sack!" Women were thus considered an important and skilled labor force, and their wages were the major expense in the hop business.[10] Of an estimated $178 per-acre cost in 1882, the $60 picking costs were the largest item. The faster the women picked the crop, the less waste occurred and the greater the profits. But Euro-American women soon withdrew completely from the fields, as growers began to bring in the urban unemployed males. By the 1880s Eastern women were already replaced with a new reserve army of Western women in Washington.

The accompanying 1867 print from *Harper's Weekly* shows three separate groups of pickers and four tenders taking down poles with hops on them. Two young children are helping with hop baskets, and one young girl is holding another young child. Most of the women are standing and working, though some appear to be resting on boxes. They wear full skirts and jackets with long sleeves; most have sunbonnets on with long backs coming down over their shoulders. There appear to be other women visiting in the fields wearing dresses

Hop Picking—A Western New York September scene. Source: Harper's Weekly, *September 28, 1867, Library of Congress.*

and hats, lounging, talking with the pickers. The picture conveys the feeling of a lively and happy group enjoying their work.

The second picture, an 1880s photograph, is rather stiffly posed. The boxes have changed little, but no men appear in the picture. The women are carefully dressed in blouses, skirts, and aprons; three have wide-brimmed hats, while the fourth wears an old-fashioned bonnet. Although other photographs do exist that include tenders, one senses that this picture is meant to convey the propriety of single women working together in the hops fields rather than a friendly neighborhood group. The first picture is romantic; the second, somehow Victorian in tone.

In contrast, the 1904 picture of the Yakima Indians resembles the 1867 print. Here men, women, and children are again shown together in the fields. The women still wear long skirts, one wears a bonnet, and one has two children by her side. There appear to be no boxes. Instead, the women pick on to a blanket from which the hops

Hop Picking, 1880s, Otsego County hop pickers. Source: Smith-Telfer Collection, copyright, New York State Historical Association, Cooperstown, N.Y.

are apparently transferred to baskets and then boxes. The picture seems startlingly contemporary. Migrant workers in the fields; it is a twentieth-century minority working-class scene.

Indians were already picking most of the Washington hops by 1882. In that year 2,500 came from Puget Sound, British Columbia, and Alaska, some three hundred miles by canoes; others came by land. E. Meeker, a Washington hop expert, wrote of the Indians arriving in Tacoma that they were "inveterate and reliable workers, going to the hop-field as soon as they can see to work carrying their dinners with them, and remaining until pitch dark." They drove hard bargains, he said, and were "masters of the situation." Even paying the Indians $1.00 a box, growers could still clear $100 per acre. Meeker predicted the state of Washington would soon eclipse New York as the hop-producing center.[11]

Meeker's prediction was correct: today Washington produces more than 60 percent of the nation's hops.[12] But Meeker was incorrect to assume that his own Puyallup Valley, near Tacoma, would be the favored site. Hop-growing soon moved eastward over the Cas-

Yakima Indians in the Hop Fields, Washington. Source: Library of Congress, Photograph Collection 16055.

cade Mountains to the drier but irrigated Yakima Valley of central Washington. The first hops were planted in the Yakima Valley in the 1870s, but until 1910 hop-growing there was uncertain, at the mercy of fluctuating market prices. In 1911, however, an upturn began. Some hop growers received forty cents a pound and averaged a yield of a ton per acre, nearly four times the dwindling Eastern yields.[13] Other Yakima farmers took note of the profit from hops, and soon hop-growing was well established. Today more than 90 percent of Washington's hops are grown in the Yakima area.

American Indians followed the hop migration from Puget Sound to central Washington. Every year they came from all over the state, from many different tribes, to pick hops at Yakima.[14] Everyone came:

men, women, children, dogs, and horses. Meeker had marveled at the size of the migration to Puyallup, commenting that it looked "as though they had come to 'stay all summer.' "[15] Yakima residents lined the streets to watch the colorful parades of Indians arriving each year for the harvest.[16] The regional historian L. V. McWhorter first interviewed the former Nez Perce warrior Yellow Wolf during the hop harvest of 1908, and he added to the narrative yearly for the next twenty-four years as Yellow Wolf and his band made the annual trek from the Colville Indian Reservation in northeast Washington to pick hops in Yakima.[17]

Hop-picking was a social occasion, characterized by late-night parties, horse-racing and gambling. As Louisa George, a Nooksack Indian woman, recalled: "I heard singing and shouting where the gambling was going on. Oh, I wanted to go. . . . That's what I used to go to Yakima for. I used to go to the gambles and stand behind them and coach whatever side I wanted to win."[18]

The Euro-American residents of Yakima regarded the yearly Indian gathering with mixed attitudes. On the one hand, hop harvest was an exciting time, especially for those whites who were involved in the harvest themselves. But some people disapproved to the late-night Indian gatherings. One Yakima resident, Margaret Keys, remembered:

I heard my dad telling they had a lot of trouble with the Indians gambling. The squaws and young ones would pick in the very early day. The men didn't pick much. They had to sleep in late in the morning because they'd gambled til late the night before. Oh they'd live it up. And then they'd try to get the money away from the squaws and sometimes it wasn't so easy. And then somebody would come up to where dad worked . . . and he had to go down and settle the fight.[19]

While Euro-Americans viewed the Indians merely as a somewhat picturesque labor force, the experience viewed from the Indian women's side was often starkly necessary. Louisa George yearly made the trip from northern Puget Sound to Yakima, taking her children with her but leaving her husband behind. Sometimes she only picked hops; sometimes she remained to pick other orchard crops as well. She made the trip because she needed the money to feed her family. She remembered:

Indians on West Yakima Avenue on their annual trek to pick hops.
Source: Photograph Collection, Yakima Golding Hop Farms, Manu-
script and Special Collection, Washington State University Libraries,
Pullman, Washington.

One of my girls was very sick; she had tuberculosis. I told her that I
thought we should go home. I said, "You're too sick to be out
here." She said, "No, mom. We have more to eat when we're out. If
we go home we'll be starving." She wouldn't go home, so we went
over to Yakima. She got so sick that I had to put her in hospital.
They just kept her there until she died.[20]

Although hop growers could count on the yearly migration of
Indian workers, they were always afraid that they would not have
enough pickers. So, like the earlier growers in New York State,
Yakima growers recruited local women and children to supplement
the Indian work force. For women, hop-picking was an opportunity
to earn extra money for things such as school clothes or Christmas
presents. Families often made an "outing" of it, camping in tents near
the hop fields. They picked together, sharing boxes (later sacks), hop
poles, and other picking implements. For the children, hop-picking
time was a somewhat confusing mixture of play and work. Margaret

Keys recalled that obliging older relatives picked into her box, when she was a very young child, so that at the end of the harvest season she had a five-dollar gold piece to show for it. As she got older, she had to pay more attention:

> I remember playing house in those . . . boxes when you didn't have to work. You could turn them upside down and have a hidden house and people would have to lift them up to come in or you turned them on the side and were more friendly to the people calling. But when they were full of hops you'd stay completely away from them because they dumped the hops in the box you have to have a box full. And if you shook them a little bit, particularly if it was war, the hops would go down. And any kid that run by and shook the box got clobbered.[21]

She concluded, ruefully, "There was a lot of no-nos if you were a kid in the hop yard."

But there were special pleasures, too. There were the pleasures of camping out in a tent, which everyone who lived more than two or three miles away did. At the yard where the Keys family picked, the owner grew a field of potatoes for the yearly harvesters. But that was all: Washington growers did not provide accommodation and food, as had New York growers. The pickers supplied themselves with food or bought from commercial wagons. Margaret Keys remembered:

> The wagons would come through, a watermelon wagon, and a meat wagon that had lunchmeat and things and the bakery wagons. . . . Some parents would buy and some wouldn't. I knew one family [where] the man was [picking] for his winter underwear. . . . His name was Mr. Williams. He was not a willing picker. He didn't show up til the season was almost over. His wife kept threatening him, "If you don't get enough for your underwear, you just gonna go cold this winter." We used to worry about Mr. Williams' winter underwear—he was a great one for pop and things from the wagon.[22]

Children were so important to the hop harvest in Yakima that the opening of school in the fall was delayed until after the hops were picked. For parents the challenge was to find a way to get the children to work while still allowing them time to play. Margaret Keys's mother set a quota system: one big barrel had to be filled each morning and afternoon. When the barrel was full, the children could

Swedish Immigrants Hop Picking in Yakima area, camping out with children. About 1916. Gerda Lunstrum, Anna Narboe, Anna Carlson, Hugo Carlson, and Edna Narboe. Source: Family Picture Album of Florence Wick Martin.

go and play—and of course the sooner it was full, the more playing time there would be! Another effective parental method was to give the hard-working child five or ten cents to spend at the food-wagons.[23]

For the Euro-Americans, as well as for American Indians, hop-picking was a social work experience. In the early period there is no evidence of much contact between the two cultural groups, either while picking or in the night-time activities. By the early 1930s, however, a Yakima grower was reporting participation by both whites and Indians in dances and movies. There were tribal games and ceremonies as well.[24]

By the late 1930s the yearly crowds in the hop fields dwindled.

Mechanical hop pickers, large rotating drums that stripped the hops from the vines, were introduced. The hop vines were now cut by truck-driven teams of workers and transported to the mechanical pickers, rather than being picked in the fields. Far fewer workers were needed, and much of the work was too dangerous for young children. Family groups, both Euro-Americans and American Indian, left the hop fields. Today, hop-picking is highly mechanized, and only the low-skilled job of feeding the hop vine into the picker is still done by women.[25]

In 1883, at the very beginning of the hop industry in Washington, Meeker had fretted about a possible labor shortage: "We could raise hops enough to supply the world: Just how many can be picked is a problem that will be speedily tested by the increased acreage being planted."[26] The size of today's hop industry would astonish Meeker, and so would the small number of hands needed for harvest. Mechanical picking has brought an end to the multicultural family-centered activities that used to characterize the hop harvest. Today most people have no idea of the history of hop-harvesting or its importance for women's work, in both Indian and Euro-American cultures.

7 Southwest Monuments of the Salinas

THE SALINAS NATIONAL MONUMENT LIES SOUTHEAST of Albuquerque, New Mexico, between the Rio Grande and the Rio Pecos in the Salinas Valley.[1] The Salinas Valley is part of the Estancia Basin, which was formed from a great prehistoric lake that once covered this part of central New Mexico, and archaeological sites in this Estancia Basin are among the oldest in the country. The Salinas Monument marks the sites of three prehistoric Indian pueblos and seventeenth-century Spanish missions—at Quarai, Abo, and Gran Quivira. Most importantly for the history of rural women, the Salinas Monument preserves a part of the remarkable building skills of indigenous women, specifically the Pueblo women of the Southwest.[2]

Today, these skills are being revived by Hispanic women who trace their heritage of the arts of plastering and fireplace-building to these early Pueblo women. Known as *enjarradoras,* these women practice the skills of their grandmothers who had the responsibility for the final plastering and yearly replastering that repaired erosion of wind and water and kept adobes from disintegrating. It was a skill passed down from early Pueblo women and kept alive in Indian pueblo and Hispanic villages where women took part in construction of *jacales,* shelters constructed of poles and mud, helped make adobe

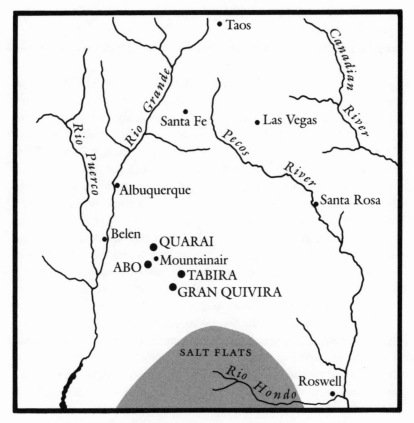

Map showing location of Salinas Monument sites.

bricks and construct adobe buildings, and functioned as masons. The recreation of that tradition has also helped me to see the monuments of the Salinas as monuments to the skills of women as well as to the religious and architectural ventures of men.[3]

Friars oversaw the ambitious building projects that form the basis of the Salinas Monument. Men designed them on the model of European churches, but Pueblo women used their traditional building arts to create the churches. Alonso de Benavides wrote in 1626 that the women and children had built more than fifty "sumptuous and beautiful" churches and that the women had laughed when the men enlisted by the friars to build the walls had run away. The walls of the missions at Quarai, Abo, and Gran Quivira still loom impressively above the visitor, carrying the eye up to what is now the open sky. They are a monument to the art of their builders and a reminder of the ways in which the lives of indigenous women were affected by European colonization.[4]

The history of Pueblo women's building tradition extends far back into the early history of the Salinas Valley. For the first four thousand years Paleo-Indian women were probably satisfied to construct shelters from animal hides. When intensive hunting led to the disappearance of larger animals, these early groups scattered to hunt smaller animals and gather wild foods, leaving few traces of their cultures. Later people built, successively, pit houses below ground, above-ground jacales of wood and mud, and then masonry structures. The old pit houses eventually became ceremonial structures, today called kivas, and people lived in their new modern structures above ground. By the late sixteenth century when the first Spanish arrived, Pueblos were living in these masonry structures. Women were responsible for most of the building. The rooms were uniform in size, of stone blocks with shared-wall construction.[5]

The stone shelters of the Salinas marked the eastern fringe of the Pueblo culture. Here nomadic tribes from the east and south came to trade. In turn, the Salinas tribes carried on trade with the Pueblos to the west and to the north, and with a major trading center to the southwest, now called Casas Grandes, in the present-day state of Chihuahua, Mexico.[6]

The Salinas pueblos formed a linguistic frontier. To the north, people spoke Tiwa and to the south they spoke Tompiro. The Spanish used the term *Jumanos* to refer to some of these indigenous peoples. I use the term *Salinas* to refer to both groups. All were part of the larger group of Puebloan peoples who numbered over 130,000 in the middle fifteenth century and who inhabited at least seventy-one villages. These people, in turn, were the remnants of a much larger and more complex Puebloan regional culture that covered most of New Mexico and Arizona before it collapsed in the fourteenth century. Now, in the sixteenth century, the Salinas peoples were in more frequent contact with the Plains peoples who had been moving westward along the rim of Pueblo territory. At the gateway to the Plains was Gran Quivira—called *Cueloze* by the Pueblos.[7]

Gran Quivira was at the center of the Pueblo-Plains trade routes. It provided a place where the two cultures that depended on different subsistence practices could come together to trade peacefully. Apaches came from the Plains to trade buffalo, deer, and antelope skins. Pueblos came to trade corn and *mantas* (blankets). Gran Quivira maintained security for the traders and stored trade goods. It was the most populous of the Salinas pueblos. The supplies stored there could maintain a larger population than other villages that made up the agricultural base for the trade.[8]

Although Gran Quivira occupied an inhospitable environment— at 6500 feet high the temperatures may drop to $-14°F$ in the winter and rise to over $100°F$ in the summer—it was successful in attracting newcomers and expanding. About 1545, the community at Gran Quivira began a major building project, creating more than two hundred new rooms. The archeological record shows the appearance of new cremation practices alongside the old and the appearance of new pottery types.[9]

These pottery styles and cremation practices have provided clues to the origin of these new settlers. Zuni villages, 120 air miles to the west, were the cultures that practiced cremation most closely related to the new practices introduced at Gran Quivira. Pottery styles also came from the Zuni. The Spanish had not yet appeared in the Salinas Valley, but they had already begun to disrupt the Pueblo cultures to the west. Zuni was visited by the Spanish in the 1540s, and smallpox epidemics may have followed as they did in other Indian populations who had no immunities to this virulent new disease. The newcomers in the Salinas Valley may have been refugees from that village. The women continued to manufacture their own cookingware but began to make decorated pottery in the style of the newcomers. Each group apparently continued its own mortuary practices, as both the older and newer styles existed side-by-side. Whatever the cause of the new infusion of settlers, the cultures continued to develop and expand. By the mid-sixteenth century Gran Quivira was the center of a thriving trade. People grew cotton as well as corn. They manufactured cotton mantas and had surplus corn for trade, as well as salt for those who did not wish to gather their own from the salt lakes farther north.[10]

The women of Gran Quivira had well developed skills as Pueblo builders and potters. The architecture was similar to that in other pueblos where women did the building. They built many small ten-foot-square storage rooms, as well as plastered limestone living rooms of about fifty-five square feet. The rooms were arranged around a central plaza and joined by common walls two to five feet thick. Women may have also built underground kivas used by men for religious rituals. The women used special pits for mixing mortar and plaster (three feet in diameter and six inches deep) and for firing the pottery they made.[11] The women made their own cookingware. They had a wide variety of pots, but their favorite was the *olla*, a pot eight inches high and twelve inches in diamter, with a short neck and a straight outflaring rim. Gran Quivira women imported a special glaze-decorated ware from nearby Abo.[12]

In addition to building and pottery making, women ground corn. While men raised most of the crops, the women were the possessors of this essential skill that turned tough corn kernels into useable meal. Later Pueblo women used an average of three quarts of meal a day and liked to keep thirty to sixty quarts on hand. They ground an estimated twelve bushels of corn a year per person in their household and kept another twelve bushels of corn per person in storage. In addition, they prepared extra cornmeal for ceremonies and for exchanges at the time of marriage. Such meal was important both for home use and for trading with the Plains Indians. It would later be sought by the Spanish explorers and settlers.[13] Salinas women used the same flat slab metates with mealing bins used by other Pueblo women. They arranged many of the mealing bins on the roofs of their masonry houses where they could visit and watch the younger children. As they ground the corn, they sang. Sometimes a man would accompany them on a flute. They also had *comales,* sandstone griddles with polished cooking surfaces, for making corn cakes.[14]

The women also processed hides of pronghorn sheep, deer, and bison that the Plains Indians brought to trade. The women tanned, scraped, and then rubbed the hides to soften them. They also had a great variety of awls and needles for their leatherwork.[15]

Infancy was the most dangerous time for female as well as male children. Close to 50 percent died before age three. After reaching six, a young girl was likely to live until twenty-five. Women reached their peak productive years between eighteen and twenty-five. After twenty-five women experienced higher mortality than men probably due to childbirth. If she survived childbirth, she could, like men, expect to die between twenty-seven and thirty-eight years of age. Some lived on to forty-two. Women were about the same height as other Pueblo women, just under five feet, four inches. They seem to have been healthy, competent women, who played a vital role in community survival as producers and reproducers.[16]

The social life is more difficult to trace than the economic life and material culture. People at Gran Quivira, like other Pueblos, lived in kin groups that ordered the social activities of both men and women. Like most sedentary agricultural groups, the Pueblos were not totally egalitarian. They had ranked societies but not separate public and domestic spheres. Ranking involved age, as well as kinship, sex, and skill in these societies. Most women probably lived in kin households composed of female relatives, their husbands, and children, but some women may have lived in kin groups formed around male kin. Both systems were present in later Pueblo cultures. The kin-based clans exercised control over both young men and young women. While women may not have participated in public rituals, elder clan women probably held considerable household power. In later Tewa pueblos, the oldest clan member became head regardless of sex.[17]

When the Spanish arrived in the Salinas Valley in the winter of 1581–82, there were smaller villages similar to Gran Quivira scattered throughout the Valley. Estimates of the number of villages by the first Spanish explorers range from five to fifteen. A 1638 account estimated Pueblo households had three to four married people and there were eight thousand households. The earliest census records from 1639–41 list about three thousand people in 600 households at Chililí, Tajique, Quarai, and Abo. In the 1679 census, one friar estimated population in the six largest pueblos—Chililí, Tajique, Tabira, along with Quarai, Abo, and Gran Quivira—of about 1400 households; the baptized population as a whole declined by one-third to four thousand because of smallpox and other diseases since the first baptisms and concentration of Pueblo people into villages. Given these numbers, the total of the six major villages in 1650 may be roughly estimated at a population of five to seven thousand people. Diseases introduced by the Spanish probably caused a one-third decline in the baptized population before 1640 and considering that some people remained unbaptized, there was probably a minimum of seven to ten thousand Puebloans in the Salinas Valley when the Hispanic colonists arrived.[18]

Each pueblo had its own political structure. The Spanish who arrived in the late fifteenth and early sixteenth centuries identified the Pueblo governments as "República," republican,[19] that is not monarchical. A group of male elders made decisions that were carried out and publicized by a man tested for his resistance to pleasure and pain. Two other groups of men held leadership roles—the warriors and the religious leaders.

These leaders probably represented kin groups. Pueblo elites had traditionally controlled esoteric knowledge as well as food surpluses or exotic goods that could be traded for surplus in time of need. They were a crucial part of regional exchange networks. Such leaders probably controlled mobilization of community labor, settled disputes, organized daily activities, and controlled deviant behavior. Religious groups were at the center of organizational life of the pueblos. Alfonso Ortiz, who studied later Tewa clan structures, found that while supernaturals included mothers known as "Blue Corn Woman" and "White Corn Maiden," women had relatively minor roles in these religious groups. Women could assist men and obtain ritual knowledge; but men never assisted women in rituals.[20] Males were said to contain both manhood and womanhood but women only womanhood.

The male religious elite performed the katchina dances. In these dances, men masked as Pueblo deities danced in the plaza and then performed ritual intercourse with women, often in the kivas. The leaders who controlled the dances probably also maintained communication with the leaders of other villages. Dances performed to insure fertility of crops for the benefit of the community also functioned to control the population.[21]

The descriptions of dancing by the friars in the Salinas Valley mention women only as going out to greet the katchinas, receiving fir branches that they put in their houses, and performing ritual copulation, usually with male kin. Ritual copulation with male kin was probably symbolic of the unity of the clan. The women may have had parallel rituals. Later Pueblo women participated in some dances with males and had their own dances and their own secret rituals, as well as home altars. The popularity of home altars and of the Virgin among Hispanized Pueblos may derive from a separate female religious tradition, practiced domestically, that the friars did not observe.[22]

Evidence of the power of female religion and female deities may be seen in the extraordinary stories that began to circulate in the 1620s. Friars brought an image of the Virgin north from Mexico and

proclaimed her the protector of the province. As conversion progressed, various pueblos, including some in the Salinas Valley, talked
of a woman in a blue cloak who visited and preached to them in their
own language. A century earlier in Mexico such stories had given rise
to the Virgin of Guadalupe, a particular fusion of the European
concept of the Virgin and an Aztec goddess. In New Mexico friars
first identified this mysterious woman not as the Virgin but as a
Spanish nun, Sor Maria Agrada. Fray Alonso Benavides, who returned to Spain in 1631, said that Sor Agrada gave him detailed
descriptions of the friars in New Mexico and the countryside. One
thing that puzzled the friars, however, was that this woman wore
blue and the nun's habit was brown. The blue nun may have been a
fusion of the Blue Corn Woman with the Virgin. Almost twenty
years later, in 1674, according to the friars, the Virgin herself appeared in New Mexico warning that there must be reform. *La Ma-
cana,* as she was then called, predicted punishment if Spaniards
continued to persecute the Indians and performed a miracle to convince secular authorities that her warnings must be taken seriously.[23]

Although elite males may have controlled public dances it is not
clear to what extent they controlled food surpluses and exercised
decision-making powers. If women controlled the houses and the
storerooms, males would have had to go to them to collect surpluses.
Today, among the Tewa, women also exercise considerable influence
through male family representatives who take direction from the
entire kin group they represent, including the women. Such could
have been the case among the Salinas.[24]

The Pueblos went through twenty-five years of drier than normal
weather before the Spanish arrived. They could not have had much
surplus food. According to calculations derived by archeologists
from study of tree rings, the years just before and just after their
arrival were to be the driest in over four centuries. Not until five years
after the Spanish arrived in 1581, did the weather return to normal.
Then, for seventy-five years, though winters might be cold, the rains
came and Pueblos regularly harvested crops.[25]

West of the Salinas Valley, conflict grew as the first Spaniards
made their way across the land demanding food supplies. If people
fled at their approach, Spaniards helped themselves to the food the
people had gathered and the women had stored. In one case, when
people along the Rio Grande refused their requests for food, the

Spanish set fire to one pueblo and burned the inhabitants to death. Then they garroted and shot sixteen more villagers. "This was a strange deed for so few people in the midst of so many enemies," wrote the Spanish chronicler of the expedition.[26]

Strange indeed. As word spread of the activities of the Spanish, Pueblos measured their chances. Where they could not resist, they supplied the explorers. Where they had adequate defenses, they resisted. When the Spaniards returned to colonize New Mexico in 1598, under Governor Don Juan de Oñate, women and children came with the Spanish expedition, for this was to be colonization not simply exploration. So too did Franciscan friars whose task was to Christianize the Indians. The Spanish intended to live off the Indians in this colonial venture. Indian representatives of seven pueblos pledged obedience to the Spanish crown.[27]

More than 100 mounted Spaniards entered the Salinas Valley that year and several pueblos pledged the same obedience. The Spanish returned to the Valley in 1599 asking for a tribute of mantas and provisions to prove their submission. The Salinas scornfully offered them stones to eat. In retaliation for such inhospitable action, the Spanish returned with reinforcements, set fire to one building, and shot people as they fled to rooftops. The Salinas killed the next Spaniards who passed that way. The Spaniards returned with a force of seventy armed men. Organizing several pueblos, the people fought back for six days. Spaniards killed a large number of the Salinas (they claimed nine hundred), burned part of one pueblo, and enslaved some of the people. That was the last major battle and the end of open resistance. Thereafter, the Spaniards occupied the Salinas Valley. During those seven decades of occupation by the Spanish, the pueblos of the Salinas remained as Friar Francisco de Ayeta wrote, the "veritable keys" to the provinces.[28]

Initial force and subsequent disease made it difficult for the Pueblos to resist occupation. Subjugation of non-Christians and the imposition of Christianity had been part of Spanish colonial policy from the eighth century to the sixteenth-century conquest of the New Mexico frontier. The *reconquista* tradition of suppressing native religions was joined with a Christian humanist ideal of the Renaissance. Natives were to be Christianized and Hispanized, resettled in concentrated villages (a process called *reducción*), and taught to live and work like European laborers. The goals were clear, but the methods were worked out for respective frontiers. Spanish imperialism united church and state in a centralized but flexible bureaucracy with the goal of incorporating autonomous groups of Native Americans into a global political economy. In the language of economic analysis, Spain was the core area, Mexico the dependent colonial market, and New Mexico an external region that the Spanish wanted to incorporate at the margins of this global economy. New Mexico was also an area colonized to prevent other colonial powers from occupying the area. It was preemptive colonization, costly to the Spanish government, but seemingly necessary for the preservation of the core economy and its New World colonies.[29]

At the periphery, where the Spanish began to incorporate the Salinas, was a diverse and dynamic rural society. The Spaniards used rural diversity as a mechanism of control but also created colonial societies fusing indigenous and Hispanic cultures. The Spanish policies of colonialism had to reconcile the needs of the indigenous population, the colonizers, and those directing the enterprise from Spain and from Mexico City. So successful, overall, was the system that Spanish imperialism survived for three centuries with relatively little military coercion after the initial conflict had imposed the system.[30]

Once military control had been achieved, the Spanish attempted to develop a uniform system of government. The goal was to Hispanize the population without major disturbance of the local social, political, and economic traditions of the people. Spanish authorities tended to maintain local hierarchies and simply add a layer of Spanish control at the top. Friars, who lived scattered throughout the area, were responsible for limited Hispanization, primarily converting Pueblos to Christianity, and teaching the Spanish language to young boys. They also shared secular duties, among them seeing that the local groups remained loyal to the crown. The crown supplied the Franciscan friars with food, clothing, and the necessary vestments and ecclesiastical furnishings for their churches. Frontier ventures were not profitable for the crown although officials might profit individually. The Spanish had to adapt to Pueblo culture as well as impose their own and this made the missionary enterprise central to success.[31]

The Pueblo people preferred to move out of their central villages to rancherias at different seasons. This probably made it possible to increase agricultural production and to gather wild produce as well. To control the populace, the friars attempted to concentrate people in pueblos and small villages. In the larger pueblos, friars built convents, complexes composed of a monastery, church, storage rooms, kitchen, and sacristy. In smaller villages, where small groups continued to live in rancherias, friars erected simple one room churches and established *visitas,* places where the friars only visited. The Salinas Pueblos were part of a frontier religious administrative system staffed by fifty Franciscans by the 1630s.[32]

The friars had the most frequent, stable, and direct contact with the Pueblos and the most concern over their response to Spanish control. They believed that the people were more inclined to hunt than to cultivate and therefore, as one friar reported, "it is necessary to compel them to plant." Still, in order to convert the Indians, the friars had to keep them reasonably content and within the pueblos. They tried to attract them with gentle treatment, praise, and "relieving them of all physical labor," reported one friar. If annoyed, the converts could go to live among the unconverted, "according to their whims, and in complete freedom."[33]

The friars immediately began to train converts in the new religion. They concentrated on the young boys whom they taught to read and write and to sing. By the 1630s the friars were teaching about seventy Indian boys at Abo and at Quarai. These boys served in choirs and as assistants for religious rites. While young girls were required to attend mass, they were not taught by friars. Esoteric knowledge was reserved for the males. Presumably, young girls continued their regular gendered tasks while the young boys studied.[34]

Those the friars could not entice, they depended on the secular to coerce. From Santa Fe, Friar Juan de Prada wrote that the Spanish protected the Pueblos from non-Christian Indians and put "fear in the subjected ones in order that they may not rebel and forget their obedience to the king, our lord, as well as to their ministers of instruction."[35] These officials were not entirely dependable. While a friar might serve more than thirty years on the New Mexican frontier, governors each served an average of three years.

Indian governors, men probably selected by the Spanish because they were already regional leaders, were most important for peaceful relations between Spanish and Pueblos. Don Esteban Clemente, one governor of the Salinas, spoke six languages and made frequent visits to the Apaches to exchange goods. Linguistic and trading skills allowed him to deal with the people of the Salinas pueblos but also with the various groups who came to trade at Gran Quivira. Pueblo governors, such as Clemente, were crucial in maintaining control. As long as the Indian governor was loyal, the Spanish authorities and the friars had no trouble. Governors, however, had the popularity and power among their people to lead organized regional revolts. According to later accounts, Clemente led the fourth of five major revolts against Spanish control between 1640 and 1675. All the rebellions had as a goal, said one Spaniard, "to be left in freedom as in ancient times, living like their ancestors." Clemente's rebellion extended throughout New Mexico and included plans to destroy all Spaniards. The Spanish discovered the plan for revolt and immediately hanged Clemente.[36]

Below the regional governors the local pueblo governors and kin groups were also essential for peace. Little is known about early pueblo governments, but if they were similar to other frontier areas and later pueblos, senior kin heads probably elected the governors.[37]

Kin groups, the smallest unit of local government, retained considerable power. Such decentralization made unified resistance to Spanish control difficult but the kin groups also continued to give women a role in local decision-making.

Outside of this new system were those indigenous peoples who remained hostile and unconverted, such as the Apache. While the Spanish ruled that sedentary peoples near centers of Spanish power who accepted the new religion could not be enslaved, they applied no such prohibition to the Apaches. Such distinctions increased the tensions among the different tribes who normally traded peacefully. In these conflicts, women suffered. Apaches, angered by the Spanish practice of taking women and children as slaves, increasingly retaliated in kind. In 1653, Apaches took twenty-seven women and children captive from Gran Quivira.[38]

If the Spanish system exposed women to external danger by disrupting older trade patterns, it also imposed new internal non-kin hierarchies. The friars created a new Christian Pueblo male elite to assist them in their ritual duties and mission administration, while the crown created a new secular elite. These two Spanish elites were often at war with each other. Indian women as well as men could play one group off against the other, but it was a dangerous tactic, the results of which were difficult to control.

Religion was one area of conflict. Missionaries objected to the katchina dances because of the copulation, which was performed with kin and violated European incest taboos. They also objected to the ritual offerings to Indian supernaturals, traditionally inhabitants of the underworld, whom the friars associated with the Christian devil who ruled the underworld. Spanish authorities apparently considered the dancing as part of the Pueblo culture and one that should not be disturbed. Perhaps they recognized the important role of the elite in controlling the labor of the community, something upon which they depended. Conflict over the dances was clearly conflict with local power structures and led to growing hostility toward friars. By the 1660s friars had ordered the katchina dances halted, the kivas and ritual objects destroyed. All of the kivas at Gran Quivira were destroyed. The women then converted rooms in the pueblo for the use of the men. The male public religion became a domestic religion, practiced in the household, while the Christian religion became the only public religion.[39]

Labor was a second source of conflict, both with the friars and officials. While the crown supplied the friars with what they needed to subsist, their ambitious building program of the 1620s and 1630s put an extreme burden on the women of the pueblos. The crown's policy had always had the goal of protecting property rights and the liberty of person while making colonizing profitable through the exploitation of native labor. Missionaries did not have to pay for Indian labor; officials, technically, were supposed to pay. But both missionaries and officials were non-productive consumers and conflict between clergy and officials over the use of native labor was inevitable. Women's labor used to build churches was labor that could not be used by colonists. Building of churches in the Salinas area began at Chililí in 1613 and ended with the completion of the church at Gran Quivira in 1631. When the small churches had been completed, the friars also began construction of larger missionary complexes. Immense building projects that began at Quarai in 1629 ended at Gran Quivira in 1660. The women of the Salinas built the walls of at least three large mission complexes.

The church at Quarai, called Nuestra Senora de la Purisima Concepión and constructed between 1627 and 1632, remains the most magnificent of these structures. The walls are of red sandstone, twenty-four by eighteen inch stones, quarried from a nearby outcropping. The stone surfaces were so smooth that only a small amount of finishing was necessary. Some walls are as high as sixty feet

Pueblo Indian women plastering adobe wall, Sandoval County, New Mexico, 1936. Source: Museum of New Mexico, Santa Fe, New Mexico.

and some as thick as ten feet at the base. The church measures 100 feet in length with parts of the transept over fifty feet wide. The roofs were made of *vigas* (beams) with *latillas* (small poles) laid in a traditional herring-bone pattern on them. The women erected walls, then plastered them with gypsum one-half inch thick. They also plastered the floors with 1½-inch gypsum. When they were finished plastering, they frescoed bands of orange between two narrow black lines for trim. In addition to the church, they built dormitories, a kitchen, a refectory, and storage rooms. [40]

The church at Abo was built in the 1620s and enlarged in the

1640s. The church was twenty-five feet wide and almost eighty-four feet long on the interior with walls twenty-five feet high. After renovation the walls of San Gregorio at Abo reached a height of thirty-four feet. Like Quarai, the walls had clay mortar coverings and smooth clay floors. The interior walls were plastered with decorative patterns in red, blue, and black.[41]

San Buenaventura was the second church built at Gran Quivira. Begun in 1660, the construction of San Buenaventura reflected the growing gap between the ambitions of the friars and the abilities and desires of the Pueblo people. The convents and the storerooms were completed, but attempts to finish the church bogged down repeatedly. The planned building was also to be of massive scale. The walls facing eastward were 204 feet long and the enclosed area was 18,355 square feet. The blue-gray limestone was laid in caliche mortar and the walls were five to six feet thick. Work on the original walls went slowly and never reached more than nineteen feet high. The walls still stood at that height in 1670 when the Apaches raided the pueblo and sacked the old smaller church, killing eleven people and capturing thirty others. The friar and some of the Pueblos abandoned the town soon after. San Buenaventura remained unfinished.[42]

There is no published account of the furnishings at Quarai or Abo. Inventories of nearby Salinas missions at Tajique and Chilili give some idea of the interiors. There were religious paintings from Mexico, *bultos* (carved statues) of the Virgin, *retablos* (paintings on copper), and carpets woven by the Pueblos. Vestments of red watered lamé and Chinese and Italian damask were in the sacristy, as well as damask chasubles, albs with drawn work, and eight-inch wide point lace, towels, and choir copes trimmed with silver. Churches had silver chalices, and probably silver dishes and cruets along with brilliantly colored cassocks for the Pueblo sacristans to wear when assisting at mass. There were trumpets, flutes, and other musical instruments. And there were canopies, banners, standards, and everything necessary to celebrate feasts.[43]

Of this richness, only the walls built by the women remain. They testify to the desires of the Spanish to create an empire on the northern frontier and to the failure of that effort when it undermined the local economy.

During the early years, when most of the missions were built, the crown allowed missionaries to use volunteer Indian labor. After

1659, the crown ordered that Indian labor must be paid for and that the friars could have only a small amount of volunteer labor. The quest of the friars for massive visible material culture to symbolize the new religion led to their efforts to recruit more and more volunteer labor and to develop commercial crops that could be exchanged for labor or for the items that local Indians could not produce. The friars tried to accumulate agricultural surplus to trade for skins to send to Mexico to purchase cloth, ornaments, and musical instruments for their churches. During the years when pine nuts were abundant, they asked Indian families to collect them. The organ at Abo and altar clothes for Quarai were purchased with the proceeds of piñon nuts sold in Mexico.[44]

Friars tried to collect food surpluses to use in case of food shortages. The old elites could not have been pleased with such control over surplus, one source of their own previous power. The Spanish authorities were also not happy, and claimed that such collecting led the friars to live wasteful lives rather than living more simply. Friars could also collect a tithe if Pueblos raised any grain and cattle on land owned by friars. Pueblos did not have to pay tithes on their native products, such as maize, beans, and cotton, but Hispanic colonists paid a tithe on all agricultural products, including cattle.[45]

Regardless of how wisely or poorly friars used the labor, it brought them into conflict with secular authorities who wished to utilize the labor of Pueblos for themselves. Officials and colonists also wanted the Salinas Pueblos to collect piñon nuts and to carry them, along with salt and corn, to the houses of officials or to other pueblos where trade items were being assembled for shipment to Mexico. In 1661 Salinas Indians presented claims for 5,365 person days in unpaid work, as well as general claims of loading salt at the salt marsh and transporting it to the house of an official who lived over thirty miles away on the Rio Grande. With the exception of gathering piñon nuts, most of this labor was apparently supplied by men, but men absent from the pueblo meant that women had to assume greater responsibility for the cultivation of crops and other tasks normally performed by men.[46]

In addition to paid and volunteer labor for the missions, Pueblos had to provide unpaid labor to Spanish colonists who held *encomiendas*. Over considerable opposition by Spanish settlers in Mexico, the crown had outlawed slavery and forced labor before New Mexico was colonized. The crown replaced forced labor with *encomiendas,* a tribute placed on males eighteen to sixty years of age within a certain area. In sixteenth-century New Mexico, the crown gave *encomiendas* to particular colonists for three generations in return for military services. These *encomenderos* collected goods from, but did not live among, the indigenous population. Twice a year, in May and October, each Pueblo household had to pay one *fanega* of maize (about two and one half bushels or one hundred pounds) and a cotton blanket six palms square (approximately fifty inches) or a buffalo or deer hide.[47]

How much of a burden was the tribute on the women of the Salinas? During the years of abundant harvests, the October payment of maize would not have been a major burden because each household produced a large amount of maize each year and villages usually produced a surplus. The May collection of blankets may have been harder on the women. Men wove the blankets, and it would have been difficult to increase production rapidly. One friar's account of conditions in San Juan in 1601 indicated that even mantas in use might be taken. He described the conditions this way: "Until this year this tribute (blankets or mantas) has been collected with such severity that it availed them nothing to say that they had nothing but what they had on. The Spaniards seize their blankets by force, leaving the poor Indian women stark naked, holding their babies to their breasts." If mantas were not available, Pueblos had to pay in hides, which were usually processed by women and would have increased their work. Other accounts indicate that some encomenderos would also take piñon nuts, woolen stockings, or Apache slaves. As the pressure to produce surplus commodities that could be traded with northern Mexico increased, women as well as men had to produce more.[48]

Even in good times the Pueblos resented the collection of tribute. The first "requisitions" by soldiers had often led to violent conflicts. Now, Pueblos no longer offered open resistance to the more formalized tribute, but its extraction caused an intensification of their labor. Previously, they had been able to trade surpluses as they wished with other villages or with the Plains peoples for the items they needed or wished. Now those surplus commodities had to be produced in greater amounts, on schedule, for men whom they saw only twice a year when they came to collect the tribute.

The tribute imposed a set system that extracted produce and commodities regardless of the condition of the village economy. Production of corn and cotton was dependent on climate and labor supply. Hides depended on trade and labor supply. The demands of building the large mission complexes and furnishing them put additional strain on the village economy. Any reduction in the labor supply or its productivity could undermine the stressed village economies that provided the foundation for the frontier colonization venture.

In their search for labor, Hispanic colonists and their Pueblo allies began raiding neighboring Apache encampments. There they kidnapped children to enslave as servants. Although Apache and Salinas Pueblos had previously traded peacefully together, relations now became strained. By 1640 the trading system was breaking down. The Spanish restricted all trading to Gran Quivira and one smaller town and ordered other villagers to stay out of the towns while Apaches were there. The formerly peaceful traders had begun to burn corn fields, capture Salinas women and children to replace those taken by Spaniards, and generally pose an external threat to the existence of the villages.

Hard times came in the 1660s. The climate moved into one of its periodic dry spells. For three years, no crops were harvested. Apaches were probably also affected by the drought and had no surpluses available to barter, but now equipped with horses and guns they resorted to increased raids to obtain the food they needed. By 1668 the land was devastated. Friar Juan Bernal wrote from Santo Domingo on April 1, 1669 to his superiors reporting the devastation. "The whole land is at war with the widespread heathen nation of the Apache Indians, who kill all the Christian Indians they can find and encounter."[49]

Gran Quivira was particularly at risk. It had lost its function as a trade center and now lay exposed on the Apache frontier. The surplus population, once fed by the trade, had no resources. Friars fed some Indians around the major missions from their storage rooms, but hundreds of Indians starved at Gran Quivira. "In the past year, 1668," wrote Friar Bernal, "a great many Indians perished of hunger, lying dead along the roads, in the ravines, and in their huts. There were pueblos [such as Gran Quivira] where more than four hundred and fifty died of hunger."[50]

Spanish officials had accumulated no surplus with which to feed the Indians. The surplus of the friars was soon exhausted. Even the Spanish ate hides to survive. Epidemics and more Apache attacks followed. Abo was sacked and burned. After the internal revolt led by the Indian governor, Clemente, was swiftly crushed, the survivors began to leave the decimated villages. By 1678 all villages had been abandoned. A mission sent out by the friars to examine the villages reported in 1681 that the pueblos were "desolate and without people."[51]

Before the final catastrophic years, Pueblo women showed amazing adaptability to the new regime they endured. When women were not laboring for the Spaniards, they bartered or sold their labor to get food for their families. According to the friars, women also appropriated food from the friars' stores, which they sometimes treated as community stores. They learned how to grow, preserve, and cook new foods and learned to spin, weave, and sew new cloth. Women still made traditional pottery, but at Abo and Quarai they also manufactured new types of pottery based on European styles for the Hispanic population. Corn rituals continued to be performed among the Pueblos in which unity with all living creatures was the focus. Women formed the center of these rituals and Pueblo female deities remained important, though many people also honored the Virgin. The Virgin became central to the Catholicism that Pueblos practiced in Northern New Mexico.[52]

The extreme repression of their traditional religion, combined with economic exploitation soon provoked a major rebellion against Spanish rule everywhere among the Pueblos. In 1680 Indians laid careful plans and successfully drove the Spaniards out of their country. When the Spanish returned in 1692, they modified their control of the Indians. They allowed the Pueblos to practice their traditional religion along with Catholic rituals and allowed them more economic freedom. Thus, although the Salinas villages were abandoned, the Pueblo cultures, along with the Salinas refugees survived.

That survival was, nevertheless, marked by a severe demographic catastrophe. By the end of the seventeenth century, the Pueblo people had been reduced to sixteen thousand survivors. It was not the conscious intent of the Hispanic colonists to destroy the Indian cultures, but early secular leaders wanted the labor of Indian women as well as men, the only resource of much value in New Mexico.

Religious leaders, on the other hand, wanted to build lasting monuments to their Christian religion. The combination of these two forces put an incredible strain on the Pueblos, particularly on women, who were responsible for maintaining much of the Pueblo culture. The fragility of the cultures of this arid land was not evident to the conquerors as they settled down to develop colonies. Certainly census figures for the 1630s, which listed hundreds of Indians around the missions, gave little indication that only the walls of the missions would one day mark these Salinas villages.

PART III

Rural Development

THE ARTICLES IN THIS SECTION USE A VARIETY OF written historical documents to analyze rural women's work in different cultures. These case studies show how historians can reevaluate traditional documents by employing new methodologies and different theoretical perspectives that emphasize women rather than men. Such methods yield rich results when applied to women of all ethnic groups, even those who had the fewest opportunities to leave written documents. With these methods, we can return women to the center of rural development studies, a place they held traditionally.

The growing literature of economic development and women's studies is the most helpful in the process of reconceptualizing the central place of women in rural development. Documenting that place depends on creating theoretical models, asking the right questions, and locating sources that can provide answers. I have used the Seneca of New York, black women on a Maryland wheat plantation, and Euro-American Pennsylvania dairy farm women to explore the issues of women in rural development and, then more broadly, the issues of women's work in the context of capitalism. Our theoretical framework is still very inadequate. The task of researchers during the next decade will be to develop economic models with women at the center, along with rural men and children, to explain how the labor of different ethnic and economic groups interacted with economic policy of political and economic male elites.

Regardless of ethnic group, rural women functioned within a developing economy that affected them differently depending on their geographic and class position within American society. Women produced within rural households that seemingly had vastly different forms of production—indigenous as with the Seneca, slave as with the women of Rose Hill, market oriented as was the case with the Pennsylvania butter makers. Yet each group seemed to intensify their labor within the developing economy. While many women retained a sexual division of labor within these households, they used their traditional flexibility of labor to adapt to changes and to initiate new divisions of labor. Using traditional and new skills, they produced commodities and services for the market, as well as items for use within the household. They also reorganized the type and amount of consumption that existed within the household and adapted ideology to their own uses.

The household is a complex institution because it is often the locus of more than one form of production and because it articulates the flow of labor and resources among them. It is this role at the center of the articulation that makes the household so crucial a nexus for class interests, conflicts, and alliances. Individual historical experiences of women, on the periphery of colonizing and at the industrial core can help in understanding the development of capitalism itself. Women were not marginal to this process of development but central to it.

8   Native American Women and Agriculture: A Seneca Case Study

AT THE TIME EUROPEANS FIRST ARRIVED IN NORTH America, and for centuries after, Native American women dominated agricultural production in the tribes of the eastern half of the United States.[1] In many of these tribes, the work of the women provided over half of the subsistence and secured for them not only high status but also public power. Yet this immense contribution to the economy and to the culture of the Native Americans has never been studied systematically by historians. We have no complete history of Indian agriculture.[2] We have no study of how women functioned in these agricultural societies. We do not know what happened to the women and their agricultural production under the impact of European invasion. Using the Seneca women, I would like to provide a prototype of what we can learn about the history of Native American women and agriculture.[3]

Several theories have recently been presented by anthropologists to describe the status of women. Peggy Sanday has suggested that there is a high correlation between female status and a balanced division of labor. She further argues that women do not only produce in agricultural societies but must also control the means of production—land, seeds, tools—and the methods of work to achieve public power. The history of the Seneca women seems to confirm both these theories and also to show that this power, once achieved, was difficult to dislodge even by the combined efforts of missionaries, government, and reformers.[4]

Unfortunately, we have no verbatim transcripts from early Native American women about agricultural production. Our only account is by Buffalo Woman, a Hidatsa who provided a lengthy description of the philosophy and techniques of agriculture in 1912. Buffalo Woman spent over a year with an anthropologist in North Dakota demonstrating in minute detail the cultivation, planting, and hoeing process. She described the cooperative work groups of the women and sang their work songs. Her account conveys a feeling of the pride and care with which Native American women performed their work. But to develop a picture of the community power women derived from this agricultural production, and the struggle to maintain that power under the impact of change, we must turn to the records of those who were the agents of change. If used critically, these records provide a starting point for the study of Native American women and agriculture.[5]

When white colonists arrived in the seventeenth century, they found many of the best bottomlands near creeks and rivers cleared, sometimes abandoned, but often filled with the neat and clean corn fields of the Native American women. An early account by Roger Williams told of the "very loving sociable speedy way" in which men and women joined together to clear fields, and how women planted, weeded, hilled, gathered, and stored the corn. In some areas, tribal women had as many as two thousand acres under cultivation, and in most areas they had accumulated surpluses that were traded to hungry settlers. Colonists were often more interested in commerce than in laborious clearing and planting, and even when engaged in agriculture many were not careful farmers. Records mention that Native American women sometimes ridiculed colonists for neglecting to keep their fields well weeded.[6]

At first colonists occupied abandoned fields or purchased cleared fields from the Native Americans. War soon added a third method by which the colonists obtained fields. "Now," said Edward Waterhouse after the Indian attack of 1622 in Virginia, "their cleared grounds in all their villages (which are situated in the fruitfullest places of the land) shall be inhabited by us, whereas heretofore the grubbing of woods was the greatest labour." During the next three hundred years the Native American agricultural societies underwent a drastic transformation as trade, warfare, and disease disrupted their subsistence economies. The Seneca, like other tribes, felt the impact of these disruptions on their economy.[7]

The foremothers of the Seneca were among the women of the League of the Iroquois whose well-tended fields surrounded their western New York villages, and whose origin myth began with a female deity falling from the sky to give birth to the first woman. Sky Woman brought earth, seeds, and roots from which wild trees, fruits, and flowers grew. The domestic plants—potatoes, beans, squash, corn, and other crops—sprang from the grave of Sky Woman's daughter. Later, according to several legends, the Corn Maiden brought corn to the Seneca, taught the women how to plant, how to prepare the corn, how to dance the corn dances, and which songs to sing at the dances. Seneca women believed that a great power pervaded all nature and endowed every element with intelligence. Each clod of soil, each tree, each stalk of corn, had life and consciousness. At a winter ceremony each year the women gave thanks for every object in nature. At springtime they offered thanks to the sap and sugar from the maple trees, which they made into syrup. Later there were planting feasts, a June strawberry feast, then a corn feast, and finally completing the cycle, a harvest feast. The purpose of these feasts was to show that life was desired and that the people were thankful for it.[8]

Seneca family life centered on the longhouse, a joint tenement shared by families of kin, the entire clan household being composed of as many as fifty or sixty people. The domestic economy of each household was regulated by an older woman who distributed household stores to families and guests. Households were clustered in compact villages of 20 or 30 houses or in larger towns of 100 to 150 houses. The more densely populated towns usually shifted location every ten years; the smaller towns might occupy the same site for twenty years or more. These compact towns proved particularly vulnerable to seventeenth-century disease and warfare. In 1668, for example, almost 250 people in one town died of disease, and, in one month in 1676, 60 small children in another town died from pneumonia. The French destroyed large Seneca towns in 1687 and 1696.[9]

Communal living, as practiced by the Seneca, provided stable care for all the children of the village. Children inherited their property and place in the clan through their mothers; and women who were childless or had few children adopted any orphan children. Seneca women showed extraordinary affection for their children, as one of the earliest Jesuit visitors observed in 1668, and children had great respect for their parents. Elders in the longhouse shared the responsibility of teaching children necessary physical and social survival skills. After their mothers had arranged their marriage, a young couple traditionally joined one of the mothers' communal households. In no case did the couple set up a separate nuclear family. According to early Jesuit accounts, most marriages were monogamous, but a few Seneca women had two husbands. If husbands were absent too long or failed to provide their share of subsistence for the household, the woman would take another marriage partner.[10]

Seneca women had possessory rights to all cultivated land within the tribal area. The women's clans distributed the land to households according to their size and organized farming communally. Each year, the women of the town elected a chief matron who directed the work. Sick and injured members of these mutual aid societies had a right to assistance in planting and harvesting; and after hoeing, the owner of each parcel of land would provide a feast for all the women workers. According to Mary Jemison, the Irish captive who spent the second half of the eighteenth century with the Seneca women, their work was less onerous than that of white women. They had no drivers or overseers and worked in the fields as leisurely as they wished, with their children beside them. The women formed Tonwisas, ritual groups to encourage the good favor of the "three sisters"—corn, beans, and squash. The leaders of these groups performed rites, carrying armfuls of corn and loaves of corn bread around a kettle of corn soup. After harvest, women braided or stored the corn in corn cribs or shelled and stored it in bark barrels. Women later ground the corn in large oak mortars with four-foot long maple wood pestles. The rhythmic sound of the women grinding corn was the first sound heard in the villages each morning.[11]

Seneca women also controlled the distribution of surplus food and—by virtue of the right to demand captives as replacement for murdered kinspeople—often influenced warfare. The matrilineal Seneca women retained a powerful position in the community through control of land and agriculture. Women had their own

Seneca Caroline Parker Mountpleasant posed in a typically Victorian manner for this mid-nineteenth-century daguerreotype but wore a dress showing the creative ways in which Seneca women adapted their traditional decorative arts to new materials and designs. Source: Smithsonian Institution, Anthropology Archives, Natural History Museum.

councils and were represented in the council of the civil rulers by a male speaker, the most famous of whom was Red Jacket. Women also had the power to elect the civilian rulers and to depose those guilty of misconduct, incompetence, or disregard of the public welfare.[12]

By the 1780s the Senecas had already experienced the most common disruptions of agricultural village life: warfare, disease, and trade. The Seneca were one of the League of Six Nations who supported the British, in part because the American revolutionaries offered them no guarantee of the peaceful possession of their territory. In August 1779, on General Washington's orders, American troops under John Sullivan laid waste to the Seneca lands. By army estimates, they uprooted, girdled, or chopped down 1,500 orchard trees; destroyed 60,000 bushels of corn, 2,000 to 3,000 bushels of beans, and cucumbers, watermelons, and pumpkins in such quantities, one major recalled, as to be "almost incredible to a civilized people." An estimated five hundred acres of cultivated crops were destroyed, along with forty large towns and villages of communal longhouses. The warriors fled to the protection of the British, and the women and children hid in the forests. Although Washington had urged the capture of women as well as men, none were taken, and the refugees crowded into Fort Niagara that winter where the British furnished meat and potatoes. The next spring the Seneca women returned to plant corn, potatoes, and pumpkins along the bottoms of the south side of Buffalo Creek at the eastern tip of Lake Erie and made maple sugar in their old way. Smallpox ravaged the communities the following year, however, and deaths led to demoralization and loss of confidence. The corn supply again was exhausted, and the people applied to Fort Niagara for supplies. The officer at Fort Niagara complained that the Seneca had improvident habits, but he sent the supplies.[13]

By 1789 trade had also drastically altered the women's way of life. They now had iron and steel hoes, awls, needles, shears, and cloth. Women had substituted cloth for fur garments and beads for porcupine quills in much of their decorated work. The estimated contact population of ten thousand had been reduced to several thousand survivors. There were about two thousand in western New York along the Buffalo and Cazenovia creeks, clustered in three or four villages.

Women retained their political power, however. When Washington sent Colonel Proctor to obtain the support of the Seneca in negotiating with other tribes in May 1791, the women intervened to urge peaceful negotiation. It was a time of crisis for the Seneca. Warriors had just brought in an Indian scalp with the story that white people were making war. The rulers had met in council and refused to negotiate. Next morning the elder women appeared before Colonel Proctor's lodge, where he was talking with a number of chiefs, and announced that they had considered his proposition:

> you ought to hear and listen to what we, women, shall speak, as well as to the sachems; for we are the owners of this land—and it is ours. It is we that plant it for our and their use. Hear us, therefore, for we speak of things that concern us while our men shall say more to you; for we have told them.

Later that day the council reassembled and Red Jacket, the spokesman for the women, announced that the women were "to conclude what ought to be done by both sachems and warriors," and that the women had decided that for the good of them and their children a peace delegation would be sent.[14]

Women also spoke during the negotiation of the Treaty of 1794 with the United States government. In 1797 they still had a dominant voice. When Thomas Morris arrived in August of that year to negotiate a land sale for his father, the women again vetoed the decision of the sachems and insisted, "It is we, the women, who own the land." Morris promised the women that if they agreed to the treaty, they would never again know want. Warriors often went to white settlements to sell furs and buy food while the women and children might go hungry, he reminded them. He said that the $100,000 offered them for the land could be put in a bank so that "in times of scarcity, the women and children of your nation can be fed." The warriors supported the treaty, because Morris promised the hunting rights would not be impaired. To the women Morris offered special gifts and a string of wampum to remind them—should they turn down the offer and then become impoverished—of the wealth they had rejected.[15]

Certainly, this was economic pressure of the rankest kind, and yet, given the difficult circumstances, it is easy to see why the women decided to sell the land. Morris's tactics were successful. "This had an excellent effect on the women [who] at once declared themselves for selling, and the business began to wear a better aspect," Morris wrote in his journal.[16]

Government and speculators had reduced the land of the women. The way was now open for teachers and missionaries to end women's domination over agriculture. The Quakers had dispatched their first mission to the Seneca in 1789 to teach the men agriculture and the women "useful arts," but the people exhibited little interest. Two years later a Seneca leader appealed to Washington to teach the men how to plow and the women to spin and weave. Washington sent a teacher; and the Secretary of State, Timothy Pickering, urged the Six Nations to fence their lands, raise livestock, and farm "as white people do." Buffalo Creek and other villages refused to admit teachers or missionaries.[17]

The leader who appealed to Washington for technical assistance was Cornplanter, who was not a traditional chief. He spoke only for his own village on the Allegheny river; there he exercised unusual power because he had received personal title to the land for negotiating the sale of Indian lands in Pennsylvania. The Quakers were quick to accept Cornplanter's invitation and soon arrived at the Allegheny village ready to retrain both men and women. At this time women were tending the fields and men were trading furs. The women refused to appear, though the Quakers proposed an incentive system, promising to pay cash to men who would raise wheat, rye, corn, potatoes, and hay, and to women who would spin thread from flax and wool. Later the Quakers conducted an experiment to prove that plowed lands produced a greater yields than fields hoed by women. It was "unreasonable," the Quakers argued, to allow mothers, wives, and sisters to work all day in the fields and woods, and the men to "play" with bows and arrows. The men warned the Quakers not to expect too much.[18]

The Reverend Elkanah Holmes reported that the Tuscarora tribe of the Iroquois told him in 1800 that among the Senecas and the western tribes women did all the field work. Among the Tuscarora, the men had already begun to substitute agricultural work for hunting, and Holmes reported them at work in the fields alongside the women planting, hoeing, and harvesting corn. In 1801 the Seneca requested oxen to plow with and spinning wheels. By 1804 a Quaker reported a large plow at work in a Seneca village above Buffalo Creek drawn by three yoke of oxen and attended by three Native American men; he reported considerable "progress" in agriculture.[19]

At Allegheny two Quaker women soon began to teach spinning and weaving, and in 1806 Seneca women promised to take up these white women's arts. Gayantgogwus, sister of Cornplanter and one of the most influential persons in the community, brought her granddaughter and another young relative to show visiting Quakers how they could knit and spin. The Quakers urged the men to spread out their farms, arguing that it was better for farming and cattle raising to be separated. The Quakers also introduced wheat and other new crops. Already 100 families had chosen to fence their farms individually and to embrace the nuclear family, while thirty new homes clustered at Cold Springs.[20]

We do not know what prompted women in Allegheny to adopt their new role so quickly. Brazilian women, moving more recently from a women's work group to a shared work situation with men, have explained that they wanted to share the burden of supplying food more equally with men whose ability to hunt had decreased with the decline in game. They also wanted consumer goods that a cash income would bring. Among the Seneca women, there was a split. Some of the older women saw the change as a threat to their strong position in the community and reasserted their traditional powers against the divisive new economy and way of life being forced upon them. Old women advised their daughters to use contraceptives and abortion and, if necessary, to leave husbands who took up the new ways. Handsome Lake, who had recently replaced Cornplanter as the new chief of the League of the Iroquois, attacked the older women. "The Creator is sad because of the tendency of old women to breed mischief," he warned. He accused them of witchcraft.[21]

Witchcraft accusations occur when social relations are ambiguous and tensions cannot otherwise be resolved. They are often an instrument for breaking off relations or withdrawing community protection from certain individuals. The older Seneca women formed a rival faction to the changes that Cornplanter, Handsome Lake, and the Quakers wished to institute and a power block that Handsome Lake wished to break. The accusations split the ranks of the women still further and realigned some in support of the new system and its leaders. Handsome Lake made many accusations among the Senecas and, though he opposed them, some executions did occur. In a few cases, accusations were followed with trials by council and swift execution. One older woman was reported cut down while at work in her corn field in 1799. Another was reported executed on the spot after a council decided her guilt. Four of the "best women in the nation" narrowly escaped execution at Sandusky when the executioners refused to carry out the sentence. Probably not many old women died, but the lesson was clear.[22]

As Handsome Lake, Cornplanter, and the Quakers asserted their influence more clearly over the village of Allegheny and its agricultural pattern, the witchcraft accusations ceased. Handsome Lake became the prophet of the supremacy of the husband-wife relationship over the mother-daughter relationship. Men were to harvest food for their families, build good houses, keep horses and cattle; women were to be good housewives. By 1813 Seneca women were operating spinning wheels, and two Seneca men, trained by the Quakers as village weavers, turned out two hundred yards of linen and wool that year. Well pleased with the transition at Allegheny, the Quakers estimated that the average farm had ten acres, horses or oxen, cows, and pigs. In 1821 a painted box sent from the first school portrayed Seneca girls learning to spin and weave with quotes from the Bible above their busy activity: "She layeth her hands to the spindle, and hands hold the distaff. . . . She looketh well to household and eateth not the bread of Idleness."[23]

While Allegheny seemed a model agricultural village and thus— the Quakers hoped—on its way to eventual Christianity, the villages at Buffalo Creek were still in crisis. During 1818 to 1822 there was an outbreak of witchcraft accusations at Buffalo Creek, and women were executed there and at Tuscarora. Like the women of Allegheny, the older women of these communities seemed to be opposing the new order. Jabez Backus Hyde, a Presbyterian schoolteacher reported from Buffalo Creek in 1820 that

> Their ancient manner of subsistence is broken up and when they appear willing and desirous to turn their attention to agriculture, their ignorance, the inveteracy of their old habits, and disadvantage under which they labor, soon discourage them; though they struggle hard little is realized to their benefit, besides the continual dread they live in of losing their possessions. If they build they know not who will inhabit. If they make fields they know not who will cultivate them. They know the anxiety of their white neighbors to get possession of their lands.[24]

When the New York Missionary Society requested that a mission be established at Buffalo Creek, the Seneca there called a council to debate the matter. Men and women, converts and traditionalists, agreed to allow a mission to be established, and in 1819 the first evangelical minister arrived to preach and teach. Subsidized by the government to teach agriculture to the boys and instructed by the mission society to teach all the children to work and be industrious, the new school attempted to teach girls to knit and sew. But the little girls proved especially troublesome and, when disciplined, complained to their parents. Complaints brought objections by the chiefs and a request that the children be persuaded and coaxed into obedience and, if disobedient, left to the parents to reprove. If all else failed, the child could be considered heathen and expelled. Such a doctrine of education was unacceptable, the Reverend T. S. Harris confided to his journal, because "the rod is the plan of God's own appointment."[25]

Despite Harris's severity with the young girls, the school supplied a new community focus to replace the old communal activities being destroyed by fences and isolated farming. A group of older non-Christian women soon appeared before Harris and asked to be taught as well. The minister agreed that the school would do so as soon as a female teacher was procured. Education and new skills learned in a group were attractive alternatives to the isolation of the new farmsteads and compatible with the women's new relationship to the economy. The third wife of Red Jacket—he was now leader of the anti-Christian faction—left him to join the church, and twenty persons, mostly women, asked the minister to instruct them. A number of women adopted Christian names and became members of the mission.[26]

The years between 1837 and 1845 were times of trouble for the Seneca and for other tribes who were all being pressured to move west of the Mississippi. As early as 1818 a delegation of Cherokee women had opposed westward removal and urged missionaries to help them maintain the bounds of the lands they possessed. Cherokee women took up the ways of white women to prove their worthiness to remain on their land. They learned to spin and weave and to wear bonnets and allowed their men to replace them in the fields. Their efforts were ignored by the government. When the army took the Cherokee women out of Georgia in 1839, they left a large number of spinning wheels and looms behind. Other Cherokee women fled to the mountains with a small band who refused to leave. Seminole women, deported that same year from Florida, criticized the men for allowing deportation and for refusing to die on their native soil.[27]

The Seneca would have been forcibly removed too, but for the efforts of the Quakers and the missionary Asher Wright, who had moved to Buffalo Creek in 1831. The Quakers mobilized public opinion against a treaty calling for the removal of all the Senecas, and Wright helped negotiate a compromise treaty allowing them to keep the Allegheny and Cattaraugus reservations but giving up the valuable Buffalo Creek land.[28]

When the Seneca voted on the compromise treaty, there was still no consensus, which traditionally would have meant rejection. The Quakers charged that bribery and secrecy had been responsible for the majority of the chiefs signing the first treaty and that many opposed the compromise treaty as well. The Buffalo Creek Seneca were especially bitter at the removal, held a meeting, and resolved to have nothing to do with Christian Indians, missionaries, or the gospel. Under protest, they were removed from the Buffalo Creek reservation thirty-five miles south to the Cattaraugus reservation. Their ancestral lands eventually became part of the city of Buffalo.[29]

At the time of the negotiations in 1838, the women were still working the land, making beadwork, brooms, baskets, and other articles for sale, and picking berries to sell at local markets. The women bathed twice a week and dressed neatly in beaded skirts of brightly colored calico, long tunics and leggings, and wore their hair parted in the middle and tied back loose or in a knot with ribbons. They acted and felt, remarked Henry Dearborn, Adjutant General for Massachusetts, "on a perfect equality" with their husbands, advised and influenced them, and were treated well in return. "She lives with him from love," noted Dearborn a bit wistfully in his journal, "for she can obtain her means of support better than he can." Senecas still traced descent through the females and were affectionate, careful, kind, and laborious in the care of their little children. They were "equals and quite as independent in all that is general to both, and each separately forming his or her duties as things proper and indispensable for the interest and happiness of themselves in their several domestic private and common relations."[30]

Other whites assured Dearborn that the condition of the Seneca, despite appearances, was deplorable, the men and women intemperate and dissolute and not able to raise sufficient provisions for their support. Once the flats of Buffalo Creek had been one continuous corn field, said one informant; now the fields were overgrown and the Senecas' chief subsistence was begging. Judge Paine of nearby Aurora advised emigration before the Seneca became extinct. All groups were equally wretched, the judge told the visitor, and they were causing great injury to those around by obstructing agriculture. Land values would be enhanced if the white people owned and settled the land, one trader assured Dearborn.[31]

Dearborn was skeptical about the "pretended mercies of the villainous white man," and romantic about "the noble race of the Senecas." Yet he concluded they must be forced to work and that all efforts at change must begin with the women, who traditionally tilled the land, manufactured the clothing, and managed the domestic and economic concerns of the family. First, the land must be divided and owned in severalty to be sold, devised, or inherited as with the whites. Representation must be by landowners only. Cattle and plows should be provided to the men to break up the land, and hoes, rakes, and shovels to the women. Children should be taught to read and write and premiums should be given mothers for each twelve-year-old son who regularly worked on the land or at some mechanical trade; and at sixteen, the sons should be allowed half this premium. In one generation, Dearborn wrote, in words reformers would echo through the century with each new plan to "civilize the Indians," all the Native Americans would be good farmers skilled in the useful mechanical arts, independent, intelligent, industrious, and on the march to "moral excellence and refinement." The "ridiculous" corn feast and other rites, said Dearborn, must be abandoned.[32]

Dearborn had already witnessed the corn feast where a third of the assembled people were women—teenagers of fourteen to old matrons. Five women had distributed the food—corn, beans, squash, vegetables, and deer soup—in baskets and kettles to the other women who then carried the food to their families—husbands and children scattered in groups on the grass—or home. The feast symbolized the fact: women were still in charge of production and distribution of the food.[33]

Seneca women continued their important economic role in the community. In 1846 they were reported by anxious Quakers as still working in the fields, wearing their traditional tunic and leggings, living in log huts with earth floors, and cooking a pot of venison stew for the family's main meal. Quakers urged Seneca men to withdraw their women from the fields for the domestic duties of the household and, at a council meeting with the Seneca that year, a female Quaker appealed to the women to change, arguing that "to mothers, properly belongs the care and management of the education of their children." The Seneca woman Guanaea responded that it was the earnest desire of the Seneca women in council to have their children instructed in the manner desired and to do all in their power to cooperate in and promote that goal. As a result of this meeting, the Quakers opened a Female Manual Labor School at Cattaraugus where young women under twenty were taught to card and spin wool, knit stockings, cut out and make garments, wash and iron clothes, make bread, do plain cooking, and perform "every other branch of good housewifery, pertaining to a country life."[34]

Published records do not indicate what role the women had in the establishment of a republican government with laws and a constitution in 1848. The communities had lost seventy people in a typhoid epidemic, and political dissension again divided the people. Presumably the women performed their traditional role in divesting the old chiefs of their horns, the symbol of life tenure, to allow the new constitution to be legally established. Under the new constitution men and women elected three judges to the judiciary and eighteen legislators to the council. Three-fourths of the voters and three-fourths of all the mothers had to ratify all decisions. While confirming important political power to the women, the new constitution also legitimized the replacement of consensus by majority rule among the women, thereby acknowledging the fragmentation of their power. That same year, 1848, white women were meeting less than a hundred miles away at Seneca Falls to demand the right to vote and be heard in the politics of their nation.[35]

The Seneca women were also able to continue to exert economic control over the annuities paid by the federal government from the interest on a trust fund from the sale of their lands. This was the money that Morris had promised would allow them to live forever without poverty if they gave up their lands. The Seneca annuities were first paid in blankets, calico, and yarn annually at Buffalo Creek. As with other tribes, these annuities were a main source of complaint against government policies. Native Americans often complained because some treaties had set a particular sum in gold to be paid in food and commodities, but financial fluctuations, especially inflation, reduced the quantity of goods received, sometimes by half. In addition, businesses with government contracts were notorious in their willingness to supply poor quality goods, and government officials were known for their willingness to purchase commodities that the Native Americans did not want and could not use. A cash payment was soon substituted for the Senecas, funds allotted to the heads of families, and tribal members encouraged to buy from merchants licensed to sell on the reservation. After 1834, allegedly to end frauds, Congress decided the money would go to the chiefs. Chiefs thereafter represented the tribes and received the money from the government; but among the Seneca the money was then divided by the chiefs among the mothers of the families, usually depending on their need. The women were given credit by the merchants and thus were able to retain some control over the distribution of food and commodities. The annuities were never enough to prevent poverty, however. In 1850 the Seneca received only eighteen thousand dollars. Still the fifty to eighty dollars each woman received annually was an important supplement to her earnings. The women also attempted to make the chiefs accountable not only to the women, but sometimes to white creditors as well.[36]

Nor were the Seneca women agreed on the benefits of the white woman's culture, which the Christians worked so hard to inculcate. During the 1850s Laura Wright, the missionary wife of Asher Wright, established an orphanage to care for young children and began to instruct the older women in their wifely duties. She believed women should be taught to be Christian housekeepers, needlewomen, and laundresses and planned to buy material and teach them to make garments for sale. She began by sponsoring dinners at which she gave lessons in making clothing, housekeeping, and child care. But during these dinners, the non-Christians—still at least a third of the women—would gather outside in an opposition meeting to ridicule the converts. They considered sewing a ruse to break down the old religion and insisted on observing the old rites.[37]

Later Ms. Wright borrowed eight hundred dollars to invest in material and contracted to supply the government with 650 duck coats and red flannel shirts for the western tribes. Several women even purchased sewing machines on credit, hoping to pay for them with the proceeds from the contract. After a long wait, the government finally paid for the garments, but the amount was so small that the women did not consider it worth their time to continue sewing for sale. They did, however, continue to sell their beaded work, baskets, and berries to nearby whites, and they continued to farm.[38]

By all evidence, the Seneca women still had a strong political, religious, and economic role in the 1850s. It is surprising, therefore, that when the Victorian anthropologist Lewis Henry Morgan began his studies of the Iroquois in 1846, he did not perceive the importance of the economic role of the women. It was not that he believed the Native American women were unproductive. He noted in his journals of 1862, while visiting the western tribes: "Among all our Indian nations the industry of the women is proverbial." But he encouraged the women in domestic manufacture, the products of which could be purchased by government agents to reimburse the women for their labor. The women then would support the whole tribe, he suggested, and after a time the men would unite with them in labor. Such a plan might have been good half a century earlier, but industrialization had already made it unlikely that women would continue domestic manufacturing, as Laura Wright had found out. Among the Native American women only traditional manufactures, such as pottery and blanket weaving in the Southwest, ever provided much of an income and even then it was very low.[39]

Like other American men, Morgan continued to place his main hope for the progress of all women in the "affections" between the sexes, in the perfection of the monogamous family, the education of women, and private ownership of land. After a visit to the Iroquois in 1846, he claimed that the males considered the women inferior, dependent, and their servants—and that the women agreed. Later Morgan wrote of the power the Iroquois women exercised through their clans, but he never mentioned the economic functions of the women as he meticulously traced their kinship systems. He certainly did not agree with Frederick Engels, who drew upon Morgan for *The Origin of the Family, Private Property, and the State,* but who concluded that the only way to liberate women was to bring them back into public industry and abolish the monogamous family as an economic unit.[40]

By the end of the nineteenth century, Morgan's goals had become those of most reformers in America who were concerned about the "Indian problem." In the 1870s the federal government began encouraging the training of a few Native Americans for "higher spheres," that is, to teach common school. Some Seneca women from the Cattaraugus orphanage, now named the Thomas Indian School and financed by the state of New York, went to Oswego Normal School or Geneseo State Normal School. Most, however, went to Hampton Normal and Agricultural School; there from 1878 Indians were taught in classes separate from the black students, though both groups were expected to become agriculturalists, mechanics, or teachers. Hundreds of young Native Americans were educated in the East in "rigidly organized society," anthropologist Alice Fletcher wrote, so that they could resist the restless experimenting and energy of the West when sent there as teachers. The Carlisle Indian School in Pennsylvania was founded on the same principles as Hampton, with the difference that its founder did not believe Native Americans should be exposed to black students and accepted only Indians.[41]

In 1881 Secretary of the Interior Carl Schurz praised the Carlisle School for keeping the girls busy "in the kitchen, dining-room, sewing-room, and with other domestic work." The education of Indian girls was particularly important, he wrote, because he felt that the Indian woman had only been a beast of burden, disposed of by her husband alternately with "animal fondness" and "the cruel brutality of the slave driver." Attachment to the home would civilize the Indians, he predicted, and it was the woman's duty to make the home attractive. She must become the center of domestic life and thus gain respect and self-respect. "If we educate the girls of to-day," Schurz predicted with the reformer's usual assurance, "we educate the mothers of to-morrow, and in educating those mothers we prepare for the education of generations to come."[42]

Reformers quite commonly ignored the agricultural traditions of the women and insisted that Indians had all depended on game for subsistence. The reformers argued that the Indians had no right to the land because they had simply roamed over it like buffalo. Reformers always saw the key to civilization in the family, a family in which the man held the land. Individualism, private ownership, the nuclear family—all were marshaled to defend the breakup of reservation life. Tribal government meant socialism to many and thus had to be destroyed. Daughters, the reformers were fond of saying, must be educated and married under the laws of the land instead of sold "at a tender age for a stipulated price into concubinage to gratify the brutal lusts of ignorance and barbarism." Coeducation would lift Indian women out of servility and degradation, said Thomas J. Morgan, so that their husbands and men generally would "treat them with the same gallantry and respect which is accorded their more favored white sisters." The plan for education remained the same: cooking, sewing, laundry work, teaching.[43]

During the years while reformers spoke long and piously of breaking up tribal life, the Seneca women struggled with disease and lack of food. Cholera, smallpox, and typhoid fever swept the reservations in the 1880s. A drought caused the loss of the corn and potato crop, and the orchards produced little fruit. The government further reduced annuities. When Laura Wright died in 1886, after fifty-three years of missionary work among the Seneca, she was still giving out meat and flour and trying to devise a plan for a Gospel Industrial Institute where women could learn to cook and sew and clean.[44]

At the Thomas Indian School, the old educational goals of the early nineteenth century were translated into modern terms by the whites and continued into the twentieth century. In the classes of 1907 the boys were taught agriculture, the girls "household science." The school reported with confidence in 1910 that girls needed instruction in the comfortable, sanitary, and economic arrangement and management of the home. They were trained for general laundry work and scientific cooking, for their homes and for the homes of others. During vacation they might earn as much as four dollars per week as domestics in one of the local homes in Silver Creek or Buffalo. The most intelligent young women were also channeled into teaching and targeted to teach on other reservations. Many, however, dropped out of Hampton and returned to the reservation. Some were ill, others were needed at home.[45]

White educators expected most Seneca women to marry and settle on the reservation. Many women did marry and continue to live on the reservation. Others taught for a few years or cleaned and washed dishes for Silver Creek families. In 1910 the Census recorded 2,907 Senecas, all but about 200 in the state of New York. Over 60 percent of the 1,266 males were gainfully employed, mainly as farmers and farm laborers, although a few worked in the railroad, chemistry, and building industries. Less than 12 percent of the 1,219 women were gainfully employed, although girls were more likely than boys to attend school and 75 percent of them could read and speak English. The women's occupations were reflective of their place in the white world: twenty-three were servants, six were dressmakers, and six were teachers. Still, thirty-one were listed as farmers and eight as basket makers, reflecting how tenaciously the older women had maintained their traditional occupations.[46]

According to the Census of 1910, 85 percent of all Native American men twenty-five to forty-four years of age were gainfully employed while over 80 percent of the Native American women of the same age were not. Of the 19.6 percent of Native American women who were gainfully employed, almost one-third were employed in traditional white women's work—as servants, laundresses, and teachers. More than two-thirds were employed in home industry—manufacturing baskets, pottery and textiles—or as farm laborers and farmers. These two-thirds, while engaged in occupations considered traditional for the Native American woman, were actually in new occupations geared to the market economy and reserved for working-class women of certain ethnic groups. Black, German-American, Swedish-American women, along with Mexican-American and Japanese-American women, were still in the fields. Immigrant women still stitched in their tenement houses. A Cherokee woman in the fields of an Oklahoma farmer, a Navajo woman weaving outside her Arizona hogan, a Seneca woman cleaning the home of a white New Yorker— all were accepted in practice as working women but considered exceptions to the ideal that the Native American woman's place was now in the home.[47]

The policy of the federal government, of missionaries, and of reformers to move the Native American woman from her traditional role as farmer into the accepted white woman's role as housewife and mother and to move the man from his traditional role as hunter and warrior into the accepted white man's role of farmer seemed to have been successful. Native American men had developed a functional relationship to the dominant white man's economy and Native American women had retreated to a dysfunctional relationship with the economy, that is, they expressed their productivity indirectly through the home and husband.

What Carl Sauer has called the "Neolithic agricultural revolution," the domestication of plants by women, was ending in North America approximately five thousand years after the revolution of the plow began in Mesopotamia. Whether or not plow culture began as the German geographer Eduard Hahn suggested—with sacred oxen drawing the ceremonial cart and pulling the plow, a phallic symbol for the insemination of the receptive earth—the husbandman had taken over agricultural operations in many areas of the world, and the women had retired to the house and to garden work. Male hierarchies prevailed where cattle, plowed fields, and wagons became dominant. Wherever the plow was introduced, women lost their old relationship to the agricultural economy. The process in North America was now almost complete.[48]

In spite of the disappearance of their traditional economic function, Native American women continued to be active in tribal organizations and to display independence and strength in arranging their lives. In addition, they kept alive older traditions that conflicted with the new ideology of private property, profit, and subordination of women to men. Many reservation lands were lost and divided, but some tribes clung to their communal lands, refused to divide land into separate plots permanently, refused to give up their annuities, and continued to believe in the Native American culture as a better way of life than that which the white Americans had offered to them. The U.S. Commissioner of Indian Affairs (1910) reported that he was still trying to get rid of the Seneca annuities, but the tribe had refused. They still held lands communally and their tribal organizations were strong. The Seneca tribe had maintained its control over the reservation and its internal government. They refused to recognize the white man's marriage laws. Marriage was often cohabitation and divorce separation at pleasure, complained one government official. Such conditions were "abhorrent to the finer sensibilities of civilized mankind," he told the U.S. Commissioner of Indian Affairs.[49]

Seneca mothers had not lost their reverence for the land. Though agriculture was now male and the plow dominated and some Seneca men participated in the industrial, large-scale, technological, and profit-oriented agriculture, the older attitudes from the matrilineal subsistence agriculture survived. Their relation to the land had made the women strong and enabled them to keep alive the belief that the purpose of land was more than just to bring profits to those willing to exploit it.

9 Rise Up Like Wheat:
Plantation Women in Maryland

IT WAS A QUICK DEATH. ON THE NINTH OF MAY, RA-
chel suddenly became very ill. The doctor came but gave little hope
for Rachel's recovery. The next day Martha had Rachel's bed brought
down to the kitchen so she could nurse her better. Martha tried all
the usual remedies but Rachel could not swallow any of them, nor
could she speak. Rachel died there in the kitchen. Years earlier Rachel
had nursed Martha through a severe illness. Martha recalled Rachel's
nursing the night she died. That night Martha wrote in her diary:
"My loss is great but I trust it is her gain."[1]

How could Rachel have gained by her death, Martha lost? The
words had a double meaning. Christians often spoke of death as
release, as gaining a spiritual reward, but the words did not only
mean that. Martha saw Rachel into her grave the next day but not
into the family plot. Rachel was buried in another space, in another
part of the plantation near a horseshoe of pines with her "people."
Rachel was black and a slave. Martha was her mistress. That may be
why Martha repeated the phrase in her diary nine months after
Rachel's death: "I trust my loss has been her gain."[2]

Rachel died in Cecil County, Maryland, in 1841. Many enslaved
African Americans had been freed in Northern Maryland in the early

nineteenth century, but Rachel spent her fifty-six years in slavery, not tied to Martha by kinship but by the bonds of slavery. Although Martha and Rachel nursed each other in illness, their concern and affection for each other was dwarfed by the fact that Rachel was "owned" by Martha's husband, Thomas Marsh Forman. Thomas might have freed Rachel but he did not. And when Thomas died, four years after Rachel, he chose not to free his other black servants either, although he had enough wealth for Martha to live comfortably as a widow and they had no children. Instead, Thomas willed his plantation, Rose Hill, and his enslaved black servants to a grandson in Georgia.[3]

By all the laws of economics, slavery should have died in Cecil County sometime during that decade when Rachel died. But slavery did not die. It stubbornly lived on. It declined gradually but by 1850 it managed to live yet, the sick man of Maryland that not even a Civil War could kill quickly. Maryland officially abolished slavery in 1864, after most of the remaining enslaved African Americans had walked away from their plantations. Forman held thirty-two enslaved blacks in 1800, by 1824 he had forty-one; in 1830 he still had forty-one. In 1850 Forman's grandson listed seventeen enslaved black people for the census. These seventeen people remained, tied to a labor system that economics could not kill, until hacked out by politics and war.[4]

This is the story of the black women who lived and worked on the Forman plantation during the decades from 1800 to 1860. It is a story crippled by the lack of documentation on their lives, for part of the punishment of slavery was to make the people under its control nearly invisible, while it made the record of the whites who held economic and political control, even white women, amazingly rich. This story could not be told at all were it not that Martha kept a diary from 1814 to 1845 in which she recorded the activities of the black women at Rose Hill.[5]

Rachel's life and work spanned most of the years that Martha kept her diary. We know more about Rachel than any of the other hundred or so women who probably lived, died, and left the eight hundred acre plantation from its settlement in the mid-eighteenth century until 1860. Rachel was born in 1785, the daughter of twenty-year-old Rachel Burk. Although young Rachel helped her mother occasionally at spinning and sewing, she was primarily a field hand and was still in the fields when Martha arrived as a bride at Rose Hill in

1814. Martha must have paid attention to the black women who worked in the fields as well as those who worked in the house, for she became aware of Rachel's intelligence, industry, and capability. Martha brought Rachel from the fields into the house and taught her to bake, make candles, spin, hackel, and cut out clothing for the other black people. Rachel was certainly the most skilled woman at Rose Hill even before Martha decided to begin sending butter to Baltimore in the 1820s and Rachel became dairy maid. In the 1830s Rachel continued to produce large quantities of butter for sale, as well as to manufacture clothing, process food, and manufacture candles. "I miss her in everything," Martha mourned months after her death, when Rachel's replacement as candlemaker had produced inferior ones.[6]

Martha praised Rachel at her death but she told us almost nothing of Rachel's personal life. She recorded the work of Rachel sewing, spinning, taking wool to the factory, sewing a scarlet waistcoat, a greatcoat of brown cloth, making paper window curtains, making shirts, pantaloons, frocks, whitewashing, cleaning house, and making candles. Although a field hand when Martha arrived in 1814, Rachel was already working in the house. Forman wrote to Martha in 1814, just before their marriage, that thirteen of his enslaved black people, probably a third, were engaged in serving him. He had a coachman, two male servants, two men attached to the garden and stables, a cook, chambermaid, a kitchen girl, cleaning woman, and two young girls, in addition to Rachel and her mother who were occasional sewers and spinners.[7]

This "black family," as Forman called them, were supervised by his white housekeeper Elizabeth Oakes. To Oakes, Forman entrusted the thirty keys to the thirty locks that protected his household belongings from the black women who worked in his house. Forman boasted to his future bride, "my servants are made to know their place," but he left domestic arrangements to Oakes. He wanted to maintain a housekeeper so that his bride would have time for leisure, "the book, the pen, and the visit," as he put it. Forman did not want Martha to become a "slave" to household responsibilities. The labor of the black women would allow her that leisure.[8]

Martha had a difficult first six months at Rose Hill. It was not that she was young and inexperienced; she was a widow of twenty-nine with experience at running a household while her first husband, a sea captain, was away from home. But the British invaded two months

Rose Hill in the nineteenth century. Source: Anne Spottswood Dandridge, Compiler, The Forman Genealogy *(Cleveland: Forman-Bassett-Hatch, 1903).*

after she arrived at Rose Hill and General Forman, a veteran of the Revolutionary War, spent the next five months commanding troops in the field. At first the general conducted most of the affairs of the farm through letters to his overseer but by October, he was writing that Martha would have to manage everything some day and he wanted her to become familiar with his business affairs and to manage the farm in a "military fashion," with the overseer reporting to her every day.[9]

Martha began keeping her diary the day after she arrived at Rose Hill. She did not mention Rachel during those first difficult seven months. We know from other plantation records that on December 24, 1814, Rachel Burke, then twenty-nine years old, married Henry Allen and three days later, they celebrated with a wedding dinner.

Early in January 1815, Rachel began to appear in Martha's daily accounts. She never left them for twenty-five years.[10]

Martha's frequent entries recorded Rachel's work life, not her family life. There is no mention of her reaction when Henry Allen was sold, sometime after 1824. There is no entry for her second marriage to Philip Antigua, the twenty-year-old son of Ally Antigua, on March 29, 1822. And there is no mention in the records of what became of Philip, who probably died sometime between 1824 and February 18, 1828 when Rachel is first referred to as Rachel Teger. All the hopes and trials of three marriages go unrecorded. All we know is that Rachel continued to learn and to increase her skills and that she—like Martha—probably had no children by any of her husbands. Moses Teger, her third husband, seems to have held a position of trust in the Forman family, perhaps as coachman. Martha simply recorded Rachel and Moses working at various tasks, nothing more about this couple who obviously held responsible positions at Rose Hill.[11]

The personal record is devastatingly sparse, but the work of the women is recorded in great detail. These records allow us to go beyond Rachel's life to analyze the lives of the black community at Rose Hill and to make some overall analysis of their work roles and lives at the plantation, as well as in relation to the larger community that lay outside the confines of Rose Hill.

Rose Hill lay along the banks of the Sassafras River that marked the boundary between Cecil and Kent Counties. By the 1820s plantation owners had switched from growing tobacco to the more profitable wheat. Their black workers produced and processed most of the food and clothing needed within the plantation, as well as the cash crop of wheat. Occasionally, they worked out in addition, providing labor to barter for things the Formans needed. Eventually, they would also provide a surplus of butter and other market products that could be exchanged in Baltimore for factory-made clothing and other consumer items.

The women provided much of the labor both within and outside the plantation house. A 1824 list of blacks working on the plantation is the most complete, and it lists twenty-one females. Five of these were under nine and thus probably did little work. The majority of the others worked in the household but all also worked in the fields.[12]

These women were part of an economic system that tied Cecil County to other counties along Maryland's Eastern Shore. During the eighteenth century, the economies of the Chesapeake diverged, the Eastern Shore diversifying, other southern counties remaining bound closely to the production of tobacco. By the mid-eighteenth century, wheat and corn were important crops both in domestic and foreign trade. The production of wheat linked the plantations of the Eastern Shore to ports in the South and to Philadelphia, as well as to British colonies in New England and the West Indies. Cecil County was in the forefront of this economic transition. By 1807 there were fifty-three grist and merchant mills there. Sawmills, fulling mills, and oil mills, along with the all-important grist mills, lined the river banks.[13]

Baltimore began to control the Cecil County wheat trade in the early nineteenth century. By 1815 Baltimore was the leading flour market in the United States. As flour prices increased, more farmers in Cecil County and along the Eastern Shore shifted from tobacco to wheat, but in the 1820s the boom ended and flour prices began to drop. To increase productivity, farmers then turned to machinery, to increased quality of wheat production, to further diversification, and to greater production in the household. By the 1830s plantations in Cecil County had expanded market produce to meet the demands of the growing Baltimore population and had increased their self-sufficiency. They produced more for their own needs yet became more firmly linked to the market economy. The growing number of turnpikes, railroads, and canals testified to the demands of Cecil County farmers for solid links to the market economy.[14]

Water has always been Cecil County's main link to ports of trade. Cecil County provided the shortest overland route between the Chesapeake and Delaware bays. Small towns developed along the Chesapeake in the mid-eighteenth century to act as transfer points for products and travelers. Charlestown, established at the head of Chesapeake Bay in 1742, had its own flour inspector and hosted fairs twice a year where commerce and pleasure brought together merchant, fisherman, housewife, and servant. After the 1760s, Charleston lost out to Baltimore as the main port of trade and inhabitants moved away. Thereafter Elkton became the central village because of its flour trade with Philadelphia and its ferry that carried travelers on their way north and south. Frenchtown, three miles south of Elktown, became the transshipment point after the revolution, with ships carrying freight from Baltimore to Frenchtown and then wagons carrying it on to New Castle, Delaware. Other ferry towns, like Perryville and Port Deposit, and mill towns, such as North East and Summer Hill, developed to handle the grain and flour trade, and to care for travelers. Industries developed among the small villages. At the Principio Iron Works, bound black labor made iron bar for export. But agriculture remained the principal means of wealth. By 1790 grain plantations worked by enslaved black workers had spread through the county. Rose Hill was one of the plantations developed in response to the demand for grain.[15]

Rose Hill was not alone. Thirteen other plantations in Cecil County had over 30 slaves by 1790. Although the first abolition movement swept through Maryland in the 1780s, outlawing the importation of slaves and freeing 163 black people in Cecil County, the labor of blacks remained the most valuable form of personal property. Almost 3,000 black men, women, and children remained in bondage in Cecil County after the first movement to end their servitude had died. The enslaved population continued to increase in the next thirty years as wheat plantations prospered.[16]

The flourishing wheat trade thus riveted slavery to Cecil County as it replaced tobacco as a staple crop. Only a drop in the price of flour in the 1820s brought a decline in the demand for the labor of enslaved blacks. During the 1820s some plantation owners continued to use black labor to grow wheat, but they began to utilize black labor increasingly to produce and process agricultural products for the market and for self-sufficiency while also mechanizing their farms. During the period from 1790 to 1860, the number of enslaved blacks declined 75 percent and the number of free blacks increased 1500 percent in Cecil County. The black population, however, remained almost constant over this period of seventy years, increasing only 8 percent while the white population increased by 54 percent. Blacks declined from 26 to 18 percent of the population during these years.[17]

If the black population became progressively free, why did it not increase? The answer lay in forced migration. Wheat production did not mean free labor, it simply meant fewer bound workers. Farther south, in Talbot County, Maryland, where plantations also switched to wheat and corn, slaves remained 40 percent of the population and essential to it, with slavery firmly embedded. While wheat remained the most essential Cecil County crop from 1800 to 1820, the black population declined but not as steeply as it did from 1790 to 1800 when slavery was being questioned or from 1820 to 1830 when wheat brought lower profits. Not the wheat market but the produce and processing economy spelled the real decline of slavery in Cecil County. As wheat production declined, those plantation owners who still held slaves struggled to adapt slavery to the new urban market. They kept larger numbers of women to increase household production. Planters exported to the South males and females who could not be profitably employed in the household.[18]

The slave trade was already an old institution when Maryland developed its domestic slave trade in the nineteenth century. Maryland and Virginia had entered the slave trade in the sixteenth century and by 1700 co-sponsored the largest slave traffic on the continent. During the early eighteenth century, almost twice as many blacks entered Virginia as Maryland, most directly from Africa, rather than from the West Indies or Caribbean, but the first generation of black women at Rose Hill (including Alley Antigue) probably arrived during this time. Fewer than twenty thousand black immigrants entered Maryland and Virginia from 1750 to 1769, few enough to make the revolutionary movement for emancipation in Maryland result in a law banning their importation in 1783. These were the years during which native born African Americans developed extensive kinship systems.[19]

During the next century the black population of the Eastern Shore was decimated as the domestic slave trade increased. When the heavy harvest season had ended in September, the trading season began. It continued until March when work increased again. Black workers brought an average of $262 in the mid 1820s. One historian has estimated that between 1820 and 1830, 17,500 blacks left the state. Another has estimated that about 12 percent of the 1830 enslaved population ended up on the block in the next decade, and 16 percent of these were forced to leave the state. Between 1830 and 1860, 18,500 left for other states, most from the Eastern Shore. Traders preferred male workers between twelve and twenty-five. Women were more likely to be manumitted than males, but the result was to further fragment the kin ties so patiently developed during the previous century.[20]

In the Rose Hill area sales gradually declined compared to other areas. Forman sold some of his enslaved workers. Henry Allen, Rachel's first husband was sold, as was Moses Burk. After 1820 sending blacks South began to be reserved as a form of punishment for running away. Oliver Gordon, who ran away in December, probably after his wife had died, was sold by General Forman after he was recaptured the next month. Females seldom ran away but some were sold, "exchanged," or even "given away." At Rose Hill, the one extant list of bondspeople from the 1820s is conspicuous for the absence of middle-aged females. Of the eighteen females listed, eight were eleven and under, two in their teens, and two in their early twenties but none between twenty-four and thirty-seven. Only three were between ages twenty-one and forty-seven. As domestic production at Rose Hill expanded, both selling and exchanging of black people seems to have declined. Instead, the Formans rented out their black servants to surrounding plantation owners.[21]

While women workers might be rented to neighbors, their work was still crucial for the survival of Rose Hill plantation. Women worked wherever necessary, usually in the fields. At the same time, the number of black women involved in manufacturing probably increased during this period. There are no detailed records of field production for Rose Hill. Martha confined most of her comments to the work of women in the household, but it seems evident that the responsibilities of women expanded at the same time that their work in the fields was still essential.[22]

The expansion of black women's responsibilities at Rose Hill began with the arrival of Martha in May 1814 and the departure soon after of Elizabeth Oakes. While General Forman always had an overseer for farm operations, Martha apparently got her wish to direct the domestic operations by herself. She could do so because two black women, Rachel and her sister Susan, helped her manage and execute much of the work demanded by the community of almost fifty people. The wives of overseers appear in Martha's daily accounts briefly as helping her with sewing, but her involvement in the day to day process and the work done in her absences, as well as references to everything being in order on her return, indicate that black women moved into essential and crucial roles in the daily management of the household. It was more than personalities and skill, however, for the plantation household reflected the changing market orientation of the plantation itself.[23]

The first woman who appeared in this new role was Susan Burk.

Susan was probably a second generation immigrant, born and raised at Rose Hill. Her mother, Rachel, worked in the fields and occasionally in the house spinning. Susan grew up working in the fields with her sisters and brothers. A sister, Lydia, was employed full time in the house. Susan married a man named Sudler and bore at least four children between 1812 and 1825. Emory Sudler, perhaps an older son, ran away in 1819. No other male Sudlers lived at Rose Hill, but Susan was rich in the kin of her father and mother.[24]

Soon after Martha arrived, Susan began to show up in her records; she spun, sewed, worked in the dairy, washed, as well as continuing to work in the fields when needed. For a decade Susan became the principal black woman in the Rose Hill household. When she died of typhus in 1826, Martha noted her skills at starching and pleating and as dairy maid, as well as being "a very good hand to work in the field."[25]

After Susan died, her sister, Rachel, moved into her place as principal household worker. Rachel had already assumed greater responsibility in household production before Susan died. Although Rachel still lived in the quarters, she was keeping large flocks of poultry for Martha and working in the dairy. In 1822 Martha noted Rachel's skill: "We have had as many hen eggs this winter as we could use and have made more butter this winter than any winter since I have been at Rose Hill. Rachel has the management of it, she slaps her cows well."[26]

During these years when the two sisters, Susan and Rachel, began to develop their productive skills, black women worked at many tasks. All of them worked in the fields at some times of the year. They bladed the corn, helped with the wheat harvest, hayed, husked corn, and hoed.

The primary responsibility of a core group of five or six women became expanding self-sufficiency and market surplus. They processed textiles and food, helped maintain the main house and frequently their own as well. In winter they retted, cleaned, and broke flax, carded wool, spun linen and wool, sewed trousers and frocks, made carpets and blankets, and knitted stockings. They also processed hundreds of pounds of meat each winter, salted it, and hung it in the smokehouse. During the year they produced hundreds of pounds of butter for the Baltimore market, including large orders for hotels, neatly printed with Martha's initials, "MBF." In fall, they picked and packed apples for the winter, made crab apple cider, and bottled it. They raised poultry and gathered eggs for sale in Baltimore, at the neighboring crossroads, and in the small villages nearby. They rendered hundreds of pounds of lard, made soap and hundreds of candles. They washed, cleaned, starched, ironed, whitewashed. They baked cakes, made orange puddings, mince pies, gingerbread. Their skill and flexibility of labor lay at the center of the success of the Rose Hill plantation as a social and economic institution.[27]

Despite the centrality of women to the concerns of the plantation, it remained rigidly segregated by race and class. Separation of table and gravesite deliberately marked status at Rose Hill. The General and Martha and their friends dined at the main table, waited upon by black women. White laborers and tradesmen ate at a separate table, also waited upon by black women. The women who served ate in the kitchen or in their quarters. The quarters remained the heart of the black community at Rose Hill. There the women danced, shared Christmas feasts, made love, birthed children, sickened, and died of typhus and measles, malaria and tuberculosis. And from the quarters, they were carried by kin to a separate plantation cemetery.[28]

No records exist of these women's values. The closest record we can find that reflects traits probably taken with them when they migrated to southern communities during the early nineteenth century are studies of small postwar farming communities. Women there emphasized age as an important mark of status when combined with respected personal attributes and behavior. They tolerated weakness because the community needed all its people. They maintained and passed on genealogical information, instilled the need for maintaining kinship ties, mutual aid, and closeness to same sex siblings. They demanded authority over children but performed acts of deference to male authority. They defined strength by behavior. A "strong woman" meant one who strove for moral rightness, mutual concern, and economic betterment despite adversities. She expected to be judged by her capacity for reconciliation and self-control. Women traded work roles with men frequently and maintained their own economic and social activities after marriage. They pooled their labor and exchanged goods. They created families that survived dissolution of marriage and counted their success by the quality of their children and the security in old age. Faith provided the ultimate reservoir of courage, the deepest social bond, and the touchstone of moral rightness. Such values forged in the crucible of plantation enslavement would carry the black community through the trials of plantation life, migration, and life in the rural South.[29]

The Rose Hill black community was a part of a larger free and enslaved black population that lived precariously among the white population. By 1850 this population reflected the fragmentation of the black slave community and the creation of a new free population. Of 35 households and 120 persons in the Rose Hill area, the free black population numbered only 72, of whom 50 lived in their own households and 12 lived in the households of white farmers. Eight black households were clustered together, each living in nuclear families: Araninta and Anthony Brooks and their four children; Elizabeth and John Perele and their three children; Hannah and Richard Bowser and their daughter Amanda; Sarah and Henry Brown and their three children; Matilda and James Baily and their three children; Elizabeth and David Limber and his sixty-six-year-old mother; Mary and Nathan Johnson and a young child (probably their grandson), and another young woman. Two families lived in white households and seven black men lived in a boarding house in the household of a white laborer.[30]

Other households joined black and free in one household. Next to the Forman plantation was Woodlawn, home of Mary and Thomas Ward. They lived there with their four children along with Mary Freeman, twenty-five, and her one-year-old daughter Mary. Other neighbors to Rose Hill were Henrietta and Philip Jester and their five children. Susan Rice, a seventy-year-old black woman and sixteen-year-old George Rice lived with them. In a separate household next door lived Frances Rice and her sixteen-year-old son James. Two black slaves not listed by name also lived on the Jester plantation. Mary and John Morrison had a similarly mixed household. They lived with their son William Morrison and his wife Mary and their three children. Two white laborers, John Ford and Richard Tibet lived there along with three free blacks, Barnard Thompson, fifty, Hannah Thompson, twenty-one, and Abraham, a one-year-old son. Two unnamed enslaved blacks also lived there.[31]

The free black population lived a precarious existence. Most adults remained illiterate because there was no provision for their education and most whites did not encourage literacy. One way a young black might become literate was to be indentured by the orphan's court. Two indenture records from the 1820s and 1830s indicate that boys might be taught to read and write and girls to read when they were apprenticed. But free blacks were almost as limited in their mobility as were slaves. To leave the state they had to obtain permits. Mary Hazard, who had lived in her neighborhood for twenty years and was in her sixties, had to go before the court to get a permit to visit her sick daughter who lived just across the border in Wilmington, Delaware.[32]

Free blacks were not often welcomed as members of the larger white community. Rose Hill neighbor Sidney Fisher liked hard-working Ned Kinnard, an ex-slave, but made it clear in his diary that he resented free blacks because they refused year-round work for him. He also despised the free white population when they also refused to work diligently. "Duck shooting is one cause of it," he wrote sourly in his diary. Fisher also reported slaves running away and the precarious existence of slavery. Slavery lived on, but the absence of slaves and the independence of whites drove wages up. "Ten years ago," Fisher noted in 1849, "negroes could be hired, slave or free for $50 per ann. five years ago the rate was $67; two years ago it was $80 to 85; last year it was 90; now it is $100 to $120." The value of black labor led to the greater privileges of those still enslaved, he believed.[33]

The scarcity of black labor encouraged Irish immigrants to begin to settle in the neighborhood. John and Jane McCafferty and their four children lived near Rose Hill and five young workers—four male and one female—worked on a neighboring farm. In April 1850 Fisher recorded the hiring of his first Irish immigrant woman to work in his kitchen. "The Irish are making their appearance here, and more come every year, another step onward in the progress of the neighborhood caused by the scarcity of black labor," he wrote. Fisher still had Ned Kinnard but he despised free blacks who preferred seasonal wage labor, fishing, or harvesting to full-time work for others. Fisher's mother and father had freed their slaves and though Fisher opposed slavery, it was because of its effect on whites. He believed all free blacks should have masters.[34]

In this neighborhood, Rose Hill and its owners were clearly the wealthiest in ownership of property and labor. But the Morrisons, Veazys, Wards, Eldridges, Bensons, and Roaths all held property valued ten thousand dollars and above and the Merith household was valued at twenty-five thousand dollars. Below this elite group were the King, Jester, Wensel, Gunce, Davis, and Keen households and below them farm families with no valuation on their property, such as Leatha and Henry May, who were born in Germany and who had lived in Maryland for over eleven years. Margaret and Thomas Price, a blacksmith, were the single artisan household in the neighborhood, but there were many tenant farmers and white and black laborers. These were the poor but independent people so despised by Fisher.[35]

By 1860 slavery had ended at Rose Hill, but it had not been a joyous occasion. The agonizing end lasted for over a decade, causing great distress among the black community there. General Forman began disposing of his property and giving it out to his heirs in 1841. Black women used all the skills they had developed in the past two decades in opposing the breakup of their families and community.

The crisis was chronicled in the intermittent Mount Harmon diary of neighbor Fisher. Fisher noted that General Forman had offered his heirs, "any of his negroes they chose to take" and the heirs "had the impudence to choose some of the house servants." The house servants pled loyalty to Martha and refused to leave their mistress. Field hands, who could not plead such loyalty, were the first to go. A second crisis occurred four years later when General Forman died. Martha was to have an annuity and Harriet Beeton, who had served her since a child, was to remain with her. The other enslaved blacks became the property of Forman's grandson, Thomas Bryan who lived in Georgia.[36]

Thomas Bryan, who took the General's name as a condition of inheriting Rose Hill, planned to take over the running of the plantation himself. Such a decision offered the possibility of blacks remaining at Rose Hill, even though an owner from Georgia obviously put the community at greater risk of separation. The new Forman did not move his family to Rose Hill at once, and in the meantime Martha stayed on to run the farm with the help of an overseer. Forman visited at least once and regularly corresponded with Martha, offering to buy anything that she needed to continue farming. In addition, Thomas allowed her to control the household workers, using them at Rose Hill or renting them out to neighbors. She allowed Harriet Beeton, who was married to Ned Kinnard, to make plans to move into Ned's house to live with him. Ned had been freed upon the death of his owner in 1839, and he now received a small plot of land and began to build a home. By May of 1846 Bryan had legally changed his name to Forman and arrived at Rose Hill to claim his inheritance. He began to dispose of his property as he saw fit, sending workers to his estate in Georgia and ignoring the personal lives of the black workers.[37]

Two of the women ordered South by Forman were Leonora Bayard and Sophia Sewall. Both women had deep roots in Cecil County. Twenty-three-year-old Sophia was the fourth generation in her family at Rose Hill. Ally Antigua was her great grandmother. Sophia's mother was born at Rose Hill in 1800, married in 1817, and bore Sophia in 1826. Sophia had been married to Peny Johnson for only a few months and was three months pregnant with her first child when Forman decided to send her south. Leonora too was descended from early Rose Hill women. Rachel Burk, Senior, was her grandmother, Rachel Teger her aunt. She had sisters and a brother still at Rose Hill. Leonora was thirty years old in 1846 and had worked for Fisher off and on since she was nineteen years old. She had already lived and worked for Fisher permanently for eight years when Bryan decided to send her south.[38]

Fisher recorded the response of the women's husbands. "The poor fellows," he wrote, "who heard it only this even'g are in terrible distress & have gone over to take leave of them. . . . Here these people have lived all their lives & their parents also, for generations. All their friends & relations are here. They regard the South with perfect horror and to be sent there, is considered as the worst punishment inflicted on them, & is reserved for one offense alone by the custom of the neighborhood, an attempt to run away. When to all this is added, the separation of husband & wife, parent & child, the case is very hard." Despite such sentiments, Fisher refused to help the families. "They are property, & Mr. Bryan has a right to do as he pleases with his own," Fisher wrote tersely.[39]

During the next few days the women frantically sought alternatives to the disruption of their lives. Sophia's husband, Peny Johnson, was able to get the woman who owned him to sell him so that he could go to Georgia rather than part with his wife and children. Leonora's husband was less successful. Their only hope was for her to find someone in the neighborhood to buy her and together Sophia and Leonora searched for days looking for a buyer. Finally, they appealed to Fisher. He recorded Leonora's visit to him on May 20: "She came to me on Sunday in great distress to beg me to buy her. Bryan has told them that if they could find purchasers in the neighborhood they might stay. I told her that I did not wish to buy her & said what I could to comfort her. But she seemed very averse to leaving her 'native place.' . . . It looks very hard, but is not so hard as it looks. Many things much harder & more cruel are happening every day in this wicked world."[40]

Fisher's abstract concept of justice was little solace to the families being torn apart. Forman sent away five of the women who had worked in the Rose Hill household. Martha too was distraut. Fisher wrote in his diary of Martha, "she thinks it very hard in Bryan to take them, tho really as they are his property I can't blame him, as he wants them." Leonora's husband followed her as far as Baltimore to be with her as long as possible.[41]

Sophia did not leave Rose Hill in May. She was still working for Fisher in December. The reason does not appear in Fisher's diary; perhaps the women convinced Forman to allow her to stay on at Mount Harmon until after she had her child. Her son was born in October and she named him Moses. Sometime in the winter she returned to Rose Hill, for she appears in Martha's records as sewing clothes in January and February. Then on March 27 Peny Johnson was found dead on the Rose Hill dam. Supposedly, he had accidentally shot himself. Martha gave Sophia a black frock that spring, black gloves, a bonnet, and cape. Sophia and her son Moses were still at Rose Hill when Forman arrived with his family in November 1849 to take charge.[42]

It is difficult to know exactly how many of the other black people left their Rose Hill home during the four years between 1846 and 1850. By August 1850 when the census takers came to Rose Hill, there were only seventeen black people left at Rose Hill. The gender and age balance was badly skewed. Only eight black male workers between fifteen and fifty-five remained and one seventy-year-old black man, probably Isaac Gilmore. Sophia and her son Moses were still there, but there was only one other child. Three of the remaining women were in their forties, one in her thirties, and one sixteen. Most of the women and their children had been sent south.[43]

After the young Formans arrived in 1849, Martha visited Rose Hill infrequently. She spent most of her time on her Christiana farm or boarding in Wilmington or Philadelphia. Forman never grew to like Rose Hill or to realize the potential of a plantation oriented to the marketplace. The growing resistance of blacks to enslavement and to reenslavement once they had escaped must have discouraged him in his ambitions to remain at Rose Hill with his family. Before the decade was out, Forman had moved his family and his remaining enslaved workers back to Georgia and rented Rose Hill. The black community was gone, not freed by economic or moral development but forced by property laws to migrate south against their wills and to live as slaves in Georgia until the Civil War freed them. Martha died in 1864 in Wilmington. Forman sold Rose Hill in 1867.[44]

The experiences of the black community at Rose Hill and Martha's attempts to mitigate their destruction illustrate the power of property in the early nineteenth century and the powerlessness of women and blacks against its force. The black community at Rose Hill achieved a significant measure of stability during the years from 1814 to 1841. During that period black women achieved great skill in meeting the demands of the marketplace and household self-sufficiency. Their ties to the land and to their kin were rich and deep but could not withstand the rights of property. Four generations had lived at Rose Hill. When Sophia Sewell left, she took fifth generation Moses with her.

10   Butter Making and Economic Development
in Mid-Atlantic America, 1750–1850

FOR SCHOLARS INTENT ON ANALYZING EARLY NINE-
teenth-century American economic development, rural women remain an elusive majority. Omitted from most agricultural histories
because they were not the owners of American farmland, slighted in
labor histories because their work was different from that of males,
and neglected by histories of women that concentrated on the urban
middle and working classes, rural women are barely visible in American history. Carolyn Sachs terms them "the invisible farmers."[1]

Most American women of the early nineteenth century labored
on family farms, the backbone of the American agricultural system.
Yet just how to document and evaluate the labor of these "undocu-
mented workers," whose work is absent from censuses and journals,
is a methodological and theoretical problem of major proportions.
One way to address this problem is to look at specific agricultural
tasks performed by women: butter making, for instance. The study of
butter making in the Philadelphia hinterland—a rich agricultural area
just west and south of the thriving metropolis, where rural women
labored on their own farms and the farms of others—between 1750
and 1850 has implications for the larger question of women's work
and women's contribution to the overall economic development of
the region.

Several trends emerge from this study. The first is the domination of butter making by women in its early experimental phase in the late eighteenth century. In the early nineteenth century, once butter making had proven itself as a stable, reliable source of income, a second trend emerged. A depression of prices for other farm commodities, changing farm manufacturing patterns (specifically, the relocation of textile processing from farm to factory), and the increasingly common practice of sending daughters to school intensified women's butter making activities. Butter became more profitable as agricultural commodities traditionally produced by men, especially grain and livestock, became less valuable. After midcentury, some men moved into butter making, establishing and managing creameries and butter factories on the farms. Finally, some women began to turn their attention to other farm commodities ignored by males, such as poultry raising. Although the final stages of economic development in the Philadelphia hinterland in the late nineteenth century have not yet been studied, poultry raising, like textile processing and butter making, was usually performed by women. In the parlance of the times, it was "women's work." Thus, not only was the role of women central to agricultural development in this region, but also women's flexibility and ingenuity in producing marketable products allowed these farms successfully to survive tremendous market pressures and to reproduce the family farm as well as the farm family.[2]

In 1850 the Philadelphia hinterland was a rich agricultural region marked by substantial stone houses and barns, carefully tended roads, and diversified crops. Settled in the late seventeenth century by Quaker farm families, the Pennsylvania counties of Delaware and Chester and Delaware county of New Castle had become mixed ethnically with African and European Americans sharing the labor, though seldom the property, of the region. Quakers had declined to a small minority by the early nineteenth century, but Quaker culture remained deeply impressed on the region. Through wealth, civic and political activity, and religious networks, Quakers continued to exercise considerable social influence. The region was known for its lush meadows and its productive dairy cows. The women were known for the quality of their butter. The 1850 census documented for the first time the locally accepted fact that the women of these counties produced a great deal of butter, much of it for consumption in Philadelphia homes.[3]

The transition to market production of butter began in the late

Churning. Source: Progress of the Dairy: Descriptive of the Making of Butter and Cheese for the Information of Youth *(New York: Samuel Wood, 1819). The Sinclair Hamilton Collection of American Illustrated Books, Princeton University Library.*

eighteenth century. Historian Billy G. Smith has estimated that in 1771, only 3 percent of the almost one-half of the Philadelphia free male workers he studied had cows. Each of these laborers consumed at least thirteen pounds of butter a year, to which must be added the amount consumed by women and children. The wealthy often kept herds of dairy cows at country estates and perhaps one cow for milk in town. When the Revolution cut off rural meat supplies, shortages led many urban dwellers to kill their cows for meat. By the end of the war, the city was almost totally dependent on rural women for their butter. With an estimated population of more than twenty-seven thousand in 1772 and over forty-two thousand in 1790, Philadelphia provided an expanding butter market. By the 1790s women in the Philadelphia hinterland were already producing a considerable amount of market butter. They sold this surplus to neighbors or brought it to Philadelphia to sell.[4]

How much butter women actually produced is difficult to determine because women usually did not keep written records. At the time of the Revolution, at least three-fourths of rural women in Chester County could not write. Rural males, almost all of whom were literate, tended to keep written accounts of their own farm work but not of the work done by women. There were a few fortunate exceptions. Samuel Taylor recorded in his 1798 journal: "My mother took 40 lbs of butter to Gedion Williams. Sold it for 1/6 [1 shilling, 6 pence] per lb." In 1799 Taylor recorded trips of his sister Deborah and himself to Philadelphia on several occasions to sell butter. According to his record, kept for slightly over a year, the Taylor women produced 170 pounds of butter for sale.[5]

Like the Taylor women, other farm women found a ready market for their butter. Butter sold locally in southeastern Pennsylvania for six to ten pence in the 1760s and 1770s and for between one shilling, eight pence and one shilling, ten pence in the 1790s. After the new government established its own currency in the first decade of the nineteenth century, butter sold for twenty to twenty-five cents a pound from 1815 to 1821 and seventeen to twenty-two cents a pound from 1845 to 1850. Although the American market absorbed much of the butter surplus sold by farm families, an active export butter market also developed with thousands of pounds being shipped overseas, usually to the West Indies. The new nation shipped two and one-half million pounds of butter in 1796 alone. Butter exports declined with the disruption of trade in the early nineteenth century. Still the high price of butter kept farm women eager to produce and sell surplus. Wholesale prices for firkins (100-pound tubs) of butter in Philadelphia remained over ten cents a pound for most of the years between 1785 and 1820. For some months of 1836 prices reached almost nineteen cents a pound.[6]

During these decades, then, farm women established butter as a farm product with a steady market and stable price. Many men considered butter an important part of the farm produce, mainly because it provided a commodity for use in the family and an income with which women could purchase other items needed for the household. Animal raising, grain growing, and the production of fodder crops still held men's attention as the main income-producing farm activities. Nevertheless, farm magazines continually pointed out the importance of the farm dairy for its excellent income potential. Most of these accounts assumed women's labor to be free and equipment to be already available on farms, so that a small investment in cows and fodder could bring a tidy profit. In most cases this profit was used to purchase items for the household. Many farms had what might be called dual household economy. The woman used the income from her sales to finance the purchase of household items. The man used the income from his sales to expand the capital investment in land and equipment.⁷

The shift to butter as a main farm commodity began during the economic hard times of the 1820s and 1830s. International wars contributed to an economic boom in the Philadelphia hinterland during the late eighteenth and early nineteenth centuries. When these wars ended in 1814, a recession followed. During the next two decades, butter making began to change from a craft commodity—produced for the family and sold to the market only in surplus—to a regular market commodity produced directly for sale. After 1840 the American economy developed profitable new sources of capital and industry. As a result of this boom and bust cycle, according to labor historians, northern farmers mechanized to increase their profits in a more competitive market; white males moved west into rural industries, like mining and metals, or into urban craft occupations; enslaved black women were forced to work harder by southern planters responding to the cotton market; and young women in New England began to work in textile factories. The stable demand for and price of butter made women's butter making valuable as a cushion against the instability of the market.⁸

Competition from newly settled, more fertile western lands provided another impetus for eastern farm families to reevaluate their traditional market crops. Both grain and animals could be raised more cheaply in the West and transported east by canal to compete with the crops traditionally raised by men. Butter produced in the West could not yet compete on the national market. The isolation of frontier farmers often required household women to do the extra work that kin, community, or hired labor might do in the East. This reduced the time western women could invest in butter production for the market. Moreover, to preserve butter over long miles of transport, they had to preserve it with large amounts of salt or salt-peter. Philadelphia butter makers also preserved butter with these techniques, but they could outproduce western women in the quality of their preserved butter, and they had no competition for the fresh butter they prepared in large quantities for the Philadelphia market. (After the Civil War, western women did begin to compete with eastern butter makers, but by then eastern dairies had commer-cialized and their butter had a successful regional market. Commer-cial butter makers then denounced the butter of western women as far inferior to that made in the East. They also lobbied for laws to prohibit the sale of oleomargarine, a butter substitute shipped in from the West. Their success with federal and state laws marked the beginning of a long history of political involvement by the dairy industry.)[9]

Thus in the 1830s and 1840s, men began to reevaluate the market production of butter made so successful by women. Owners of land that was not very fertile but who were close to the market began to phase out crops except fodder to feed expanded dairy herds. During these years, farmers bartered, bought, and swapped their way to better herds. By the 1840s southeastern Pennsylvania farmers had bred most of their cows to Durham bulls, which increased the quan-tity and duration of lactation and thus their milk production. In the late eighteenth century even the most ambitious farmers were satis-fied with eight quarts of milk per day per cow and cows on the average lactated for eight months. In 1844 The Farmer's Encyclope-dia reported a Delaware Durham, "Blossom," giving thirty-six quarts per day and seventeen and one-half pounds of butter per week. In 1845 The American Agriculturalist reported Durhams that could be milked for ten months of the year.[10]

The new status of dairying was already evident by 1840. Dairy products ranked fifth in dollar value among agricultural products of New Jersey, Pennsylvania, Delaware, and New York, and they were the most valuable among the animal products. In that year, Mid-Atlantic farms processed over fifteen million dollars worth of dairy products. The butter belt around Philadelphia was already well-established by 1840. Eleven counties in three states were part of that belt: Delaware, Montgomery, Bucks, and Chester counties in Penn-sylvania; New Castle County in Delaware; and Sussex, Burlington, Gloucester, Salem, Cape May, and Monmouth in New Jersey.[11]

The first agricultural census, completed in 1850, confirmed the growing importance of butter making. Butter now took its place alongside more traditional farm products, such as grain and livestock. The census of 1850 showed that 4,760 farms in Delaware, Chester and New Castle counties produced over four million pounds of butter in the preceding year. To analyze this production, I divided these farms into four categories: use (enough only for family needs), surplus, middling, and commercial. Twenty-five percent of these butter-belt farms produced only for their own use; almost 50 percent produced 200 to 599 pounds surplus; and 25 percent—the middling—produced 600 to 2,000 pounds. Commercial dairies, producing 8,000 pounds or more per year, accounted for only about 2 percent of all the butter produced in the butter belt. Similar butter belts composed primarily of family dairies surrounded other major cities, such as Baltimore and New York.[12]

The increase in butter production reflected not only the marketability of butter but also changes in the technology of butter making. Women changed both their techniques and their equipment to increase butter production. They learned to produce butter more efficiently to make it more saleable.[13]

The history of butter-making techniques is difficult to document. Butter-making techniques in the colonial period were very diverse and reflected the local practices of regions from which immigrants came. When agricultural journals came into existence in the 1830s, they often reported dairy women's suggestions for improved butter-making techniques. However, there is little indication of who, precisely, made these innovations or how they were passed from woman to woman. In particular regions, such as the Philadelphia hinterland, many women began to use new techniques at approximately the same time. Some improvements could simply be observed and copied, such as the marking and packaging of butter for easier marketing. Other techniques, such as controlling the temperature of the cream to reduce the churning time, or mastering recipes for preservation, would surely have to be shared intentionally. This oral tradition was most active among kin, religious groups, and neighbors. Since women shared a whole range of self-help information, the techniques of improved butter making could easily have been included as part of the gossip shared after Sunday morning religious meetings or during afternoon visits.[14]

Changes in butter-making tools are somewhat easier to document. Churning in the colonial period was sometimes done with only a bowl and a spoon by beating for a long time. The dasher churn, which improved the ease and speed of butter preparation, was invented in England in the fourteenth century, but because seventeenth-century American records seldom refer to churns, historians believe that churns were not used when relatively small amounts of butter were produced for use at home. By the American Revolution, however, dasher churns were quite common in the Philadelphia hinterland. Moreover, a new late eighteenth-century churn, the barrel churn, was also in use. During the early nineteenth century, both dasher and barrel churns increased in size to accommodate more cream and produce more butter. A simple dasher churn often held only a gallon of cream, produced one or two pounds of butter at a time, and took a woman three hours to churn. By 1850 farm women could choose from a variety of improved churns that held up to fifty gallons of cream and produced 100 to 150 pounds of butter in as little as one and one-half hours. For the largest churns, women employed animal power—dogs, sheep, or calves.[15]

As churns grew in size and complexity, so too did the other dairy equipment women used. Dairy women had always used flat milk pans for storing milk while gravity separated the cream from the milk. If cows gave only a quart of milk at a time, women could use a small pan. But larger milkings demanded larger pans, and by the early nineteenth century, some milk pans were as big as fourteen inches in diameter and could hold one and one-half gallons of milk.[16]

Similarly, butter-working equipment grew in size. When making small quantities of butter for home use, women sometimes used their hands to work the buttermilk out of the churned butter. However, larger quantities of butter took longer to work and even women with "cool" hands—a desirable trait for dairy women, according to folk traditions—or women who dipped their hands in cold water could not keep the butter from becoming soft and difficult to handle. Women often used small paddles to press the buttermilk out of small amounts of churned butter, but these were insufficient for large quantities of butter. Hence, large butter workers, wooden tables with levers for squeezing the buttermilk out of forty or fifty pounds of butter, became common by the mid-nineteenth century.[17]

The demand for butter production also increased the space women needed for butter making. A special tax census of 1798 in Chester County listed more than seven hundred log springhouses, located on over half of the farms, with an average size of 127 square feet. At that time, a few farms already had distinctive Pennsylvania springhouses, larger buildings with an overhanging roof in front, used first by German immigrants. Most of the tasks of butter making were performed in these springhouses, which were built over streams to allow a supply of fresh water to cool dairy products and to provide space for cleaning and storing equipment. After 1800, many farm families constructed larger springhouses of three hundred to four hundred square feet and built them of more durable stone, sometimes on the same location where the smaller log houses had existed. On some farms, at least, farm women's work space for butter making more than doubled between 1800 and 1850.[18]

Although men constructed most of this new equipment and work space, it is not known whether they or women designed them. Innovations may have been made by women as they searched for ways to process larger amounts of milk. Male family members, local potters, coopers, and builders probably worked with women in designing new equipment and produced it relatively cheaply. The fact that most dairying inventions were patented by men does indicate, however, that they were interested in the commercial opportunities that might be created by new butter-making equipment.[19]

New techniques and equipment could help the farm woman produce more butter only if she could rearrange her labor to find additional time for production. Traditionally, there had been a rough division of labor on the farm by sex. Women did dairying; men raised grain and livestock. But women also had a wide range of other tasks. They serviced, trained, and raised their children. They also sold their surplus production on the market and seasonally and during emergencies helped the men with their tasks. In addition, they produced textiles. Increased butter production necessitated reallocation of some of these other tasks. They discontinued some tasks, shifted some to other members of the family, and hired workers to perform other farm activities.[20]

Most importantly, women reduced the amount of time they devoted to the preparation of cloth. As late as 1810 Chester County farm families produced large quantities of textiles in their homes. In a census of that year, Chester County ranked third and seventh in counties producing linen (more than 170,000 yards) and woolen goods (almost 75,000 yards) in Pennsylvania. By this time, factories in Philadelphia and New Castle County had already started to manufacture small amounts of both woolen and cotton cloth. The yard goods from these factories were soon available in quantities and at a price that made it attractive for women to devote less time to textiles. The combination of available manufactured cloth and the increase in butter's profitability over domestically produced cloth encouraged women to spend more of their resources on butter production and hastened the transition to store-bought cloth during the 1830s and 1840s. The new mill towns, in turn, provided an expanded market for the sale of butter. Although new dairy equipment absorbed some of the profits from increased sales in butter, other store-bought commodities, like cloth, were also purchased with this income.[21]

The shift from textile processing to butter making also necessitated reallocation of tasks among daughters and hired assistants. Very young girls could perform fewer tasks in dairying than in textile production (where they had done numerous small and tedious jobs, such as spinning, carding, and preparation of the wool for spinning). Making cloth was easily segmented, it could be performed all year round, and it was a process to which all could contribute. Butter making was less segmented and cyclical, with the most work needing to be done in summer. Children could help with milking, scalding dairying equipment, and churning while the cream was still relatively liquid, but adult strength and dexterity were necessary to complete the churning process, to work the butter, and to prepare it for market. After the American Revolution, white girls went to school during the winter in increasing numbers. This made their assistance available for the heavy summer output of butter, but farm women turned increasingly to unpaid female relatives or hired assistants for help in the dairies throughout the year.[22]

Data to show precisely when this change occurred are difficult to find because the census of 1850 did not list most female occupations. An examination of census lists of household members, however, indicates the approximate number of female farm workers. In Kennett township in Chester County, for example, the number of women and girls between fourteen and thirty with a surname different from the head of the household suggests that approximately 30 percent of the farm households in the county included women who were not family members. Of fifty-three servants thus identified, 38 percent were black or born in Ireland, and the remaining 62 percent were native-born white women.[23]

Individual accounts by a few farm women document the search for hired women as butter-making activities expanded. Esther Lewis, a Chester County widow, left diaries and letters that give a detailed account of the use of hired female help. In 1835 and 1836, Lewis recorded sending monthly to Philadelphia seventy-five to one hundred pounds of butter produced with the regular help of a hired woman. Lewis taught her daughters to churn and prepare butter for the market, but she also used some of her farm income to send them to boarding school so that they could become teachers and support themselves if they did not marry. When her daughters were at school, she hired the daughters of other neighbor women. "She [the hired woman] does not eat much idle bread," she assured her sister in an 1833 letter. Experienced, native-born women became more difficult to hire during the next few years as the demand for their labor increased. So in 1839 Lewis hired a young, inexperienced, Irish immigrant woman who knew nothing about butter making and taught her the entire process, including how to put the lid on the churn.[24]

Thus, white middle-class farm women such as Esther Lewis could exploit the labor of poorer women for the profit of their own families. For some native-born and Irish immigrant hired women, that exploitation was temporary. They were able in turn to move on to farms of their own in which they did their own butter making and sent their daughters out to work on neighboring farms. Black women had far fewer opportunities to profit from their labor. Blacks in some southeastern Pennsylvania townships numbered over 25 percent of the population, yet almost none owned farm land. Farther south, where white women sold butter in Baltimore, enslaved black women were used to process butter. Martha Ogle Forman, a Maryland farm woman, recorded that her black dairymaid Rachel Teger made and sold 215 pounds of butter during three months in 1827. By the time Teger died in 1841, she had made thousands of pounds of butter, which the Formans sold in Baltimore to help finance their growing taste for consumer items. The control of land thus determined who used the profits made from butter production.[25]

After 1850 butter, milk, and poultry production increased. Between 1850 and 1880 butter production in Chester, Delaware, and New Castle counties rose from four million to almost seven million pounds. By 1880 the three counties produced over ten million gallons of milk, much of it transported directly to Philadelphia or to creameries for processing into butter. By 1880 the three counties also produced almost two million eggs and almost five hundred thousand fowl.[26]

During this period, men joined women in dairy production in increasing numbers. Butter making was a traditional female task, having been performed by countless women over the ages, with increasingly complex skills that were passed by oral tradition from mother to daughter, mistress to servant, neighbor to neighbor. As the demand for butter increased, however, and market competition increased for livestock and grain, men began to join increasingly in dairying with women. In the New England area men seem to have taken over milking to some extent in the early nineteenth century. Early nineteenth-century literature, however, usually did not mention men in the Philadelphia hinterland and most of the Mid-Atlantic as butter makers except as participants in experiments to test new models of churns. Although journal editors did direct instructions for organizing dairies to "dairymen," they usually made specific references to women, or "dairymaids," as the actual makers of butter. Although women continued to process some butter in their springhouses, commercial dairies or creameries managed by men produced an increasingly greater proportion of the market butter. Some women worked at these new creameries, but far more remained on the farm and specialized in processing the milk for the creameries. Many also increased their poultry production as a substitute for dairying.[27]

Such joint agricultural ventures insured the survival of the family farm in an increasingly commercialized market. American women's contribution to the farm economy of the nineteenth century has been documented by a number of scholars. Harriet Friedman, for example, has argued that family farms were able to compete successfully with commercial operations largely because family members did most of the farm work and were not paid money for their efforts, while commercial operations paid out large sums of money in labor costs. Women figured importantly in this arrangement since it was frequently women, as we have seen with regard to butter making, who trained and managed the household labor. Women's labor provided the small margin of security that kept family farms from financial ruin. Butter makers, for example, allocated their labor according to the seasonal milk production cycle, made profitable a farm process originally thought trivial and inconsequential, and hired out their daughters as wage labor at neighboring dairies when financially necessary. The surplus commodities produced by women could be marketed in barter or cash transactions and used to purchase the goods used to maintain the farm household. Because women's products were sold in local and regional markets that were relatively sheltered from national and international competition, they soon became the dominant products in the region. As men joined in the production of "women's products" or came to be more dependent on joint family incomes, the market dominance of these commodities became more firmly established.[28]

This increased dependence by men on women's labor and the products of their labor did not cause a redistribution of power within the household. Men continued to control property. Esther Lewis was part of a small minority of women who owned their own property. She had no sons, inherited her husband's farm and his personal property (including farm machinery), and could control the profits of her own work, the work of her daughters, and of hired women. Ironically, the very success of dairy operations like Lewis's drove land prices up, making it especially difficult for women to purchase land. Studies of the early nineteenth century indicate that women's control of property increased when they became widows.[29] Nevertheless, most widows in Pennsylvania did not fare well. They had no legal right to the land, the right to the income from only one-third of it, and no right to their husbands' personal property. Moreover, if their husbands had been in debt, they could be forced to sell the farm to pay creditors. Single women also controlled very little land. In the 1750s, in Chester County, for example, single women constituted 2 percent of all landowners; by the 1790s their number had increased to 3 percent.

Most women married and worked without compensation on land owned by their husbands. Under the doctrine of marital unity, Pennsylvania and Delaware women could own no real property after marriage unless they made special legal provisions to own land separately. Few did so. Reformers thought that the married women's property law of 1848 would give women more rights over property.

The law did allow women to continue to own property they brought into marriage or acquired on their own during marriage, but it gave women no ownership of the family property acquired during marriage or brought by the husband into marriage. In 1853 the Pennsylvania Supreme Court decided that the "dependent condition" of a woman "unfit her for outdoor business life," and that the married women's property law of 1848 did not mean a woman had a right to her own income and labor. The judges affirmed that a husband was "still entitled to the person and labor of the wife, and the benefits of her industry and economy."[30]

Whether or not women in actuality controlled their farms, they continued to dream of farms of their own. It is tempting to argue that they did so because they recognized the importance of their economic contributions and could negotiate control of some farm activities because of that consciousness, but because farm women's written records are relatively scarce, that argument cannot be made convincingly. What can be said in the case of butter making is that women's work brought relative security in rural communities that, at least for northern white women, were relatively more egalitarian in distribution of wealth than were urban communities. Moreover, the earliest demands for public equality emerged from rural areas undergoing this type of commercial transformation. In these areas women leaders, particularly Quakers, combined a concrete knowledge of women's economic worth with a theoretical concept of equality to demand more power in the public sphere.[31]

Regardless of the ongoing debate over how much power women had, their contribution to economic development is clear. Butter was the most ubiquitous of the "cash crops" produced by women. In the most recent study, *To Their Own Soil: Agriculture in the Antebellum North*, Jeremy Atack and Fred Bateman conclude that farm income from America's dairy production in 1860 was "almost equal to the value-added produced by the nation's textile (cottons and woolens) industry." (Value-added is the increase in value resulting from the processing of a commodity.) According to the statistical evidence assembled by Atack and Bateman, the substantial dairy output "played a reasonably prominent role in eastern agricultural activities, providing a more substantive potential even on comparatively small farms for generating income through market trade than traditionally has been recognized." Despite this favorable evaluation of dairying, the

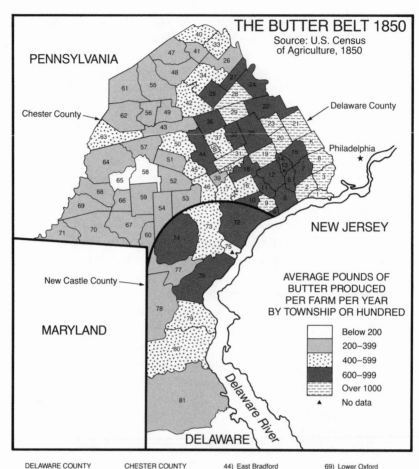

THE BUTTER BELT 1850

Source: U.S. Census
of Agriculture, 1850

PENNSYLVANIA

Chester County

Delaware County

Philadelphia ★

NEW JERSEY

New Castle County

MARYLAND

AVERAGE POUNDS OF
BUTTER PRODUCED
PER FARM PER YEAR
BY TOWNSHIP OR HUNDRED

Below 200
200–399
400–599
600–999
Over 1000
▲ No data

Delaware River

DELAWARE

DELAWARE COUNTY (Townships)	CHESTER COUNTY (Townships)		
1) Tinicum	22) Tredyffrin	44) East Bradford	69) Lower Oxford
2) Ridley	23) Easttown	45) Pocopson	70) East Nottingham
3) Darby	24) Schuylkill	46) Pennsbury	71) West Nottingham
4) Lower Chichester	25) Willistown	47) Warwick	
5) Chester	26) East Vincent	48) East Nantmeal	NEW CASTLE COUNTY (Hundreds)
6) Nether Providence	27) East Pikeland	49) East Brandywine	
7) Springfield	28) Charlestown	50) West Bradford	
8) Upper Darby	29) East Whiteland	51) Newlin	72) Brandywine
9) Upper Chichester	30) East Goshen	52) East Marlborough	73) Christiana
10) Bethel	31) Westtown	53) Kennett	74) Mill Creek
11) Aston	32) Thornbury	54) New Garden	75) Wilmington
12) Middletown	33) East Coventry	55) West Nantmeal	76) Newcastle
13) Media	34) West Vincent	56) West Brandywine	77) White Clay Creek
14) Upper Providence	35) West Pikeland	57) East Fallowfield	78) Pencader
15) Marple	36) West Whiteland	58) West Marlborough	79) Red Lion
K) Haverford	37) West Goshen	59) London Grove	80) St. Georges
16) Concord	38) West Chester	60) London Britain	81) Appoquinimink
17) Birmingham	39) Birmingham	61) Honeybrook	
18) Thornbury	40) North Coventry	62) West Caln	
19) Edgmont	41) South Coventry	63) Sadsbury	
20) Newton	42) Uwchlan	64) West Fallowfield	
21) Radnor	43) East Caln	65) Londonderry	
		66) Penn	
		67) New London	
		68) Upper Oxford	

The Mid-Atlantic Butter Belt.

authors argue that dairying was a secondary economic activity for most farms, "perceived as women and children's work, especially during peak planting or harvesting periods, and as a good means for utilizing otherwise idle family labor."[32]

Contemporary historians' designation of dairying as a secondary contributor to the farm economy because it was "women's work" perpetuates nineteenth-century men's own devaluation of women's contribution to the development of butter making. To make men's transition to a traditionally female occupation more palatable, nineteenth-century male writers often distinguished between the poor quality of butter produced by women and the butter "more scientifically" produced by men. An 1875 *Harper's Monthly Magazine* author, for example, described dairying as a relatively new specialty in agriculture in contrast to a simple traditional craft, "the oldtime churning in farmhouses, and there was the rude curdling and the ruder pressing in which our grandmothers achieved a gossipy reputation." Henry Alvord's 1899 survey of dairy development in the United States codified this devaluation of women's work: "The care of the women of the household, and the methods and utensils were crude. The average quality of the products were inferior. The supply of domestic markets was unorganized and inferior. . . . Everything was done by guess; there was no order, no system, no science in dairy operations."[33]

As my study has shown, however, the infrastructure of household dairying had in fact changed dramatically long before men entered into the occupation. Women developed butter making for the market, adopted the necessary skills and technology to increase production, and managed their own labor and the labor of children and hired assistants to facilitate the production of increasing amounts of butter. In so doing women made possible the profitable commercialization of butter making.

11 Cloth, Butter, and Boarders: Women's Household Production for the Market

IN THE STUDY OF WOMEN'S WORK, AS IN MOST AREAS of study, historical interpretations and economic theories usually coincide to produce paradigms or models. For women's work in the United States, the developmental model has tended to be the following. As the economy industrialized, households moved from subsistence to simple commodity production by the entire family. Then the men became wage workers while most of the women remained in the home producing goods and services for use. As the economy reached an advanced industrial stage, a majority of unmarried women, and then a large minority of married women, joined the male wage-labor force outside the home. By the 1970s almost half of all women in the United States were in the paid labor force. Predictions on the future vary. Some theorists argue that almost all women will become wage workers; others that at least part of the married women will remain working in the home, a reserve labor force capable of being turned out to work in time of need and returned to the home when their labor is no longer necessary for the economy.[1]

Such a summary grossly oversimplifies the complexity of the important writings on women's work produced in the last decade but it does, I think, accurately reflect the general conclusions. Housework and wage work have absorbed the attentions of most historians and economists. When a woman cares for children, cleans the house, or cooks a meal—past or present—we can categorize it. When she leaves the house for an underpaid job, we can also categorize it. But what if the woman performs work at home for the market as well as for use? Such work is not common today; it was in the past. In the early nineteenth century women in New England wove cloth and sold it to local country stores. Early in the twentieth century women in western Montana made butter, sold it for cash, and used the money to buy windmills for their family farms. In New York women of the same era took in boarders to add to the household income. Such work was simple; what it meant in the larger context of the economy, however, is so complex that it has yet to be described by historians.

The purpose of this chapter is to describe the work usually omitted from descriptions of wage work and housework—that is, work done in the household in addition to producing goods and services for use. It suggests a change in the concept of simple commodity production so that this part of American women's work in the past can be explored more fully and theories can begin to account for, and analyze, the effect of women's past work on future polities. The following analysis focuses on only a few kinds of household production for the market, looking primarily at clothmaking and butter making in rural areas, and taking in boarders in urban areas. Other labor performed by rural women, particularly the work of black women performed under slavery and sharecropping, farm women's field labor on family farms, the production of goods like canning of vegetables, and services for hired workers will not be discussed here. These jobs brought in no specific amounts of cash or credit but became part of the overall farm production. Cloth, butter, and boarders, however, brought important amounts of cash and credit into the household economy.[2] This is not meant to be a detailed description of these types of production; rather I seek to explore the historical significance of this work and to present a framework within which it can be more carefully analyzed by future researchers of women's labor history.

A word about definitions is necessary before beginning this analysis of different kinds of household production. Household production for the market is here defined to include both commodities and services that were produced by women beyond those used by the immediate members of the family. The term *home industries* refers to production of commodities for the market. *Home services* refers to services produced for the market. A *semi-monetary farm household economy* refers to a farm household that produced a small surplus of commodities for the local or regional market; *town household economy* refers to a nonfarm household that produced a small surplus of services for the local market. Using these terms, it is hoped, will eliminate some of the confusion surrounding descriptions of such work.

Sources used for this chapter are primarily literary. The examples were culled over several years from a wide range of materials on women's agricultural and economic history. Statistics are available for a few instances. Quantitative studies, for example, exist on some aspects of boarding, butter making, and sewing. For the most part, however, there has been little systematic study of these aspects of American economic history and a few comments here might help readers understand why this is so.

Farm women expected to undertake work that would bring in money to the household economy. The nature of the work varied with ethnic group and locale. In Texas Anglo women picked corn and cotton but did not work in fields otherwise. They supervised poultry, dairy, small orchard, and market garden work. Black women, on the other hand, worked at all aspects of field work and, in addition, sold eggs and poultry and engaged in dairy and poultry work at home.[3] According to Hazel Kyrk, a University of Chicago economist, as late as 1930 all farm women contributed some money to the household income. Yet census takers were often explicitly instructed not to record these women as "gainfully employed." Instructions to census takers provided for exclusion of part-time irregular employment, a definition that exactly fit the household production of farm women. The 1890 census instructed, "For a woman who works only occasionally or for a short time each day at outdoor farm or garden work, or in the dairy, or in caring for livestock or poultry, the return should be none." These census instructions tell us something about the status of women's household production but leaves a gap yet to be filled in by studying agricultural census returns and state surveys, by detailed studies of regional economies, and for the twentieth century, by oral histories.[4]

Like the income from household production by farm women, income from services performed for boarders is difficult to assess because the national census often excluded it from occupations. Sometimes, as in 1920, census takers were cautioned that taking in boarders and lodgers "should be returned as an occupation only if the person engaged in it relies upon it as his (or her) principal means of support or principal source of income. . . . If, however, a family keeps a few boarders or roomers merely as a means of supplementing or eking out the earning of income obtained from other occupations or other sources no one in the family should be returned as a boarding or lodging house keeper." Many families in nineteenth-century and early twentieth-century industrial towns did just that: took in boarders to eke out a living. Again, state and local census material can fill in these gaps. Boarders were usually listed on original census data of members living in households, and other kinds of work can be traced by a more careful analysis of the sexual division of labor. But the census problem is symptomatic of an underlying attitude that has persisted to the present. Only work that involved wage labor or ownership of the means of production outside the home was seen as important for economic change. The sheer quantity of such work, however, and the continued performance of it by women through the nineteenth and into the early twentieth century indicates that it may have been of great significance in the development of capitalism in the United States.[5]

The history of household production is still far from complete. In part, it remains incomplete because of two historical misconceptions about farm and town household economies that lead to confusion about home industries and services. These misconceptions continually appear in literature about women's work. The first misconception assumes a view of farms as subsistence or as producing nearly everything. According to this view, subsistence farms remained isolated from market forces from the early colonial period through much of the nineteenth century. The second misconception assumes a static amount of household equipment. Colonial women are pictured as candle-dipping, wool-spinning, loom-weaving, butter-churning household workers. By implication, all of the household needs were taken care of by them. The two assumptions reinforce each other. Then, according to this view, nineteenth-century industrialization quickly dominated household economies: women moved into the factories or became "housewives." Remnants of the subsistence farm remained on the frontier but gradually disappeared in the course of the nineteenth century. These assumptions promote the view presented at the beginning of this chapter. Women moved from housework into wage work.

Material Change

Such static conceptions badly distort the reality of women's economic history. Households termed "colonial" in the above view are actually late eighteenth-century households. There is accumulating evidence that early colonial households could not afford the equipment to produce their own home products. Seventeenth-century colonists had neither equipment to weave, to make candles, nor even to grind flour. Early colonists wore skin clothing, much as did the Native Americans, they used grease and rags to produce light, and at first, they ground their corn much as Native American Women had done, by mortar and pestle. Gradually hand mills replaced mortar and pestle and grist mills replaced hand mills. Wool-processing equipment was acquired. Pottery useful for food processing, especially dairying, was purchased. How the pattern varied from area to area has not yet been fully described, but it seems likely that colonial household production was relatively limited before 1750. Wealthy colonists purchased material goods or hired artisans to produce them. Poor families simply went without. Gradually, during the course of the eighteenth century, what had been inaccessible to most became accessible. Farm households gradually purchased both home industry equipment and more finished products.[6]

The change from hand milling to water-powered milling is an example of how material change could affect the labor of women. European women were not accustomed to performing their own milling and European technology was easily transferred to America and quickly improved. The preference for wheat of many early European colonists also quickened the transition from hand ground corn to stone ground wheat. Grist mills were often neighborhood affairs with a single miller working imported grind stones. The stones for hand mills most likely also had to be imported or sought in areas that had the proper type of stone. By the early nineteenth century, all wheat in the East was milled by water driven flour mills, most at local mills but some at large commercial operations that exported it or sold it on a national market. In the West, however, hand mills were still in use. In the Southwest, Native American women also continued to hand grind wheat and corn, selling both flour and cornmeal to travelers and to missionaries before flour mills became common. By 1907 few Native American women continued to process their own corn or wheat. Local mills run by water or steam power and then large commercial mills had replaced this home industry.[7]

Cloth Production

We know more about the transition from home manufactured cloth than we do about the transition in milling. Recent research on colonial Maryland indicates that the development of spinning and knitting was a response of upper-income plantation households to stagnation in the tobacco economy about 1680. Within the next century, according to a study of one Maryland county, the percentage of households that had wool-processing equipment rose from less than 10 percent to 80 percent, as the processing of wool spread to the poorer classes. There is, as yet, no comparable study for the New England colonies where many textiles were imported, but by the early nineteenth century, textiles were a major home industry in a number of states and surpluses were often bartered or sold.[8] The ideology of self-sufficiency of the New England farms in 1800 was based to a great extent on the ability of women in the household to provide a surplus for the local market. The factory manufacture of yarn and cloth undermined this rural way of life. Farms in southern New England and the northern mid-Atlantic states disappeared first, with whole families moving to mill towns. In northern New England, farm families hung on by using the wages of farm daughters to pay off mortgages.[9] Farm families elsewhere either commercialized, developed new ways women could bring cash into the old farm economy, or moved west where land was cheap. By the Civil War, few women did any spinning or weaving within the household except on the frontier. By the end of the 1870s, the price of yardage had dropped so low that store-bought calico had begun to replace homespun everywhere, even in the remote areas of the Southwest, where it destroyed a small local trade in cotton articles manufactured primarily by Native Americans.[10]

Even then there were exceptions to the generalizations that women no longer wove in the home for the market. Cloth for clothing was

Installing a loom in the attic where daughters could weave was a common way that New England farm families extended their incomes in the late eighteenth and early nineteenth centuries. Source: RG86–G–6J3, Woman's Bureau, National Archives.

now purchased, but factory manufactured rugs had not yet captured the national market, and surplus from local markets filled the void. Mormon women wove large quantities of rugs for sale in the 1880s. Navajo women also produced rugs for a specialized eastern market, primarily able to compete because of a depressed local economy and domestic sheep production. By 1903 Navajo women were producing forty thousand to fifty thousand hand woven rugs a year, selling them commonly for one dollar a pound, and using the money income to buy commercially ground flour and factory manufactured cloth. As farm women added textiles to the items customarily purchased with cash or barter, they found new ways of bringing in an income by producing other items in demand on the local market. Rural women sometimes made clothing or performed household services for single males but a more significant contribution to the farm economy was in the production of butter.[11]

Butter—A Rural Industry

Nineteenth-century farm women produced large quantities of butter, often marketing it in the same way as cloth had been marketed earlier, by taking it to the local country store where they exchanged it for needed commodities. Stores then shipped it to urban distributors. Agricultural censuses regularly reported production of butter, and references to women's dairy work are scattered but numerous. By 1840, 14 to 23 percent of agricultural income in New England and 5 to 17 percent in Middle Atlantic states came from dairy products, many of them produced by women. According to the 1850 record of one country store serving a Louisiana parish, women from 285 farms brought in 24,000 pounds of butter that was shipped to urban areas. One region of Delaware in 1850 had 256 farms producing an average 602 pounds of butter per farm. Within a decade, the farms of this region were producing an average of 1,193 pounds. In this area, butter making was still considered women's work. One quantitative study of marketable butter surplus produced by 21,000 rural households in the northern United States listed in the 1860 agricultural census concluded that income from sales of butter on small farms provided a significant addition to the income of farm families and a substantial potential for generating income through market trade. Any farm over 20 acres could produce this marketable surplus with farms of 20 to 49 acres being capable of producing forty-three pounds of surplus butter per year. On the 20 percent of the eastern farms of 100 to 499 acres, as much as 40 percent of the income could come from the sale of milk and dairy products.[12]

By the Civil War some women on southwestern and western farms had also begun to produce butter for the market. Guri Olsdatter, a Norwegian woman in Minnesota, wrote in 1863 that with three cows she produced 230 pounds of butter one summer for an income of sixty-two dollars. Native American women of the Osage tribe in Oklahoma and the Yakima tribe in Washington produced twenty-four thousand and twenty thousand pounds of butter respectively in 1890. The western market for farm butter continued to exist well into the twentieth century in some areas. Elinore Pruitt Stewart, a Wyoming homesteader, wrote in 1913 that from ten cows she sold enough butter to pay for a year's supply of flour and gasoline. The butter making of other Wyoming women has already been mentioned.[13]

Farm families successfully fought the introduction of butter substitutes, scornfully called "hog butter." Through their Granges, women and men generated enough pressure to force Congress to pass a stiff regulatory law in 1887 to control the manufacture of processed oleomargarine. The law decreased production of oleomargarine for almost a decade, but by the turn of the century production had increased once more. Moreover, new dairying equipment—especially mechanical cream separators—and centralized marketing techniques allowed the commercialization of butter making in the early 1900s. Wyoming women on the frontier were among the last to depend upon butter making for a substantial income.[14]

Other Farm Production

Rural women's contribution to the semi-monetary farm household economy of the nineteenth century through the making of butter was not the only one. Black and white rural women also developed truck farming to supplement their household income. The garden had traditionally been part of women's work on the farm and the word "truck" became associated with their gardens in the colonial period. By the late eighteenth century, English visitors had already described the little patches kept by Euro-American farm women in which they raised "truck" for local markets.[15] There is some evidence that Afro-American women in the South also developed truck gardening and trade under slavery and considerably more evidence that as freedwomen even more of them moved into truck farming. Frances Harper, a well-known black abolitionist lecturer who went south during reconstruction, mentioned black South Carolinian women as providing the majority of truck farm produce in that state and, moreover, using this as an economic base to allow black men greater freedom in their political activities.[16]

Farm women often provided incomes from combinations of sales and services. Native American women sold herbs, berries, nuts, and in the West provisioned the army with fodder and vegetables in the late nineteenth century. In addition, they sold pottery, baskets, weaving, and bead work that sometimes, as in the case of Navajo weavers, almost reached mass production.[17] Euro-American women put together incomes equally varied. One Nebraska farm woman, Mary Harpster, kept an account for the years from 1884 to 1886. Some of her entries were as follows:

> May 16, 1885—Joe paid for his sewing, 70 cents
> May 18, 1885—George paid for his sewing, 70 cents
> June 19, 1885—Sold milk, Joe boarding, $3.50
> December 21, 1885—Made three shirts, 25 cents each, for McLains
> November 24, 1886—Washed, 60 cents
> November 27, 1886—Washed, $1.00
> November 28, 1886—Ironed, 30 cents
> November 29, 1886—Sewed, 25 cents
> November 25, 1886—Knit mittens, 20 cents

By November 1886 Harpster was bringing in from $4.35 to $4.80 a week and had purchased a knitting machine. Her experiences were similar to those of women in other rural areas in the Midwest and West. Wisconsin women sold dairy milk to dairies that were developing a regional market for cheese. Mormon women in Utah managed small cheese factories in the late nineteenth and early twentieth centuries.[18]

Economist Ruth Allen, who studied 975 Texas families in 1928–1930, concluded that household production for the market could still be an important factor in the lives of these families. Although Allen's published data are difficult to use because of small samples (usually twenty to thirty) on individual questions, her study indicated that women's contribution could be significant. In one sample of Euro-American farm women who did not do field labor, one-fourth produced a money income. Over a third of the women who were in farm-owning households produced a money income, and a fourth of the women in tenant farming, where women did work in the fields, also produced a money income. At a time when the average farm tenant's cash income was barely over $100 a year, one Scottish tenant woman made an income of $175 from eggs and chickens. Allen estimated that the average money income from production in the home for sale and use exceeded the income from wage labor. The farm woman could make more in sales alone than in field labor. The reason not all women chose to produce poultry or eggs for the market was that black and Hispanic women, as well as some Euro-

American women, did not have the facilities, the skills, or the finances necessary to engage in home production for local distribution. Wage labor was easier to handle and to calculate. Even among most Euro-American farm women, almost none had a system of books that analyzed home production. Nonetheless, home production was so important that Allen estimated women's work of this type probably brought in more income than the entire family's cotton crop.[19]

An ideology of economic self-sufficiency underlay this process of home production. The economic philosophy was neatly formulated and inscribed on the overleaf of a Nebraska farm account: "1. Spend as much less than you receive as possible; 2. keep savings for emergency plus something; 3. pay as you go." Self-sufficiency was absolutely necessary for the early stages of a developing economy but at odds with the shift to rural credit-based capitalist enterprise and the development of the farm-tenant credit system in the South. Most male farmers abandoned this philosophy long before farm women did, however, because of the commercialization of field crops. On many farms there then existed a dual economy—the women and children providing for living expenses and keeping these expenses on a cash basis while the man handled the field crops, using the income to pay for mortgages and the new machinery. Sometimes the women's cash income helped pay the mortgage and provide cash for capital improvement as well.[20]

As commercialization of farming accelerated in the twentieth century and women lost more and more of their local markets to centralized marketing networks, the semi-monetary farm began to disappear. The concept of the dual farm household economy persisted, however, with many farm men unwilling to invest income from field crops in machinery or furnishings for the house. The country life reformers of 1900 to 1920 attempted to provide new avenues of income for farm women and urged men to be responsible for the upkeep of the house, but for those farms that commercialized their field crops, men controlled the means of production, thus leaving women on the farm in a vulnerable position. As long as farm income remained low, women's contribution was important. Their income from production of commodities combined with production of use items gave them status and some independence within the farm family.[21]

The farm depression of the 1920s and 1930s accelerated the

long-term movement of people off the farm and completed the transition to a money economy of those left behind. Thirty million people left rural areas between 1929 and 1965 and between 1940 and 1970, the farm population declined from thirty to ten million. Those women who remained on the farm, while still active in the daily operation of the farm, were less likely to produce either goods for use or for sale. Middle-class women saw themselves as rural "homemakers" rather than as farm women. Their daughters joined Future Homemaker clubs. Poor women began to commute to urban areas, taking poorly paid wage work.[22]

Boarders—An Urban Solution

While farm women experienced the impact of commercialization on their work, similar changes affected urban women. Both immigrant women and native born migrant women who had left small farms for urban areas had performed farm work in addition to "housework." Once in town, single farm women often went into domestic employment or into factories, but married women found the opportunities for household production much fewer than in the country. Space was often lacking for gardens and animals, and regional urban based markets usually provided milk, eggs, and poultry. While women could take in washing or do home sewing, an even larger number may have taken in boarders, as this was one of the service sectors that was the slowest to develop on a commercial basis. Particularly in towns in the process of industrializing, urban married women most commonly earned money by taking in boarders. Boarding was widespread among both native born and immigrant households until the 1930s.[23]

Abundant records exist to document boarding as an important way in which working-class families in almost every industrial town eked out a living. There were two national studies done on urban areas, one published in 1892 and another in 1904. In addition, federal and state census returns included boarders, and the Women's Bureaus conducted several surveys. Because boarders became an object of criticism by middle-class reformers during the progressive era before World War I, there are many literary documents which, if used carefully to allow for bias, can give us an idea of the importance of the income from boarding in working-class families.

Boarding seems to have paralleled the process of industrialization, increasing greatly after 1850 and probably peaking around 1910, but varying from region to region. A town like Barrington, Rhode Island, in the process of industrializing from 1885 to 1895, showed about 25 to 30 percent of the families taking in boarders, while a stable farming community like Foster, Rhode Island, had perhaps 3 to 4 percent of the families with boarders. Other communities studied in the late nineteenth and early twentieth centuries show 15 to 30 percent of the households taking in boarders. As late as 1920, in highly industrialized Rochester, New York, 16 percent of the married women contributed to the household income by taking in boarders.[24]

Until we have more detailed studies for individual cities and states it is difficult to say precisely how economic factors interacted to create the divergent percentages of women taking in boarders that was reflected in state studies published by the Bureau of Labor in 1892 and 1904. Among 2,132 cotton-worker households in seventeen states studied in the 1892 report, most of them native born American, 27 percent of the wives took in boarders. Families taking in boarders ranged from highs of 44 percent in Virginia to a low of .07 in Rhode Island (See Table 1). In the 1904 study of 25,444 working-class families in industrial centers of thirty-three states, 24 percent took in boarders or lodgers. The rate of boarding per household ranged from a high of 40 percent in Maryland to a low of 3 percent of households taking in boarders in South Carolina (See Table 2).[25]

What seems to emerge fairly clearly from the studies is that boarding could be as profitable, or even more profitable, for working-class wives than other forms of women's work. In the 1892 study, citied above, where 27 percent of all the wives took in boarders, 16 percent of the wives worked at other jobs with only a 2 percent overlap where wives did both. Overall, women made 42.65 percent as much as their husbands when they took in boarders and 45.52 as much as their husbands in nonboarding type work. In a state like Massachusetts, annual boarding income could average $225.25 while other types of women's income averaged only $184.47. When one looks at the 4,559 New York households studied in 1904, it becomes clear that income from women's work at home and outside the home there was critical. Assuming the women were seldom doing both, women provided 32 to 35 percent of the gross family income.

Table 1:   Cotton Worker Families Income by Type of Work 1892

	Percent Boarding	Percent Non-boarding	Percent Both
Alabama (N = 43)	28	19	0
Connecticut (N = 149)	22	20	.03
Georgia (N = 198)	25	22	.04
Kentucky (N = 19)	21	26	.05
Louisiana (N = 10)	10	0	0
Maine (N = 163)	21	19	.02
Maryland (N = 163)	40	.03	0
Massachusetts (N = 399)	23	26	.03
Mississippi (N = 33)	21	21	.06
New Hampshire (N = 118)	32	21	.03
New York (N = 186)	31	.07	0
North Carolina (N = 147)	27	.07	.01
Pennsylvania (N = 212)	31	.03	0
Rhode Island (N = 54)	.07	.11	0
South Carolina (N = 32)	19	28	.06
Tennessee (N = 68)	32	.07	.01
Virginia (N = 123)	44	18	.05
United States (N = 2132)	27	16	2

SOURCE: U.S., Bureau of Labor, *Seventh Annual Report of the Commissioner of Labor* (2 vols.; Washington, 1892), II, Pt. 3.

Moreover, the average income of women working at nonboarding occupations came to only 24 percent of the husband's wage, but the income from boarders was 37 percent of the husband's income in native born and 43 percent of the husband's income in foreign born households. The survey showed that a foreign family averaged $277 annually from boarders against $230 in native-born families. Thus, boarding was particularly attractive for immigrant families because the husband's income was likely to be less than among native-born workers. Women may have taken in boarders not only because they could increase the family income but also because that income may have been more than they could have obtained in the low paying jobs available outside the home.[26]

According to these survey figures, the wife's income from boarders in 1904 in New York, even in native-born families, could pay for the house rent, clothing, and part of the fuel while the husband's

Table 2:   Working Class Families Income by Type of Work 1904

Area	Percent Boarding and Lodging	Percent Non-boarding
Alabama (N = 297)	23	20
California (N = 507)	19	5
Colorado (N = 197)	11	0
Connecticut (N = 810)	25	8
Delaware (N = 196)	30	10
District of Columbia (N = 100)	31	10
Georgia (N = 298)	38	17
Illinois (N = 1633)	23	8
Indiana (N = 601)	32	13
Iowa (N = 332)	29	9
Kansas (N = 196)	14	1
Kentucky (N = 335)	27	8
Louisiana (N = 193)	18	17
Maine (N = 366)	17	7
Maryland (N = 616)	40	16
Massachusetts (N = 2577)	32	1
Michigan (N = 887)	24	6
Minnesota (N = 398)	29	4
Missouri (N = 794)	17	4
New Hampshire (N = 299)	32	3
New Jersey (N = 994)	18	4
New York (N = 4559)	21	15
North Carolina (N = 198)	17	4
Ohio (N = 1800)	19	4
Pennsylvania (N = 3702)	19	4
Rhode Island (N = 475)	30	13
South Carolina (N = 200)	3	37
Tennessee (N = 199)	32	6
Texas (N = 197)	19	8
Virginia (N = 386)	29	9
Washington (N = 200)	17	2
West Virginia (N = 199)	21	7
Wisconsin (N = 699)	25	7
United States (N = 25,440)	24	9

SOURCE: U.S., Bureau of Labor, *Eighteenth Annual Report of the Commissioner of Labor* (Washington, 1904); 50, 260.

income could cover the largest expenditure, that of food, and other incidental expenses. In either type of family, the household ended the year with less than thirty-one dollars saved, the difference in the foreign-born man's salary being just about made up by the greater income from children working and boarders in the immigrant family.[27]

Detailed studies are available for only a few cities as yet, but the important role by women's home services is evident in a 1908 study done by Margaret Byington in Homestead, Pennsylvania. Almost 43 percent of one group of families kept lodgers and in half of the households with boarders, that work provided over 25 percent of the total income. Byington also found that the families that took in boarders were families where the husband made less than twelve dollars a week. Since 85 percent of the East European men made less than twelve dollars a week, these women were more likely to keep boarders. Among East European women, almost 64 percent kept boarders. Taking lodgers, Byington concluded, "was a deliberate business venture on the part of the family to increase the inadequate income from the man's earnings."[28]

In one group of families in Homestead, Byington also found 53 percent of the families depended entirely on the husband's wage. Other cities may have had similar but changing patterns, for the 1920 Rochester, New York, survey concluded that 55 percent of the families relied solely on the husband's wage. Since Rochester was a predominantly working-class town, where 28 percent of wives contributed to the household income, other towns may have had similarly high contributions by wives.[29]

While there is no indication that a negative ideology developed around the farm wives' household production, boarding-house services and home manufacturing in urban areas came under increasing attack from two sources: unions and reformers. Unions concentrated primarily on sewing and manufacturing in the homes but progressive reformers, beginning in the last decade of the nineteenth century, mounted major campaigns against lodgers in what became, according to some scholars, a rhetoric of "demonology." These attacks were framed in terms of progressive attitudes about childhood. Children in these homes were seen not only as neglected by overworked mothers but also as exposed to the sinister influence of young, single, working-class men. In practice, however, not only was this income crucial economically for the households, but also boarders could provide rich psychic returns to householders who were older and whose children were working or already gone from the home.[30]

Immigrant households may have taken in more lodgers proportionately than native-born households after the turn of the century. If boarding had once been a way middle-class households survived evil days in the early nineteenth century, and a way both native-born and immigrant households survived the industrializing process of the late nineteenth century, it may have been that native-born women moved away from taking in lodgers before immigrant women were able or wished to do so. It seems likely that progressive anti-lodger rhetoric affected native-born working-class households before immigrant households. More careful study of the ideology may provide insight into its function in terms of class and ethnic groups.[31]

What can be said with certainty is that the practice of boarding was an extremely important source of income for married urban women as a whole in the century from 1840 to 1940 and that by neglecting it, one overlooks an important economic element in the lives of the urban working class, the working lives of working-class women, and in the developing industrial economy itself.

Theoretical Implications

Most of income produced by women was from manufacturing, processing, or services requiring little capital investment. Large-scale capitalist enterprises did not grow from their work. Nor was capital accumulated and invested by women performing this work. Instead, money was absorbed into the household economy to make it more productive, with any surplus reinvested in male-directed economic ventures. This was particularly the case with the income of farm women. Alternatively, other income was reabsorbed into the urban economy through household purchases, either barely maintaining household subsistence or raising the standard of consumption of the family and raising its productivity within the wage-labor sector. The goal of women's household production remained to make ends meet rather than to consciously make profits. The goal was to raise a family, if the woman was a widow, or to contribute to the household income. Women were able to use skills developed within the household economy to support themselves and their families but inevitably became wage workers or housewives as further economic development made household production unprofitable.[32]

Household production was a stage between subsistence and wage labor that did not lead to entrepreneurship. Rather than become entrepreneurs with highly capitalized business ventures, women fell back into the role of providing raw materials or labor for the new enterprise or they became new consumers for the product. Thus, although household production was a transition stage, it was not transitional to capitalism for individual women.[33] Males tended to divide into three groups, those who owned the means of production, those who did not, and those who provided the ideology and support system for this division or mediated between the two groups. Women, however, never divided in this way in that they directly participated only in the last two groups. Women almost never controlled the means of production under capitalism although they may have provided the social context within which those men who controlled the means of production functioned as a group.[34]

What was the importance of this household production? It allowed high productivity by both adults in families. It allowed families to care for their personal needs by having women provide services we now call social welfare. Women could provide these services, as well as produce commodities for use in the home and, in addition, produce services and commodities for local and regional markets. Rural men could increase production of field crops for the growing urban areas without increasing food costs. Low food costs combined with taking boarders allowed the males of American urban families to work for lower wages than they might have required had women not contributed to the family income. At the same time, families could afford to buy commodities that raised their material standard of living and forwarded the development of a complete market economy.

The 1920s and 1930s were important decades in the transition of women from household production to wage labor. To maintain the standard of living that women's work in the home had previously allowed, they now began to work outside the home at wage labor. Work at home was no longer productive because the services and commodities that women had produced had become commercialized—capitalist structures could perform them more cheaply than could women. This shift occurred at the same time that a greater emphasis was being put upon keeping children off the labor market and during a period of economic dislocation caused by the depression. As a consequence, the locus of production by married women began to shift from the household to the capitalist workplace.

How well does Marxist theory explain these historical developments? Marx did not describe home production in detail in *Das Capital*. He did, however, identify, what he called the petty mode of production where the workers owned their own means of production. He saw this type of production as being joined to agriculture, both being held together in a bond of union that was broken by the introduction of capitalist production. The centralization of capital annihilated this old system, concentrated the scattered means of production, and resulted first in a modern type of domestic industry and then manufacturing in factories.

Thus, Marx identifies simple commodity production as an important stage in economic development. Ernest Mandel, in *Marxist Economic Theory*, elaborated on this type of production, again identifying it as a transitional stage between a society governed by labor cooperation in a society governed by the economic laws of capitalism. He pointed out that the money acquired by this type of production was employed to acquire items for use that in turn prohibited the accumulation of capital. Once this simple commodity production was subordinated to capital in a money economy, production for distant markets destroyed the small producer, giving rise to domestic industry and then to factory manufacturing.

Simple commodity production, as seen in this classical Marxist sense, can accommodate the development of women's work here if it is expanded to include services produced in the home and to explain how the sexual division of labor affected the historical transition. In the United States, farm families could move West to remain on the land or switch to production of a new commodity—usually butter. Town families could accommodate household services to the expanding industrial economy. By responding to market changes, women's production was a crucial economic factor in both rural and urban families, for it maintained within the family the older mode of production. When the older type of production ended, women moved into wage labor in greater numbers and shifted the locus of their work from the home to the workplace.

If Marxist theory incorporated all examples of women's work, including simple commodity production, it could more accurately describe both the past and predict the future. A model that incorporated the realities of the lives of women's past—that they at one time produced for the market at home as well as produced for use—could illustrate how the development of capitalism has affected American women. Such a model may even challenge overall theories about the development of industrialization in the United States.

When one combines the household production of women in rural and urban areas, it is too important to be ignored. It contributed to the developing capitalist economy and at the same time was critical in the service and commodity product sectors that remained underdeveloped the longest. Women going to work outside the home today is, in reality, part of a continuing process in which women are and have been shifting their workplace and moving from a household income to a wage income as commodity production, technology, and the development of the service sector displaces their jobs. The New England women who sold cloth, the Wyoming women who sold butter for the farm windmills, and the New York women who boarded lodgers to allow the household to survive were not so different in motivation from the women who today go out as clerical or service workers. The political implications of that process, however, are likely to be far different. Since World War II, for the first time in American history, large numbers of married women have moved out of the simple commodity mode of production and into the capitalist mode by becoming wage laborers. The fact that women are not only leaving the household but also leaving a transitional mode of production may have an important impact on the development of capitalism and on women's reaction to it.

PART IV

Rural Social Welfare

WELFARE POLICY AND INSTITUTIONS HAVE LONG BEEN a contested terrain in American society. Since the colonial period when Europeans transferred their public welfare systems, the clients, the providers, and the public policy shapers have vied over the formulation and implementation of policy. In these contests of ideology, politics, and economics, the clients have often lost out, out voted and out talked by the more powerful decision makers. Often rural women have received unequal access to unequal institutions and unequal ability to shape those institutions to their needs. Still, the rural clients of public support, where it existed, were able to influence the delivery of care. In this section, I explore the extent to which public institutions provided for the welfare of rural women and the extent to which they were on their own.

Health, education, and welfare, and the federal agency whose name bears these words, do not adequately suggest the complexity of the American system and its history. Most welfare—including health and education—has been provided by family, kin, and local community for most Americans for most of United States history. The states gradually assumed more responsibility in the nineteenth century, first for education, then for health, hardly ever for what became known as welfare, the support of dependent people without family, kin, or community to support them. While various reformers urged the development of federal policy in the nineteenth century, the states remained the primary public entities responsible for the welfare of citizens. Most states failed to provide for the welfare of their rural majorities. Southern states failed most visibly to provide adequately for rural inhabitants, particularly if they were black, but other states reflected controversies over how to provide delivery systems to reach Americans equally. Ethnicity provided a convenient way to justify reluctance of wealthier citizens to deliver welfare services to those in need. The rural poor woman was at the end of the welfare chain. She received the least, particularly where she belonged to an ethnic group that had no political power.

The Wisconsin case study looks at the welfare institutions from the standpoint of rural poor women. It discusses welfare mainly and touches on rural health only briefly. There is much to be learned about the health of rural women. The studies undertaken by the Children's Bureau on infant and maternal mortality rates began to explore the conditions of rural health in the early twentieth century. Historians have not added significantly to those early studies.

Scholars have given more attention to education than to health. Access to education has always been severely limited for rural women, particularly after the age of fourteen. The need for large numbers of lowly paid teachers in rural areas has been the major factor in allowing access for some women to continuing education. Since the early nineteenth century most rural schools have been staffed by rural women who have constantly fought to achieve better schools, better education, and better pay. Adult education was severely limited in the nineteenth century. Chautauqua provided the best opportunities for rural women. Thousands of women attended Chautauqua lectures and took correspondence courses to obtain education beyond elementary school. Agricultural education for adults, which began with farmer's institutes in the late nineteenth century, used many Chautauqua techniques to transfer new technology and skills to the rural population. It was, however, an education severely narrowed and focused. It was practical self-help with an overlay of reforming ideology that emphasized the sexual division of labor and the importance of homemaking skills for women. The section on the first years of extension service in New Mexico evaluates the successes and failures of this system.

Rural Social Welfare

Inadequate schools, health care, and welfare plagued the lives of rural women. Most struggled to provide family, kin, and community substitutes, but most had to rely primarily on their own resources. Many managed to survive and to stay on the land but each succeeding farm crisis sheared off another group unwilling or unable to exploit their families and themselves to stay on the land. Recently, the last of the survivors have become more vocal in their protests over agricultural policy and their demands for rural policy that will focus less narrowly on profits and more broadly on the welfare of rural people.

12 On Their Own: Women
on the Wisconsin Frontier

WHEN I FINISHED *LOOSENING THE BONDS: MID-*
Atlantic Farm Women, 1750–1850, I had answered a number of
questions that I had about those women. I had proved to my satisfaction that farm women had not had less work on the farm during the
transition to commercial agriculture but more. I had confirmed that
farm women had not left much in the way of writings because most
of them had probably remained illiterate until the 1770s, and that
while they had rapidly achieved literacy in the first decades of the
nineteenth century, farm work had left little time for married farm
women to leave accounts or letters before the 1840s. I had also
become convinced that women developed the dairy industry upon
which the farms of the Mid-Atlantic based their prosperity after it
became uneconomical to produce grains in the 1830s.

Every research project brings new questions in place of the old.
While there were few German women in the areas that I studied,
there were many German women in nearby Lancaster County. Much
had been written about the Pennsylvania Germans but, I found very
little about the women. I had noted a similar lack of research on
German farm women elsewhere, despite the fact that Germans composed the largest non-British Euro-American ethnic group not only
in Pennsylvania but also in states such as Texas and Wisconsin.

I wanted to know more about these German farm women. I also wanted to know more about what farm women were doing in the late nineteenth century, especially in dairying areas. And, I wanted to find a different geographical area to work in. My new research project became defined as German women, late nineteenth and early twentieth century, but I needed to find an area.

The choice of an area was difficult. I had started doing family history research on my German Wisconsin grandmother who came to this country in the late nineteenth century from the Austro-Hungarian Empire. Although Wisconsin seemed a natural choice, I was concerned that family history might bring me too close to my history. I wondered if I could distance myself enough to tell the story dispassionately, not without emotion but with insight. My hesitancy came in part from the fact that my grandmother, and my mother as a child, had been desperately poor. My mother did not give me many details. Her father had left the family and she never mentioned him until his death in 1947. She had quit school after the seventh grade when someone in the family became ill and she had to stay home to nurse. Her feet were crippled because she had to wear whatever shoes she could get, usually ones that did not fit her feet. She had a passion for, as she said "nice things," that I never quite understood. And a hatred of farm life so intense that I was drawn back to the land almost in reaction to it.

There was risk there. No doubt about it. To go back to Wisconsin was to go back to painful memories of my mother. When I began to retrace my family history I had only a name, "Schopp," and a town name, "Medford." On my first trip, I just drove around the countryside wondering where she might have lived. There were words that came back—Dorchester, Rauscher, Gaebert. I remembered how my grandmother, in her seventies when she lived with our family would talk in her still broken English about being "by Gaeberts" or "by Dorchester." Never having learned German I just wondered about the strange syntax. That was grandmother's way of speaking, that was all. To begin to sort out what was grandmother, what was mother, what was Wisconsin culture, what German culture was something that took me a long time to decide to do. By 1986 I had tentatively decided that I would settle on Wisconsin. When Gerda Lerner asked me to go to the University of Wisconsin at Madison as a Visiting Professor in Spring 1987, I knew that I had to go back.

There is a sense in which daughters do complete the visions of their mothers. This was a symbolic way of finishing the education my mother so desperately wanted when she was a poor farm girl.

I brought one major question with me when I began my research on Wisconsin farm women. It was a question that drove me back day after day to the Historical Society seeking an answer. It was not the only question but one that came out of my past and that I had to answer as a historian. Why, in the first decades of the twentieth century, in Wisconsin, a state not known after all for its poverty, could a family know such hard times? Why, as the oral traditions of the family inform me, did children have to go to school hungry, with only an apple in their lunch pails? Why did a mother of eight have to say she wished her youngest, born in 1909, had never been born because there was so little for her to eat? How could this have happened in a country that I was brought up to consider a land of plenty? I wanted to know why my mother went hungry to school and why the family had no one to help them.

I began with the welfare structure of the early twentieth century in rural Wisconsin. What I discovered was that there was none. The first comprehensive state welfare law to cover all rural children was not passed until 1929. Correspondence in the state records indicates that this legislation allowed counties to provide rural social welfare agents but did not require it. Citizens advisory boards were to take the responsibility, but in the four rural counties I chose to study—Marathon, Clark, Taylor, and Lincoln—only one had a board by 1934. Both counties and state refused to appropriate funds. Not until the depression of the 1930s brought massive infusions of state and federal monies was a uniform system of child welfare in homes established in rural counties.[1]

Without a systematic monitoring of rural needs what was available for poor families? Let us start at one extreme with the oldest institution, the county poorhouse. Established in the nineteenth century by the middle class, the working poor dreaded rural poorhouses, which had become a symbol of defeat. Poor families considered institutionalization of the family, or part of it, recognition of failure to provide for their families. Women did everything they could do, including starve their children, to stay out of these places. The state also had a system of county asylums where the mentally disabled could be cared for. In other words, the most dependent people were cared for, however badly.[2]

In April 1902, Matilda Rauscher Schopp posed in front of her 18 × 24 foot log house for this picture by an itinerant photographer. Her first husband had died in August 1901 and she was about to marry again. She bore five more children and raised them in this log house. Source: Family photograph.

For families that could not provide for children, there was the State Public School at Sparta. Established in 1885, by the early twentieth century the home had been transformed from a place of temporary refuge for children of families in time of crisis to an institution that broke up poor families. According to a study done in 1924 by the Children's Bureau, children placed in the Sparta home were indentured out, usually to farms, where children were worked very hard and often deprived of an education. Moreover, children with mental disabilities were indentured along with normal children. If the family in which the child was placed wanted to adopt the child, this was done without notifying the family. Children were sometimes kept from communicating with members of their families. In 1920 the state Supreme Court held that the practice of adopting out state school children without a separate adoption proceeding was unconstitutional.[3]

Wisconsin was one of the first states, in 1913, to provide aid to dependent children in their homes. But this 1913 law was not mandatory. A second 1915 law required counties to provide aid and established a minimum amount to be paid to families. Counties also ignored the 1915 law. The state had promised to pay up to one-third reembursement but did not bear its burden, and so rural aid to dependent children continued to be uneven and sometimes absent until the 1920s.[4]

For young women who bore children out of wedlock, there was little help available. A 1925 study showed that 43 percent of young women in Wisconsin who bore children outside of marriage were from rural communities and 54 percent from communities with populations under five thousand. A fifth were domestics, frequently from rural areas where the custom dictated that marriage would follow pregnancy. But marriage frequently did not follow for these rural women whether in towns or in the country. Young women could be cared for in a state home for girls but officials in the home encouraged women to give up their children, did little to attempt to have the fathers (who were frequently known) contribute to the child's support, and often took children before the six weeks to two months that social workers felt as necessary for the health of the child. Mortality rates of children born out of marriage were much higher than those born in marriage, and evidence seemed to point to early adoption as the cause for this, as well as poor care for young women because of hostility in their communities.[5]

Instead of caring for these children, communities ostracized them and their unwed mothers. In the 1920s, laws still referred to these children as "bastards." Moreover, it was almost impossible for young women and their families to use the legal system to enforce child support. Three-fourths of the young women never attempted to get judgments against the fathers. Those 20 percent who did found the district attorneys arrayed against them and in league with the fathers' attorneys. An old rural practice, that of gangs of men coming to the assistance of the alleged father by swearing to intimate knowledge of the promiscuity of the mother, resulted not only in failure to establish support but also in robbing the young woman of self-respect and morale in her community. Norway had established the practice of having anyone who claimed intimacy sharing support, and several counties later used this technique to stop the practice. But the custom of accepting the testimony of these gangs was common in many rural areas. In the minuscule number of cases, 7 percent, where support could be obtained, it was usually inadequate and there was no means to enforce the court's decision. Investigators also reported some young women as victims of family abuse and some who were of "limited intelligence" preyed upon by gangs of young men.[6]

Welfare investigators noted an important difference between white and black communities in attitudes toward children of unwed mothers. In black communities, children were always taken in and raised as a part of the family with the community also accepting them. White communities would not accept the woman or her infant; instead communities assumed harsh treatment and public disgrace would check the conduct of young women. To defend themselves from the ostracism of the community, families frequently would not help their own daughters. Many of these daughters fled to the cities to escape the opprobrium of small towns and farm communities.[7]

If the public structures did so little to help families, then did private agencies do more? Although welfare agencies had been established by various denominations, particularly Catholic and Lutheran, these agencies tended to be located in urban areas. None operated in the four counties that I am studying, although I have yet to examine church agency records. Parish priests did not, apparently, take welfare as one of their charges. The extent of their parish duties was to visit families where there was marital discord and counsel patience. I suspect that churches, when they took care of families, took care of village families. Even a 1926 list of child-caring institutions showed none for these four counties. The Children's Home and Aid Society of Wisconsin, based in Milwaukee, listed no boarding homes in these counties for 1920.[8]

If not public or private agencies, then why not kinship networks? Rural women have traditionally tended kinship networks for just such cases of need. I do not know why these did not work. I suspect that these were hard times for all immigrants, and that they had little to share. These immigrants had not settled as a community but as fragments of families. Kinship networks were incomplete. My grandmother Matilda Schopp, for example, had no mother or mothers-in-law in the neighborhood. Her mother died in Austria. Her first husband's mother died in 1920; her second husband's mother, who was not married when he was born, never came to the United States. Matilda's father lived with the family for a while but he was elderly and died in 1902. She had come to the United States with a sister and two brothers. Her sister, who lived a few miles away on a farm, helped by sharing farm-grown food, but she had little to spare from the struggle to feed her own family. One brother died in 1907, and a second moved to California after serving in the military during the Spanish-American War. A sister-in-law also died in childbirth in 1908. Of the two kin remaining nearby, both had mortgages on their farms by 1910. Kinship support networks did not survive migration and the first generation of settlement.[9]

There was one important effort on the part of organized women to reach these rural women during World War I. The Woman's State Council of Defense organized eighty thousand women in Wisconsin during 1917 and 1918. While the ostensible purpose was to help win the war, child welfare became a part of their program. The Children's Bureau urged state councils to weigh and measure children under six in an effort to find out the health of young children in the nation. Children were a natural resource according to progressive reformers, and this was to be a sort of national referendum on the health of the nation's children. The posters that promoted the weighing and measuring showed a band of children of all nationalities trudging up a hill, their faces toward the sun, under the legend: "The Health of the Child Is the Power of the Nation."[10]

Weighing and measuring was not as narrow as it might seem. While volunteers were trained to do the actual weighing and measuring, they had rural nurses or doctors present to do checkups and to inform parents of any diseases or problems that could be corrected. Rural areas were not disease free. Tuberculosis, venereal and other communicable diseases, as well as malnutrition were present in most rural areas and the Children's Bureau hoped this great national weighing would focus attention on the needs of the nation's children.[11]

The women of Wisconsin weighed and measured a larger percentage of children under six than any other state. An estimated 165,000 Wisconsin children, 65 percent of all under six, were processed during the great weigh-in in May to July 1918. Of the four counties I studied, Taylor County examined 1,330 children and had them screened by nurses; Clark completed its health canvas of 5,000 children in thirteen townships with doctors in attendance. In Lincoln, 2,246, almost all the children in the county, were weighed and two-thirds examined by physicians and nurses. Marathon County was one of the few counties that refused to participate. The men of the county council of defense informed the women that it was not essential and voted to postpone it. Apparently, the election then absorbed their interest, the influenza epidemic followed closely, and Marathon children remained unweighed.[12]

Women volunteers reported that the weighing was one of the most popular activities in which they participated. Rural women were eager to find out about the health of their children. In Lincoln County, rural women brought children to school houses where nurses checked them. In Clark County women volunteers followed up their efforts by attempting to have a rural nurse appointed. Most of these areas had no doctors, and thus a rural nurse was an important aspect of health care. In Clark County, however, the woman superintendent of schools blocked volunteer attempts as unpatriotic. She wrote to the Women's Council of Defense: "We feel that during this war time we should and can do the necessary work relating to the health of our children. Our population is a rural one and the health of our children very good." It took little opposition for the men to settle quietly back and ignore the welfare of the county's children. In La Crosse, one of the counties successfully organized, only an impassioned plea by a volunteer before the county board of supervisors reversed their decision to turn down a petition signed by six hundred rural women asking for a rural nurse. After being berated for their callousness, the men changed their votes to give the women their nurse. Ten counties appointed rural nurses as a result of the council's work, but some counties, including Clark, remained without.[13]

All these babies and tots being weighed and measured, this record of national resources, meant something different for farm women than welfare workers. It meant better health for their children, hope for the future, and reassurance. Regardless of whether it meant anything in scientific terms, in symbolic terms it meant that someone cared about them and their struggle to raise healthy children. The thousands of women who brought their babies and toddlers to schools for that weighing were making a statement of confidence and trust that the system could be of help.

One farm husband wrote in to the state council disgruntledly that if children were fed whole grain bread and milk they would not have to be weighed. But that begged the question. In fact, as my grandmother knew, farm children could be malnourished. And that is what the state council determined after the great state effort at weighing. "The young children of Wisconsin quite generally are not properly nourished," the state council committee on child welfare concluded. Health care professionals had told them that malnutrition had caused a great majority of the physical defects found during the health screening.[14]

Many women who headed the state council wanted to remain organized and continue reconstruction work. It seemed to them that eighty thousand women organized could be a force for great change. They had organized women in areas where no women's groups had existed. The women's club, which claimed twelve thousand members in the state, for example, had only three rural clubs. The Women's State Council of Defense (WCD) had organized primarily through small towns, but it had asked that women be appointed in every township so that the network spread throughout the state. They had a potential delivery system that could have been used by state or federal officials had they wished to help rural women. The WCD formed a network that enlisted home demonstration agents, Red Cross, county and state officials, and women's groups where they existed. Despite the important work that women had done during the war, few but the state leadership, and then not all of them, wanted to continue the work. When polled, most groups voted to end their work when peace was signed. Those who did wish to continue were not always most concerned with the welfare of women. The Taylor chairman, for example, scrawled on her questionnaire that they wanted their group to continue "until Taylor County becomes Americanized." Considering that Taylor was one of the counties with the most prosecutions of dissenters and the most extra-legal activity directed at German-Americans, this was not a good omen.[15]

And so the WCD disbanded, leaving rural women on their own to struggle with the postwar reconstruction as best they could. At the beginning of the 1920s, some home demonstration agents in some states did help with rural health problems. In New Mexico, in the 1920s, they helped get rural nurses hired by counties, got milk for malnourished children, and established hot lunch programs in rural schools. I hope that such a thing also happened in Wisconsin in the 1920s.[16]

I am only planning to take my research of rural Wisconsin women up to 1920 because I know that many rural daughters, like my mother, abandoned their farms about that time. Some young men came back from the war to work on their family farms and some farm daughters married them. But there was little there for poor rural women. The war left them becalmed on the land as they had been before. The war had made work harder and had stripped it of much of its cultural significance. Even in the counties where there had been little overt harassment of German-Americans, their culture and language had been devalued. Work was no longer a way to transmit values, it was only a way to transmit poverty.

Did wartime schools give these young women a vision of the American way of life? Certainly they must have. But the only road to that life was through urban life. And so the exodus began. The farms needed cash and young women could provide it by going to the cities to do domestic work. The link with their mothers was broken, not permanently, but somehow irreparably. A folk culture was broken. Mothers could not pass on their culture to daughters as they had previously. Popular culture would become a substitute for traditional culture and provide rules for these farm daughters to live by. Many young women, like my mother, chose to leave their farm homes rather than to endure poverty. To not abandon an impoverished world would have been to choose their own impoverishment. They found homes within themselves and emerged into a type of fierce quiet selfhood. They escaped from what was mean, forbidden, and cramped. They escaped to a world that promised some freedom, no matter how difficult. They had nothing to gain from the land and everything to lose. So they turned their faces toward the city and never looked back.

13 Crossing Ethnic Barriers in the Southwest: Women's Agricultural Extension Education, 1914–1940

THE EDUCATIONAL PROGRAMS OF THE AGRICULTURAL Extension Service were, inevitably, reflective of the public policies and practices of the various agencies involved in delivering those programs. Created in 1914 as part of the progressive reform movement in the United States, the Agricultural Extension Service (AES) was involved in both the idealism of that movement and the realities of American life that committed it in most areas to rigid gender and ethnic segregation. Because AES was both national and local, it became the crossroads where public policies of various levels of government met, clashed, and changed. At the national level, officials attempted to maintain systematic policies; at the local level agents attempted to adapt them to local conditions. The success of these programs must, in the last analysis, be judged by how they worked at the local level, educating the poorest, female ethnic women. Educating ethnic women and girls in rural communities in New Mexico, the focus of this essay, can thus be seen as more than just an isolated example of how public policy was implemented. How well agents crossed the ethnic barriers in the Southwest as well as other areas of

the country is one key to judging how well agricultural policy functioned in the United States.

This essay looks at the way in which the New Mexico AES
(NMAES) dealt with the question of ethnicity in its educational
programs for women during its first twenty-six years, from 1914 to
1940. I use the counties of Doña Ana in southern New Mexico and
Santa Fe in northern New Mexico to test the success of AES in
delivering educational programs to non-English speaking, Hispanic
communities. My criteria for success are: ability to adapt national
and state programs to local economic and social conditions and needs
of these constituents, the amount and quality of transfer of technology occurring, and number of rural people able to remain on the
land. Measured by these criteria, despite the ethnic and gender discrimination inherent in the program, agents were quite successful in
Santa Fe in delivering an educational program to Hispanic constituents. In Doña Ana agents were almost totally unsuccessful.

All New Mexico counties shared certain geographical and demographic characteristics that made educational programs difficult to
implement. The region in 1914, indeed to a great extent today, is
large, sparsely populated, and divided by mountains and deserts that
are practically impassable during parts of the summer and winter.
While much of the farming population was, and is, concentrated in
the valley of the Rio Grande, a fertile swath that cuts through the
center of the state from north to south, other rural communities are
scattered along the Pecos and Gila Rivers as well as numerous smaller
rivers, in mountain valleys, and on the eastern plains. In 1910 a few
years before the AES began, over 80 percent of New Mexico women
were living in these rural areas, on farms or ranches. In 1940 almost
70 percent still lived there.[1]

Economically, most rural women in New Mexico were poor.
Some were so poor they could not afford the few cents necessary to
buy commercial patterns or material necessary for clothing projects.
In 1940 almost half of the state's eighty-four thousand farm women
lived on farms under 50 acres and over three-fifths on farms under
175 acres worth just over four thousand dollars each. Over one-third
lived on subsistence farms producing primarily for their own use and
almost three-fourths lived on farms that produced less than one
thousand dollars worth of products to use or sell.[2]

In 1914 at least 60 percent of all rural women were Hispanic.

Most read and spoke only Spanish. By 1940 the number of rural women who spoke and read English had greatly increased but most women still were not completely comfortable using English literary sources. Moreover, Hispanic women had their own separate cultural traditions. Their strongest ties were to kin and village community. Mother-daughter and neighbor ties were particularly strong. Public activities usually revolved around religious holidays and there were few nonreligious, community-based, public activities. Women did not often accompany men on trips to town, nor did they migrate to work there. Women took care of the small subsistence farms while men and children, usually boys, worked off the farm to bring in a cash income. There was, however, a tradition of village cooperation, frequently kin-based, with labor exchange among women common.[3]

The Hispanic culture was well-adapted to deal with changing conditions. Communities had successfully adapted to major economic and political changes since their arrival as colonists in the late-seventeenth and early-eighteenth centuries, primarily through family-based change. There was also a tradition of distrust of outsiders, developed over several centuries. Some outsiders thought they understood the problems of rural people and wanted to help; others wanted to exploit. Sometimes the difference between the two types seemed minor as rural people attempted to develop survival strategies that would allow their families to remain on the land.

Staff officials recognized the need to recruit bilingual agents early in the new program. Few Anglo-Americans knew Spanish, however, and administrators had no strategy for training Spanish-speaking agents except through the regular college agricultural and home economics programs. Few rural people had the necessary education to complete these programs or the economic and social support necessary to do so. The early home demonstration staff was small, underpaid, and undervalued. Men assumed that the agricultural agents could organize home demonstration activities but that home demonstration agents could not organize agricultural activities; that if only one agent could be funded, that one should be a male agricultural agent. On this premise, both the AES administrators at the land grant college and the county officials agreed. If the population was mixed, the agent was almost always Anglo. Only in overwhelmingly Spanish-speaking counties, where county commissioners stipulated that a Hispanic agent be supplied in their funding agreements, were agents Spanish-speaking. Before 1929, except for World War I, home demonstration agents served in only two to four of the state's thirty-one counties. From 1929 to 1937 only eight to sixteen home demonstration agents served and not until 1938–40 were there seventeen to twenty agents in the state. Of these, only one Hispanic agent, Fabiola Cabeza de Baca, was employed for any length of time, from 1929 to 1940.[4]

World War I provided a small exception to this poor record of support for home demonstration agents before 1929. The state voted emergency funds during the war and these, together with expanded federal funds, allowed the AES to hire extra home demonstration agents. During 1917 Gertrude Espinosa was hired with emergency funds, and in February 1918 a Spanish-speaking Anglo agent was added. Espinosa began to translate bulletins on cooking, sewing, and poultry raising into Spanish. She spoke to parents before organizing children, something she knew was absolutely necessary. During 1918 these two agents gave 162 demonstrations in Spanish in seven counties and visited over three hundred homes of Hispanic women. Informal canning demonstrations went on in the homes of women where, as one agent wrote: "the native women come with black shawls over their heads, roll their cigarettes and smoke as they stand about the table where the demonstrator is working." The first state-wide Mother-Daughter Congress, held during the war, featured demonstrations in Spanish as well as English. Only a minuscule part of the Hispanic majority was reached, however, and after the war funds for Spanish educational programs for women were dropped. The few male Hispanic agents retained after the war provided some guidance, primarily for girls and boys in clubs. The female Hispanic majority was largely unreached during the 1920s even in the few counties that did retain a demonstration agent.[5]

The assumption that agricultural agents were more important than home demonstration agents, and that no one person could be trained to perform both tasks led to instability that greatly weakened the home demonstration program. Sarah Van Vleck, the only Spanish-speaking agent, took over Doña Ana County in 1918 at the end of the war. She stayed for seven years, but after her term neither a permanent nor a Spanish-speaking agent replaced her. The next agent stayed for only two years. Her successor stayed for over four years, but when she left in June 1932 she was not replaced until June

1937. During these five years, no work was done with women. Girls were enrolled in cooking or clothing clubs but little attention given to their work. It took the new agent over a year to reorganize the women, and then in two years, she left. Thus, the program suffered from the lack of an ongoing program for English-speaking women as well as for the Spanish-speaking majority.[6]

With the exception of Van Vleck, none of the agents spoke Spanish or gave much time to organizing the Spanish-speaking majority. A few girls had been organized into clubs since World War I. At least one woman in San Miguel, Señora Rodriguez, described by the agent as the "most cultured and influential lady in the town," became a club leader. In Old Mesilla, an Anglo teacher organized Hispanic girls there into an award-winning club that canned, did needlework, and gave concerts. When it came to organizing women during the 1920s, however, the agents chose to work primarily through the local Farm Bureau rather than directly with farm families, and the Farm Bureau was organized primarily of Anglo agricultural developers. As Van Vleck explained in 1924, "While natives and Mexicans make up about 50 percent of the population, the American people take the lead in all agricultural affairs, and determine the policies to be pursued."[7]

Doña Ana County had a Hispanic majority but not as large a majority as in the northern counties. Hispanics had lost political control in Doña Ana by the late nineteenth century and they had lost much of their land as well. The census of 1910 showed that two-thirds of the farm families were still Spanish surnamed, however. Almost one-half of them were born in New Mexico, another one-quarter were naturalized citizens who had immigrated from Mexico, and one-quarter Mexico aliens who frequently rented land and worked as farm laborers. Most of the Anglo minority were citizens, but almost all had migrated to the county from other parts of the United States. This Anglo rural minority had successfully engineered the development of Elephant Butte Dam in the early twentieth century. When completed in 1915 the dam resulted in high water assessments that many poor Hispanic farm families could not pay. Anglos also successfully pushed for other public projects in the county that raised the tax base on land. The state land grant college and thus the state AES was located in Doña Ana County, but the college, the AES, and the Farm Bureau were dominated by Anglos. All three groups considered Anglo male farmers with their agricultural development projects as their primary constituents.[8]

The decision to work through the Farm Bureau simplified the work of the overworked, underpaid HDAs. It also meant, however, that they would spend most of their time working with the Anglo women already organized in the Farm Bureau, most of whom assumed their roles to be narrowly domestic. No complete records of the county Farm Bureau exist for the period after 1917, when it was formed. A liberal and quite progressive Jewish-New Mexican businessman headed the Farm Bureau during these years. He lobbied successfully for federal projects favorable to western farmers, including irrigation. However, no Spanish surnames appear on county lists of male or female officers. Only once do the records of the agent note meeting at the home of a Hispanic woman for a demonstration. One meeting was held with blacks in Vado in 1927, and a food preservation meeting for "colored girls" took place in 1937, but except for these references, one would not know that the rural majority was Hispanic or that there was at Vado a vigorous community of black farmers who would later organize a branch of the Southern Farm Tenants Union. There seemed to be a total lack of understanding of Hispanic women and what was needed to engage them in the programs. As the agent reported in 1927: "There are a great many Mexicans in the valley but little work has been done with them, tho they are always invited to the meetings."[9]

One agent did initiate an outreach program in the northern part of the county in 1922. With the help of the state Director of Child Welfare, Dr. Janet Reid, Van Vleck began a study of nutrition of Hispanic children. A state nurse spent six months surveying health conditions with Van Vleck and they found an appallingly high infant mortality rate—an estimated 50 percent in the village of Salem—and widespread malnutrition. Few families had cows, and adults fed children what they ate—tortillas, beans, and chile. The two women took action at once. A dairy donated goats that they loaned to the mothers of the most malnourished children. With the aid of the Red Cross the women obtained milk supplements for the schools. They organized clubs to can food and cook school lunches. They also succeeded in getting the county to hire a full-time health physician and a nurse. The nurse then took over the health work in rural areas.[10]

These projects, however, were undertaken for the poorest rural population, those who lived in jacals (chinked wood huts) in the *bosque* (brush around the river), and who were really below subsistence. As for those Hispanic farm women who were struggling to continue subsistence farming, or to improve their farms, there was no explicit mention of attempting to reach them. The strict gender segregation of clubs may have contributed to this lack of contact. Poorer families needed to have projects that contributed to the income of the family. Most Anglo farmers, as the HDAs repeatedly noted, were well educated and fairly prosperous. While the prosperity of Anglo farmers was probably exaggerated by agents, the comments did reflect the fact that those women and children who organized into clubs had different interests from poorer Hispanic farm women and daughters. Anglo daughters could afford material for sewing and cooking projects; many Hispanic daughters could not. The agent did not encourage mixed vegetable or poultry clubs, thus girls tended to be organized only in cooking and sewing clubs. When the new agent arrived in 1940, she noted that at Mesquite "the Anglo and Spanish-American girls were separated because they did not work well together." When this new agent tried to visit the Hispanic Club, she drove all over Mesquite before finally giving up. "We have hopes of locating the girls and their leader early and really doing some work with them next year," she reported. The old agent had managed to work with one group of Hispanic women on sewing for three months, but when few women showed up during the summer the new agent disbanded the group. The new agent apparently did not understand why these women might not be attending during the summer and abandoned further attempts at education.[11]

Late in the 1930s the agent reported that the Hispanic boys could not afford livestock projects and thus were being organized into handcraft groups. Nowhere was there discussion of organizing girls into vegetable or poultry groups or of helping to provide livestock to children who might develop projects. Goats were loaned to starving families but little was done to help other families improve their situation. The gender segregation both reflected and increased the ethnic segregation already institutionalized in the county AES program.[12]

As a result of the indifference of the agents and their lack of understanding, there was little help in countering the drastic economic influences of agricultural development on Hispanic farm families. Most families turned to farm labor and housework to survive. When the New Deal came into the county, agents worked with federal representatives, but they opposed programs that might have helped the poorer farmers. The Farm Bureau blocked an attempt to establish a migrant camp in Doña Ana because farm owners feared it might become a center for farm workers to organize. The agricultural agent also opposed resettling poor share-cropper families on land of their own under the rehabilitation program of 1935. He believed that people were rehabilitated if they were placed back in their former status of farm laborers or share croppers. "It is doubtful," he wrote, "if it is possible to rehabilitate most of these clients beyond the point where they were at the time of the beginning of the depression." In fact, most New Deal programs in the Mesilla Valley benefited middling families or wealthy farmers.[13]

The situation in Santa Fe County was a direct contrast to that in Doña Ana County. Stability was the most important factor. There was no HDA in the 1920s, but from the time that Fabiola Cabeza de Baca was appointed in 1929 the program grew steadily under her guidance. From 1929 to 1932 De Baca served both Santa Fe and Rio Arriba Counties; from 1932 through 1940 she worked in Santa Fe County alone. Except for a period of hospitalization and recovery from an automobile accident, between December 1932 and September 1934, and relatively short vacations, De Baca devoted her full energy and time to serving the Hispanic, Anglo, and Indian women of the county. The women's support for her was so firm that even during her illness, the women continued their organizations. When De Baca returned, she was able to rebuild momentum swiftly. This decade of stability was a very important factor in building rapport and trust within the Hispanic community. The agricultural agents also remained the same in both counties for the entire period, both welcomed her work, and found that her organizing of women assisted them in organizing the men. As the agent in Rio Arriba reported, his organizing among the men was much easier after De Baca arrived: "She has helped materially in establishing much better cooperation among farm homes, with the results that men farmers have reacted more readily to better farming practices."[14]

Thus, much of the credit for success among both men and women belongs to this unique woman who pioneered agricultural extension

Fabiola Cabeza de Baca Gilbert after retiring from her Agricultural Extension work. Source: Agricultural Extension Service Records, New Mexico State University.

among Hispanic farm families. De Baca had grown up on her grandparents' ranch near Las Vegas, New Mexico, after her mother died when she was five. She studied with the Sisters of Loretto, then taught in a rural school before receiving her degree in Home Economics from the agricultural college in Las Cruces. Her clearly written reports provide an extraordinary record of how AES educational programs were implemented at the local level.[15]

In some ways, the lack of organization by a Farm Bureau or similar organization was an advantage to De Baca. It enabled her to organize new groups in communities of Anglos and Indians, as well as Hispanics. By 1938, she had helped organize thirteen adult clubs, and estimated that she was reaching 80 percent of the farm families. De Baca also organized women to act as volunteers for children's clubs, both Anglo and Hispanic, teachers, and farm women. She did not encourage strict gender segregation in children's clubs. By 1937, for example, she had organized some 373 children, 112 boys and 261 girls. Of the girls a majority, 191, were in traditional food and clothing clubs but an additional 70 were in agricultural clubs with the 112 boys. Many girls were in home gardening and poultry clubs. De Baca began by encouraging women to undertake gardens and can or sell surplus, to learn nutrition as an adjunct to preparing this surplus, to exchange field labor with neighbors to obtain the foods they needed for their food preservation projects, to engage in poultry raising, to learn handicrafts to sell as well as to improve their homes, to sew better constructed garments, and to undertake home repairs. For those she could not reach directly, with group demonstrations or individual home visits, she provided a "Ciencia Domestica" column in the weekly newspaper *El Nuevo Mexicano* and bulletins in Spanish.[16]

De Baca also encouraged transfer of technology among poor Hispanic women. During the early 1930s, she helped them obtain— both cooperatively and through family saving projects—canning equipment such as pressure cookers, tin can sealers, jars, and second stoves that could be placed outdoors where it was cooler. Later, she helped them obtain sewing machines, purchased patterns for collective use (fifty to sixty women used each of the patterns collected in her office), taught them how to repair their sewing machines, and how to modify the commercial patterns. She encouraged the women to barter labor for material and sewing supplies, shop for inexpensive yardage, and encouraged their efforts to improve the appearance of their children and themselves. By the late 1930s, 95 percent of the women had home gardens and 90 percent had sewing machines. The children were well nourished and well dressed.[17]

By this time women were also redirecting savings into the appearance of their homes. De Baca reported in 1938, "Nearly every woman in club work has carried on some repair work in her home." New Deal projects were bringing in cash to the families through husbands, and children and women were saving this cash income to purchase needed building materials. This pattern had been established long before, however, for even in hard times of drought, she had encouraged men and children to pool family resources to help the women buy pressure cookers to improve the family food supply. Then families had helped with the purchase of sewing machines to be better dressed. Now women planned and organized more elaborate building projects. Women usually depended on men for adobe brick-making, carpentry, and putting up walls, but they assumed responsibility for plastering, painting, and finishing houses, additions, and storage rooms.[18]

Women also began to take a new interest in the interiors of their homes. De Baca encouraged this first through development of handicrafts, which she hoped would supplement family incomes. Outlets for crafts had been established in Santa Fe for native crafts during the

1920s, and De Baca encouraged women to supply articles directly to these stores. She noted that although women usually had good taste in selecting materials and colors, when purchasing ready-made items they often selected garishly colored items because they wanted to be up-to-date. De Baca told women to trust their own traditions, to produce products of hand-dyed and woven materials, and to contine to do their traditional colcha wool embroidery.[19]

The work of De Baca is a good example of what could be done with extension education when agents successfully crossed ethnic barriers. Her ethnicity allowed her to know how to work with Hispanic as well as Anglo women. She worked to decrease ethnic and gender segregation. She encouraged women in their traditional farm work, labor exchanges, and handcrafts, at the same time that she introduced new technology. She began with what people wanted most and then introduced other programs as they saw their relevance to their survival and prosperity.

When the depression of 1932–33 and the drought of 1933–34 hit Santa Fe farm communities, the work of De Baca bore fruit. Although there were few federal programs in existence at the time, families were already expanding family gardens and knew how to can. When the federal government finally arrived with its program to purchase cattle, the families were able to butcher and can the healthiest animals. In 1935 over 90 percent of the farm families preserved enough food for the following year. They also canned large amounts of food cooperatively for families unable to do so. Through educational work De Baca helped change attitudes and practices while retaining much of the fabric of Hispanic culture. She kept families on the farms for a decade, thus enabling families to remain on the farm through the severest drought and depression in New Mexican history. Once established, the pattern continued through World War II, with cash from soldiers going directly to the women who maintained the family farms. Ultimately, the war did cause disruption of rural communities. It brought heavy casualties of New Mexican men and few rural jobs for those men who returned. After the war New Mexican women entered a new phase of the struggle to remain on the land. That struggle has still not ended.

14 Keeping Down on the Farm:
Farm Women in Farm Crisis

IN OCTOBER 1986 I ATTENDED A CONFERENCE ON American Farm Women in Historical Perspective at the University of Wisconsin, Madison. I came away from that conference with a great sense of urgency, of anger, and of determination on the part of women to "Keep Down on the Farm."[1]

I came away from the conference with three distinct impressions. First, the women did not want to leave their farms. Second, they did not think they were "bad managers" or that they were to blame for the farm crisis. They were angry with officials—federal and state—who told them they would just have to do something else. Third, farm women questioned farm policy. They complained about farm policies that paid huge subsidies to wealthy producers who lived on so-called "family farms," while smaller family farmers were being asked to quit. Nor did they unanimously support the assumptions of many agricultural colleges—both administrators and faculty—that the only solution to the farm crisis lay in employing increasingly technological methods on farms. They had questions about new biotechnological methods and about what are now considered old chemical practices. There was talk about "sustainable agriculture," methods that used science to reduce intervention. The Indian woman who spoke about traditional attitudes toward the land was given a very respectful hearing.[2]

If you think the question of agricultural research and methods is not a hotly debated issue, then you are not in touch with agricultural colleges. When we had the first Farm Women in Historical Perspective Conference in Las Cruces, New Mexico, in 1984, nothing set off tempers more than just raising the question of chemical use. And at the University of Wisconsin recently, when students posted notices on campus vending machines to discourage consumption of milk from the University of Wisconsin dairy herd because of the university's use of BGH (Bovine Growth Hormone), the response from the dairy science department was swift and sharp. One professor called the student protest "deplorable," and the Wisconsin Guernsey Breeders Association added its abhorrence that individuals and groups used "emotion and scare tactics to stop progress."[3]

But of course, that is the issue that some students as well as some farm women are raising. Is the new research inevitably leading to progress? Will huge dairy herds, with their input and output computer-monitored, provide the best solution to the farm crisis?[4]

Farm women are raising other questions about policy. Because the policy seems to be to encourage them to get out of farming, those who refuse are finding themselves suffering to an extent that they do not believe Americans should endure. Farm families, already under stress because of economic concerns, are now finding that there is not much of a rural safety net. Farm women talked over lunch at the conference of the stress of driving automobiles without insurance, of having to drop insurance on barns because of uncontrolled rises in insurance costs. They worried about husbands who seem prone to accept the verdict that they are "bad managers" if they are having hard times. People involved in new efforts to help farm families cope reported that inevitably it was the farm woman who called for assistance for her husband who would not seek help.[5]

The task that these farm women gave to scholars at the conference was to deal with these human issues. If agricultural research seemed dedicated to fewer dairies with more cows, farm women wanted our research to focus on keeping them on the land. The task for historians was to find out what women had done in the past to deal with farm crises. The question was not that of the old song "How You Going to Keep Them Down on the Farm," because that

Children's Work in the Fields, Aroostook County, Maine, 1942. John Collier, Farm Security Administration Photograph. Source: Library of Congress.

was not the issue any longer but "How Are We Going to Keep Down on the Farm."

Historians already know a great deal about how women have done this in American history. The first thing historians of rural and farm women have found is that this crisis is not new but almost as old as the colonization of North America. There has been a constant migration off the farm and a constant migration from one piece of land to another. Land has always been getting scarcer in some areas, land values have always been going up, population has been increasing, some soils have been depleted, there has always been increasing market competition from farmers somewhere else. There have been sunset farms and sunrise farms, to borrow a current popular phrase regarding industries.

This quiet crisis has been punctuated by periods of extreme crisis in specific regions and with specific commodities. In the Northeast in the 1830s, farm families faced falling grain prices. In the area of Pennsylvania that I studied this was brought on by soil depletion and competition from Western grain growing families that had more fertile land. In the 1880–90s farm families in the South faced declining cotton prices, and farm families in the Midwest faced declining wheat prices. A farm crisis occurred in Northern Wisconsin in 1900–10 because lumbering, which farmers had depended on as their "cash winter crop," ended and families could not support themselves on the land. This was the crisis that my own grandmother endured. From 1920–35, there was not only a drought in the Midwest but continuing declines in market prices.[6]

These crises involved different places and different people but there has been a constant struggle by women to stay on the land. Because this is such a big, diverse country, with a variety of people and a variety of crops, this constant crisis has often been masked. One can always find boom and bust in American agriculture. Before 1910, when the rural population was still the majority, those crises were usually met with rural solutions, and I would argue that women have been crucial in developing these solutions. Women have been central to the ability of the farm family to survive on the land.

Collective ownership of land was one solution that Indian women maintained. In many agricultural tribes women were responsible for a system of allocation of land for use. In matrilineal societies this was common, and the system has been retained by many tribes. It has kept Indian women the most rural for the longest period of American history. Although one of the largest Indian "nations" is now Los Angeles, where approximately 65,000 Indians live, the reservation remains the link with the land. And the reservation system is supported by the women. Indian women do not live well on most of these reservations, but they have held on to their land, kept it as a home for children who ventured out, and made it a base for their survival in a nation that expected indigenous peoples to become extinct by no later than 1900. Almost 100 years later, after that target extinction date, Indians are very much with us and are a growing part of the critique of land policy in the United States.[7]

"Cotton tenant farm family earns $50. a year," Dorothea Lange
scrawled on this Entaw, Alabama, Farm Security Administration photograph in 1936. Source: Library of Congress.

Keeping alive the memory of living on the land and rural cultural
values, even when individuals have had to abandon that land, is
another contribution rural women have made that has helped others
to stay on the land. There was no land reform in the United States for
blacks. There was labor reform when slavery ended; but only a few
blacks were able to obtain land and therefore to retain claim to that
land. When black women and men began to withdraw their labor
from the southern cotton system to move north, they took with them
a whole cluster of rural survival traits—reliance on kinship, community, work, a language of assertiveness. When Alice Walker writes
about searching for her mother's garden, or of the deepest values of
love among rural women, she is reclaiming that rural survival tactic
and making it available for all Americans.[8]

Although black women have been the most notably successful at this reclamation of the American landscape, it is also being done by Indian women writers, such as Paula Gunn Allen in "Shadow Woman," and Hispanic writers such as Estella Portillo de Tremblay in her recent novel *Trinie*. These women have questioned the whole ethic of reducing land to its bottom line of profit and separating it from the human dimension, the human qualities that have been associated with the struggle to remain there.[9]

Those black, Hispanic, and Indian women who have remained on the land have done so by remaining poor. There are some exceptions to this, at least in New Mexico, where a few Hispanic families have been able to retain large ranches. Most, however, have been poor, and most have exported their children to urban areas to bring back cash to remain on the land. Mainly these people lost out to the wealthy and worked for them as farm laborers—in household and field. They have remained on the land by selling their labor, and it has not been a very good life as American lives go, at least in material terms. Hispanic farm women in the Rio Grande Valley of Texas have, however, retained their ability to organize and to look after the welfare of their families.[10]

Most people do not usually focus on these Indian, black, and Hispanic women when they speak of farm women in farm crisis. Although these women were in the past the majority in many areas of the country, we have come to focus on that other majority, the Euro-American women who struggled, sometimes at odds with these other women of color, to remain on the land. How have these middling Euro-American women kept on the land? They have used a wide range of strategies, including changed patterns of reproduction and production.

By reproduction, I do not just mean bearing children but the whole complex of managing, maintaining, training, and planning in a farm family. These cannot be easily divided from the production of food and fiber, plants and animals, that goes on in family farms but I will try to separate them here for purposes of explanation.

If reproduction is more than bearing children, it is first of all just that. Farm women have consistently reduced their fertility over the last two hundred years. This reduction has been greatest in areas just behind the frontier, where agriculture is a main crop. Once an area has turned to other ways to make a living, the relationship between fertility and land is not as evident. Some historians think now that fertility decline in rural areas may even have preceded urban decline in fertility, but all agree that the rural decline is tied to the availability of land and its price. The desire to obtain land for children was so strong among Quaker farm families in eighteenth-century Pennsylvania that they consistently reduced the size of their families more than other religious and ethnic groups. They probably married late, weened late, developed concepts of marital cooperation, and perhaps were even the first Euro-American women to use artificial birth control.[11]

Denying daughters access to land and exporting them to cities or to other farms was another solution embraced by farm women. Women also often socialized their younger sons to accept denial of land and exodus from the land. Women have socialized children to survive in cities, convinced them that there is no place on the land for them and, frequently, attempted to prepare them by getting a longer period of education, usually at the state land grant college. Keeping girls in school longer was a technique that began early in the nineteenth century.[12]

Farm women also developed kinship and community ties that provided social welfare in rural areas where government did not provide it. Women frequently used their churches to provide welfare. They also elaborated family rituals, oral traditions, and helping customs. Rural governments seldom provided rural welfare in any systematic way until the 1930s. Poorhouses were not an acceptable alternative for any but the most desperately poor farm women. Farm women wanted help within families, not institutionalized welfare, but they seldom got it. In Wisconsin, considered a progressive state, they did not get it either. My grandmother certainly got no help and when kinship and church failed her, she resorted to exporting her daughters to the city. They sent money back. Later, bootlegging by her son also helped the farm survive.[13]

Whenever possible women also developed strategies of mutuality with men. They consistently included men in social structures, for entertainment, and, whenever possible, for welfare as well. Rural women became fund raisers and organizers in their communities. They got money from men by entertaining them and feeding them, and they used the money for their own welfare projects. Women applied this principle to politics as well. They were among the first women to gain access to national organizations, such as the Grange, to political organizations, such as the Farmers' Alliances, and to parties, such as the Populists and Socialists. Because of these strategies of mutuality, rural men were the first to consistently embrace expanding political power to women through suffrage. (I should add that this worked most successfully in the Midwest and West and apparently did not work well in the South, but that is a complicated story.)[14]

Farm women not only planned and managed, but they also maintained. They often did this by subordinating their interests to the unity of the farm family. They reduced levels of family consumption when necessary. They increased absorption of stress, developed mental flexibility, and as later women said, "made do." They asked only for success of the farm family in reproducing itself, of passing the farm on to the next generation.[15]

In addition to this work of reproducing the farm family, women were central to successful production on the farm. They exhibited a willingness to perform the labor of men, all types of labor. They increased the hours of their own work to take the place of hired men during harvest and family and farm crises. They gave up the labor of their daughters if they were first born and the husband needed them in the fields. They allowed their children to be worked harder and longer than they knew was healthy. They mobilized and made bearable this child labor. This flexibility of family labor gave the family farm its durability and made it more productive than large commercial farms in the nineteenth and early twentieth century.[16]

Women also developed what we might call "women's cash crops." They provided not only supplies for the farm family but produced considerable surplus commodities, especially chickens, eggs, and butter, as well as vegetables. They also, apparently, established a custom of maintaining discretion over the income from these sales, using it to strengthen the farm family. They not only strengthened the farm household but also freed other capital for further investment in farm commodity production.[17]

Historians are also now coming to see women as playing a large role in experimentation in farm commodities. They developed new crops not yet commercially viable. They spent their own time and money to develop experimental crops. A woman would say, "I think I'll try a few cherry trees this year." If that worked, she might put in a few more the next year. In one area near where I live, the valley is known for its cherry orchards, but few know that it was women who did the first experimentation and started the later profitable business.[18]

These are the past patterns that seem most clear. New patterns are emerging. Women are no longer supporting the denial to daughters of access to land. Instead they are attempting to develop a more flexible family labor force that includes sending daughters to agricultural school and supporting their partnerships in farms. These daughters, in turn, are beginning to question the curriculum in agricultural schools. Women are beginning to question the policies of extension agents, experimental agents, and faculty. They are insisting on greater policy-making roles in the household, community, and at the state and federal level. They are insisting on rural services as their right. They are insisting on laws to protect their right to land and ownership. They are making alliances with other women, extending networks to scholars, urban women, and land reform groups.[19]

And, I might add, this is not easy, nor is it possible for all farm women. There are real differences that have not been addressed previously. Women are insisting on a voice in traditionally male-dominated farm groups. They are beginning to write about the land in a way that reaffirms the importance of a rural way of life, not romantically or just as a way to make money, but as a part of a way of life that can provide other incentives to remain on the land. There is a revolution going on out in the back country, a quiet one. There is not much rhetoric but a lot of organizing in traditional ways, and a new-found voice to express what was expressed most often in action in the past. Women are coming to grips with what it means to have lived on the land and to want to continue that tradition in the face of almost insurmountable odds.

PART V

Rural History

RURAL HISTORY HAS SEVERAL ROOTS. AGRICULTURAL history, the discipline that developed in the United States during the 1920s, provides a source rooted in field crops, commercial production, and the white males who controlled them. The publication of *Agricultural History* in 1929, gave a name to this field and reflected its concerns. A second source was the social and peasant history that began to flourish on the European continent, of which Marc Bloch's *Feudal Society* became the exemplar. Europeans saw rural communities, particularly in the Middle Ages, as complex and rich cultures worthy of careful—even loving—explanation. Where agricultural history looked at one part of rural life, social history told a broader story of the interaction of rural economics and society. After World War II European social history became more abstract and theoretical, but it continued to provide a framework within which rural society could be studied effectively. European social history, like American agricultural history, seldom focused on women.

When women's history became a part of the academic study of history in the 1970s, it focused on urban women. Still the discipline raised important questions about women's work in production and reproduction. It asked broad questions about the role of women in household and community, in private and in public.

When a few historians began to study rural women in the 1980s, they found other disciplines helpful. Since the 1920s rural sociologists had looked at the part of culture that agricultural historians had not, the families and communities within which rural people lived out their lives. New studies approached people not just as rural but as black, Hispanic, Indian, or Asian, as specific groups with a separate history. Historians also found economic studies that looked at rural development, the economic context within which rural folk struggled. Anthropologists, sociologists, folklorists, had all studied rural people. The history of rural women is an interdisciplinary field that attempts to bring all this research together, test the results, determine the gaps, and pose new questions.

When we say rural women are central to this history, we do not mean that men and children are not, but that women can provide the core of rural studies, the missing link without which we cannot understand how rural people lived and struggled, how they stayed on the land, and why they left.

These last essays are attempts to look more closely at what historians have written and what they should consider writing about rural women. For one particular region and time—the Philadelphia hinterland from which I have learned so much—I have looked in detail at what has been studied and what we still need to know. In the last essay I have ranged more broadly in an attempt to sum up what we know about rural women and what the role of scholars should be as interpreters of the past and providers of information crucial to the formulation of public policy. Rural historians have three specific audiences. They write for the broad public to inform them of a collective experience within which they can see their own family and individual experience. They write for each other to share specialized knowledge upon which the discipline can grow as a part of the humanities. And they speak to policymakers who wish to formulate contemporary rural development policies. The narrow definition of agricultural history and policy will evolve into the broader concepts of rural history, rural studies, and rural development policy. The history of rural women will be central to that evolution, just as the women themselves were central to rural life in the past.

15 *"You May Depend She Does Not Eat Much Idle Bread": Mid-Atlantic Farm Women and Their Historians*

THE WORDS ABOVE WERE WRITTEN BY FARMER ES-
ther Lewis, in a letter to her daughter and son-in-law in 1837 about
the work of her hired woman. As a widow, Lewis had many responsibilities, managing both farm and household. But her words, in
many ways, seem to sum up the industriousness of Mid-Atlantic farm
women in the antebellum period.

In the past fifteen years, scholars in many fields have vastly increased our understanding of the importance of work performed by
women along the eastern coast before 1850. Because women's work
has not been the explicit focus of much of this research, however, the
implications of this growing body of scholarship are not yet clear.
Consequently, the research has not been incorporated by historians
in their broader interpretations of the economy. Edward Pessen, for
example, has offered a major reinterpretation of the predominantly
rural antebellum economy without mentioning women's work. This
chapter provides an analysis of recent historical literature relating to
the work of rural women in the Mid-Atlantic from 1750–1850 that
should be considered in any overall evaluation of the rural economy.

Some historians say that the Mid-Atlantic is everything left when you take away New England and the South. There is some truth to this view, enough, at least, to have to begin a review of the historiography of rural women in the Mid-Atlantic by enumerating what states are included. I have used the states defined as the Middle States by the United States agricultural census in 1850: New York, Pennsylvania, New Jersey, Delaware, and Maryland. In many ways parts of Delaware and Maryland seem distinctly southern in their heavy reliance on tobacco as a field crop and enslaved black workers as a labor force. Yet for all their many economic and social divisions, these states formed an entity so strong that all remained in the Union even though some still sanctioned slavery in 1860. The Mid-Atlantic states were known for their diversity, and in some ways that diversity defied boundaries. The new research on this area, taken as a whole, points to an emerging historiography of rural women's lives there.[1]

No overall guide exists for the historical literature of women in the Mid-Atlantic region. Douglas Greenberg's 1979 review article, "The Middle Colonies in Recent American Historiography," reflected the then current lack of interest in women as a separate group with a separate history and the neglect by historians of rural history in general. The omission of women in his article helped mask what was even then available on their history. A more recent bibliography by Elizabeth Steiner-Scott and Elizabeth Pearce Wagle on New Jersey women and Trina Vaux's *Guide to Women's Resources in the Delaware Valley Area,* are focused primarily on urban women, and provide only general references to women's history for the Mid-Atlantic region. The few available bibliographies of rural women's history are seldom detailed enough to include specific studies on the Mid-Atlantic. There is, on the subject of rural women, little old ground to clear away.[2]

Culture is a fundamental category for analyzing women's work in the Mid-Atlantic area. As an ethnically heterogeneous area, the Mid-Atlantic cannot be discussed without a basic understanding of cultural differences. The gap is especially evident in ethnic immigration studies. Kathleen Neils Conzen has pointed out for another region what is also true of the Mid-Atlantic, that rural immigrants have just not received as much attention as their urban counterparts. Nor has agricultural history or rural sociology paid much attention to immigrants. Most early immigrants borrowed and contributed to the cultures of those already in America in rural or small town settings. They also maintained distinctive ethnic traits in direct relationship to the presence or absence of an ethnic community. Ethnic churches often provided rallying points, followed by schools, voluntary associations, and a press. Since women gradually became caretakers of community as well as family culture, their history is central to that rural ethnic history.[3]

The Mid-Atlantic has a rich ethnic history. The history of its Native American population alone is extremely complex. Besides the much-studied Seneca, many tribes of Indians inhabited the area, all gradually displaced by Europeans during the seventeenth and eighteenth centuries. Their cultures varied immensely and the women fared variously in different areas of settlement. Several anthropologists and historians have provided preliminary studies of Seneca women. Nevertheless, much remains to be done using archaeological and historical sources to document the lives of Indian women in the cultures that survived after 1750, particularly on the western frontier.[4]

The Swedes and Dutch also left a visible historical imprint as separate cultures in most of the Mid-Atlantic, at least until the early eighteenth century. Susan Klepp has traced the disappearance of Swedish culture in Pennsylvania in the late eighteenth century and the role of intermarriage by Swedish men with English women in that disappearing culture. Such studies of intermarraige are essential in tracing the fortunes of the cultures that disappeared from the area.[5]

The Swedes and Dutch, of course, were replaced by a complex mix of Northern Europeans and Africans. Irish, Welsh, Scots, and English from Great Britain and Germans from the continent, along with a few French and a large population of Africans in the southern tier, settled in the Mid-Atlantic during the eighteenth century. Thus, by the beginning of the nineteenth century, the Mid-Atlantic had substituted a diverse European and African immigrant population for the diverse Native American population that had once inhabited the region.[6]

Several recent studies have begun to analyze the emerging black culture and to look at the important work of black women in rural areas. Jean Soderlund has clearly pointed out the early excess of men over women in rural black communities in Pennsylvania and showed that information is adequate to begin assessing women's experiences in black families. Merle G. Brouwer has reminded us of the way in which slavery interfered with family ties among black Pennsylvanians. Black women, it should be remembered, were a large minority of the female population in parts of southeastern rural Pennsylvania by 1850—13 percent of Kennett township in Chester County. Kent and Sussex counties, in the slave state of Delaware, both had large rural free black populations. Hundreds of community-based black churches developed in rural Pennsylvania and Delaware in the early nineteenth century. In late eighteenth-century Maryland, black families took form and increased but remained fragile and subject to disruption by white owners. Demographic studies of these communities are establishing the basis for further study of black rural women.[7]

Much has been written about the predominantly English Quakers. They are one of the most visible Euro-American cultural groups in eighteenth-century Pennsylvania. Because Quaker meetings were at the center of community networks, new studies that describe gender and class patterns within these meetings provide an important context for women's lives. Research describing the survival strategies of Quaker families—how many held slaves and for how long, and how they decreased fertility to cope with problems of increasing land costs—also help define cultural concerns. The ways in which women participated in these changes and their work lives have yet to be explored by historians. As ministers, doctors, teachers, and reformers, rural Quaker women were among the first to participate in public life and were key actors in the first women's rights movement in New York and Pennsylvania. We need to know more about the communities and families out of which these rural Quaker women emerged, how they created their new public lives, as well as what ideology made it acceptable for them to act as leaders in carving out these new spaces for themselves in American life.[8]

Historians now believe Germans numbered at least a third of the population of Pennsylvania by 1790 as well as a sizeable part of other Mid-Atlantic states. For all the attention given to the Pennsylvania German material culture by historians, they have yet to explain the ways in which German women created, used, and passed on that culture. Earlier out-dated studies of German communities tell us little about women, but fine new studies, such as those by Marianne Welkeck of Pennsylvania Germans and Elizabeth Kessel of Maryland

Germans, are no different. Three hundred years after the first German women settlers arrived to help found Germantown, we still know almost nothing about them despite numerous celebrations to mark the tricentennial in 1983. The research provoked by those celebrations began to ask new, more relevant general questions about the cultures of these people but not specific questions about women.[9]

These omissions do not occur because the material is lacking. In addition to quantitative sources, there are many literary sources. In Pennsylvania, German opposition to common schools was based on the fact that an effective German language school system was already in place. Literacy was widespread, apparently among women as well as men. Regardless of who read the German publications of the late eighteenth and early nineteenth centuries, they reveal much about women's work lives. Unless the 588 German almanacs published in Pennsylvania between 1750 and 1850 are vastly different from the roughly 2,400 almanacs published in English, they contain anecdotal material that helps explain popular attitudes toward gender relations. Pamphlets, such as *Die Berg-Maria,* describe individual German women whose lives gave rise to popular legends. Instructional booklets, such as those for midwives, also exist. One *Weiber-Buchlein* published in 1808 at Euphrata, Pennsylvania, contained instructions for midwifery and for dying cloth. When used by historians who have studied the new methodological techniques developed by historians of women, sources such as these can yield important insights about German women.[10]

Information on family and work for the non-Quaker immigrant—for the Scots, Scotch-Irish, Irish, and Welsh, as well as the Yankees, is so scanty that we can still say little about women's work in large areas of the Mid-Atlantic. Some students of Irish immigration are now calling into question earlier generalizations that principally Irish men immigrated during the early nineteenth century. As revised estimates of female immigrants and migrants appear, the task of recreating women's work roles can go forward.[11]

Even without the necessary cultural studies, elements of a new framework are emerging from the studies of rural women and the family in the Mid-Atlantic. Two subjects seem particularly important, the physical reproduction of the family and the cultural reproduction of the life-patterns for the family. Both are central to the management strategies of farm families.

Fertility studies are one way historians have begun to look at women's reproductive work in various cultures. Historians now estimate that land ownership patterns affected fertility rates in Pennsylvania until 1850. Several historians have built on the groundbreaking studies of Robert V. Wells that document declining Quaker fertility. The links between fertility, land ownership, and culture are also explored in a recent cross-cultural study on York County, Pennsylvania, by Daniel Snydacker for the period from 1749 to 1820. He concluded that among those families that kept their land, a large number (76 percent) excluded one child from an equal share. Quaker families were able to avoid excluding children as their holdings shrank by decreasing their family size. Snydacker also found that Presbyterians and Lutherans not only sold their land far more frequently than Quakers but also reduced their fertility much less. Germans who kept their land imposed contractual obligations to avoid excluding children. Presbyterians depended on the maintenance of skills and passing on of tools to achieve the same goal. Those without land excluded far fewer children (22 percent). Snydacker concluded that only Quaker families used family limitation as a strategy to avoid excluding children. Quakers also divided their land into smaller parcels to keep their children from leaving the community, and families loaned money to others in their meetings. Such family strategies demanded different roles for mothers and daughters in these families that need more careful analysis.[12]

New York appears to share this relation between fertility, availability of land, and culture. Mark Stern's work on rural Erie County, New York, for example, is an important new study that begins to provide a comparative base from which to build a picture of women's household work. Stern argues that rural New York native-born Anglo American women, particularly owners as opposed to tenants, restricted fertility to a much greater extent than German women. He maintains this was done not only because of the lack of land but also because of a cultural expectation that they would have fewer children.[13]

These studies merely point to the importance of women's reproductive work as a factor in understanding broader social changes. Closely related to the question of reproduction are ways in which women birthed and reared children. Seasonality of conception, for example, still remains largely unstudied for this region. And scholars have only just begun the task of documenting childbirth and child care practices that can help historians analyze the process of physical reproduction as well as its rate.[14]

The cultural reproduction of the family has been studied primarily through colonial and state family laws that set the boundaries on women's participation in America's developing economy. At one time, scholars believed colonial and early nineteenth-century American women had relatively greater access to property than English women. The research by Peggy Rabkin and Norma Basch on New York, and by Marylynn Salmon on Pennsylvania law, has shown that women were severely limited in control over property in these states. So far there are few studies, such as those of Suzanne Lebsock or Linda Speth on Virginia, Toby L. Ditz on Connecticut or Susan Admussen on English villages, that analyze inheritance patterns of Mid-Atlantic women in the eighteenth century. New research by Gail S. Terry, Jean B. Lee, and Lois Carr for Maryland; David Narrett for New York; and Carole Shammas, Lisa Waciega, and Marilyn Salmon for Pennsylvania, will provide a much more secure base for historians who wish to discuss the extent to which women had access to both real and personal property.[15]

Studies based on the extensive probate records of the Middle-Atlantic states, especially wills, can enable us to analyze the role of kinship in women's lives and women's role in preserving property for male members of the family. It is hoped that these studies will lead to more precise ways of measuring women's roles in family survival strategies. Once into the nineteenth century, there are sufficient literary sources for scholars to begin to analyze the development of rural middle-class family life as Mary Ryan has done so brilliantly for urban Oneida County, New York.[16]

The wide range of work performed by women is evident through studies of slavery, indenture, and wage work. The decline of slavery in New York and Pennsylvania has been well documented, but the conditions of the black women still enslaved has not. There is strong evidence that work conditions for bondswomen declined where slavery continued in Delaware and Maryland, even though in important material ways the lives of all black workers improved in the late eighteenth century. Indentured labor, a form of labor that coexisted with slavery, also decreased in the late eighteenth century, as Sharon Salinger has pointed out. Rural areas north of the Mason-Dixon line may have had difficulty keeping women indentured as well as enslaved. Farley Grubb argues that by the 1770s immigrant servitude in the Mid-Atlantic had shifted from rural agriculture to the urban service sector. Just as surely, the number of native-born servants hired by the year for wages, as seasonal workers, and as migratory workers increased. Lucy Simler and Mark Stern have both argued that ownership of land was not as widespread in the Mid-Atlantic in the late eighteenth and early nineteenth centuries as historians have believed. Greater attention to women's labor, including their wage labor and tenant labor, should help correct the idea that this area was one of land-owning, self-employed farm families.[17]

Changes in technology and material culture indicate that not only did women's wage labor increase, but also that women's labor changed dramatically. British historians have carefully documented the revolution in labor from 1750 to 1850 as women moved out of fields during the transition from sickle to scythe and cradle harvesting. Although we know that transition also occurred in America, we do not know when or how it occurred in the Mid-Atlantic. Travelers' accounts of the presence or absence of women laboring in the fields can only be accepted for the limited areas they actually visited and then must be used cautiously. Account books are more precise guides although they have not been used extensively as yet. Accounts for the Philadelphia hinterland place some women in the field, particularly at harvest time, even after the increase in the use of scythes and cradles at the end of the eighteenth century. Analysis of inventories of household tools, made at the time of death of the males and widows, is allowing historians to glimpse the scope of women's work in processing food and fiber as well as providing service within households. Historians have already documented the important transition to textile production on Maryland plantations in the late seventeenth century. My own study of dairying tools also indicates women increased household production in the late eighteenth century. Clearly, studying process and change in tools will be increasingly useful in the analysis of women's work.[18]

Material culture studies also indicate an increase in women's work because of increased household consumption. The work of Jack Michel for the early Delaware Valley and Lorena Walsh for the Chesapeake area, points to a drastic increase in consumption in the second half of the eighteenth century that was probably colony-wide. Material culture, as anthropologist Mary Douglas cautions, should

Pickers in the Strawberry Fields of New Jersey, 1867. Source, Harper's Weekly, *July 3, 1867, Library of Congress.*

not be read too literally as resulting from rational, practical needs, or as merely frivolous expenditures, but as the language of culture and group values. Regardless of the cause, the increase in material culture signaled a great increase in the work of women. Whether relating to textiles, food processing, or service, creation and maintenance of the material objects all required time, attention, and skill. The growing number of looking glasses and clocks indicate an increasing consciousness of appearances and the time used to maintain them.[19]

For women unable to labor in their own households or those of others, the poorhouses remained a last refuge. The aged, the physically disabled, the mentally ill, and the unemployed all sought refuge in rural poorhouses during the early nineteenth century. Rural poorhouses records are particularly rich for the early nineteenth century, and the few that have been studied show an increasing number of women without families to care for them living in deteriorating conditions. Employment patterns seem to have determined both use of and conditions in poorhouses. Counties that offered jobs for males, such as Seneca County through which the Erie Canal passed, had poorhouses filled with males. But elsewhere, for much of the early nineteenth century, women and their children accounted for the majority of inmates. Communities provided for these inmates with mounting reluctance. Joan Underhill Hannon calls the period from the 1820s through the 1850s in New York State "a period of perhaps unique stinginess in the public relief system." In New York, Hannon argues, expenditures per resident on poor relief sank to 11 percent of the earnings for common labor in 1835 to 1839. She concludes that poorhouses may have consciously decreased the level of care to avoid serving the unemployed. While the cause of this stinginess is still being debated, a pattern of neglect of poorhouse inmates is emerging from studies of rural Pennsylvania and New York. These conditions probably instilled a great aversion in poor women to entering the poorhouse unless all hope of independent work vanished. When it did, dependent rural women often spent time in rural poorhouses under brutalizing conditions within a public support system that declined in effectiveness as commercialization and industrialization dislocated workers and their families.[20]

Despite deteriorating conditions, studies of rural Pennsylvania, Delaware, and New York indicate a rise in the number of dependent poor women. Poorhouse stewards also increasingly labeled many of these women "deranged," "idiot," or "simple." Seventeenth-century English doctors had already noted the disproportionate number of women with mental problems. Were women more prone to mental illness than men? Or was society simply labeling women's social deviance as mental illness? Nancy Tomes and Ellen Dwyer have provided models of the study of urban asylum inmates. We need more study of the "madwoman" who was not in the urban asylum or in the attic of the middle class but in the basement of the country poorhouse.[21]

Rural women also may have been subject to an increasing assortment of urban-based prescriptive literature in the early nineteenth century that advised them to emulate a "true womanhood" inconsistent with the realities of their rural labor. The study of prescriptive literature is an important part of women's history, yet there are few regional studies of how this urban-based literature made its way into the back country and was transferred regionally. Leonore Davidoff has done a superb study for the English countryside of East Anglia. Many areas of the Mid-Atlantic could be studied similarly. This literature also needs to be examined for what it says about women of ethnic groups other than Anglo-American. Where foreign language presses existed, particularly the German language press, the output needs to be examined for prescriptive statements about women.[22]

Studies of literature, however, must be grounded on an understanding of agricultural development. Historians cannot assume that urban economic models apply in rural areas. What commodities a farm produced, what work women performed in their production, and how these products fared in the marketplace are major questions that must be answered. In hard times, farm families reorganized their work and developed different attitudes toward women's traditional work. These changes were in response to commodity production for regional, national, and international trade. Careful studies of regional agricultural production are absolutely essential. Ellinor Oakes's work on dairying provides one such study. The work by Fred Bateman on income from dairy products, central to many Mid-Atlantic farm incomes, points to the importance of women's work in the survival of the farm. Much work considered "traditional" women's work—in dairy, market garden, orchard, hop field, and poultry yard—has not yet been studied. After 1808, for example, when upstate New York farm families discovered the profitability of growing hops, women became a majority of the hop pickers as well as providers of important household services for the entire seasonal work force. Each major city in the Mid-Atlantic—New York, Philadelphia, and Baltimore—had a butter belt surrounding it, where the work of women was crucial in milking, processing, and marketing butter. Knowledge of general agricultural conditions and an understanding of the economics of specific commodities is necessary for describing rural women's importance to agricultural development.[23]

Beyond these general studies of economic change, we must have studies of how these changes affected individual women. Biographies of individual rural women are difficult to find because biography seems most appropriate for "notable women" whose lives are well documented, and women tend to become "notable" through their work in urban areas. Yet many "notable" women, such as Susan B. Anthony and Mary Shadd, grew up on farms or in rural areas. Short biographies and collective biographies can bring together scattered and brief information on farm women who did not leave for cities or become famous. Unless we know more about the majority of women who stayed down on the farm, who did not go public and become famous, we cannot understand the small minority who did.[24]

When rural women moved into the public sphere, it was most frequently through religious activities. Religion is one of the topics for which new studies have opened up major questions about rural women. Recent studies of Quakers and of evangelical women point to the importance of religion in the lives of women. English studies have shown that women were attracted in large numbers in the seventeenth century to new sects, such as the Puritans and Quakers. When Puritans refused them the right to preach, a number of women turned to Quakerism, and when Quakers controlled their lives too tightly, from Quakerism to utopian communities. Quaker women were among the first women to emerge into public life as ministers and then beyond the meeting house as active leaders in rural communities. By the early nineteenth century, an evangelical brand of religion was also burning through the Mid-Atlantic, leaving abundant church and private records that make it possible to document leadership, membership, female bonding, education, and missionary work.[25]

Most widespread of women's religious groups were the evangelical maternal associations that spread through the New York hinterland between 1815 and 1860. Richard A. Meckel calls these Protestant voluntary associations a type of "shadow ministry" in which women would preach and evangelize without formal recognition. Revivalists now abandoned Paul's dictum that women must be silent and encouraged them to speak out at prayer meetings. Maternal associationalism swept rapidly through the Presbyterian and Baptist churches, receiving much of its support from the lower middle-class. Mary Ryan has provided a rich case study of how these women's groups functioned in Utica, New York. There must have been many others, for all major towns and most outlying villages and settlements along the Erie Canal had these associations by the early 1830s. The movement traveled eastward from frontier to city.[26]

Another outlet for women's religious fervor was the pious memoir. This act of "self-reading" marked not only a new level of literacy but also a consciousness of spiritual autonomy and self-improvement. In the evangelical culture of early nineteenth-century America, rural as well as urban women expressed themselves in pious memoirs. They too, as Joanna Gillespie has noted, had "full permission to bloom within their station, if not to transgress its boundaries." Women still had a restricted ministry in these evangelical churches but they spoke at Sunday school rallies, stood up to speak in church meetings, and exhorted congregations before and after the sermons. Such activities moved rural women to claim a new spiritual equality with men.[27]

Sunday schools were a natural transition for many evangelical women. A public yet restricted space, the Sunday school seemed an acceptable place for women who were unready to claim full freedom in public. Conversion was central to Protestantism and women in Sunday schools assumed major responsibilities for that crucial event in the lives of young people who now provided most converts for evangelical churches. Mid-Atlantic rural women staffed thousands of these Sunday schools gladly, often receiving no pay but an enhanced status in the community.[28]

Secular school teaching provided an even more public role than religion for women. Anne Firor Scott has documented the influence of the feminism of New York's Troy Female Seminary. Rural Quaker seminaries were important training centers in Pennsylvania. Keith Melder has emphasized the oppression of seminary training, but the potential for liberating literacy was certainly there as well and recognized by the early women who had access to this new higher education. The ideologies of Republican mothers and teaching daughters both flourished in the Mid-Atlantic. Why they flourished and who benefitted needs to be documented more precisely. After all, if a rural mother could not write (and Alan Tully has shown that most women in rural Pennsylvania could not at the time of the Revolution), they could not educate their children as citizens. The move to both functional and liberating literacy of rural nineteenth-century women was an incredible accomplishment. The consequence of the transition from an oral to a written tradition for women was of enormous significance and cannot easily be dismissed as a leap into oppression.[29]

Last, but certainly not least, women participated in secular volunteer reform. The importance of black people in moving white reformers from abolition to anti-slavery is now quite clear, but beyond sketchy biographies of Sojourner Truth, Harriet Tubman, and Mary Shadd, little is known about the work of black Mid-Atlantic rural women in this first black liberation movement.[30]

On the other hand, studies of white reformers have progressed far enough to pose intriguing questions. Abolition, temperance, and women's rights continue to hold major research interest, but charity and asylum reform are receiving some attention. Gerda Lerner, Ellen Du Bois, Nancy Hewitt, and Judy Wellman have expanded our understanding of the early relationship between abolition and women's rights. The gap in the 1830s, when the abolition activities of white women declined, has still to be explained. What were the reforming women doing? The development of prohibition reform into militant activities by white women is one possible explanation. Temperance began to be politicized in the 1840s. Several studies have concluded that women fused the more popular prohibition crusade to the emerging women's rights movement. The confluence of militant temperance and women's rights in the late 1840s and early 1850s may prove to be more significant than historians have thought. The women's rights movement, like the temperance movement, was extremely popular with nineteenth-century white rural women. Abolition—even more anti-slavery—was not, except with a small group of radical church women.[31]

The question of constitutional rights concerned some early nineteenth-century reformers. Clearly, during these years a few rural women took their first tentative steps along the road of legal reforms that would lead in later years to demands for full equality. Rural women and their male allies demanded the right of petition. Despite efforts of the United States Congress to convince women that they did not have this right, some women at the state level continued to exercise it. Temperance petitions from women in Pennsylvania testify to the persistence with which women there claimed this right. Demands for married women's property laws that breeched the wall of the doctrine of marital unity opened the way, as legal historian Norma Basch has reminded us, to create a new class of disfranchised property owners—rural as well as urban. In early 1848 forty-four women from Genessee and Wyoming counties in New York petitioned their state legislature for equality as woman citizens rather than as wives. These petitions from the New York hinterland indicate a major change in the way some rural women were beginning to look at themselves. They saw themselves as citizens with political rights equal to those of men.[32]

Historians need to grapple more fully with this question of the reform activities of rural women, for it may provide an important key to understanding the emergence of the women's rights movement. The Seneca Falls and West Chester women's conferences of 1848 and 1853 took place in rural areas and attracted rural women. The breeding grounds for early feminism may well have been the back country during rapid agricultural development. Early nineteenth century feminists demanded legal, political, and occupational rights but still had qualms about dealing with relationships in the family. The fact that their movement was rural and family-based may help explain those qualms.[33]

The new research on rural Mid-Atlantic women points to the need for a drastic revision of traditional history that excluded them from discussion of antebellum economy. Rural women were central to that history rather than marginal to it. Indoors and out, upstairs and down, their labor was essential for the survival of the farm economy. As Esther Lewis wrote of her servant woman, they ate no idle bread. Their industriousness must be recognized in any analysis of the development of agriculture in the Mid-Atlantic. Historians who continue to treat women's work as irrelevant to agricultural history risk weakening, distorting, and undermining their analysis of rural development.

16   The Role of Farm Women in American
History: Areas for Additional Research

RECENT CHANGES IN WOMEN'S PROPERTY AND CRED-
it rights and the intensification of women's political activism may
affect farm women more than urban women in the next two decades.
Family farms have traditionally demanded from women both hard
work and the subordination of their interests to the interests of the
family farm as a unit. The role that women have played in American
agriculture is still not adequately understood or appreciated, nor is
their role in the development of some major U.S. institutions. Since
women on the land will take an increasingly important role in shaping
the future of farm policy as the country goes through the economic
transition of the next two decades, and they will play this role with
greater self-consciousness and visibility, they will demand greater
attention from policymakers to their present lives and from scholars
to their past lives.[1]

Historians still have an incomplete and fragmentary knowledge
of the work roles that women have played, of the support networks
that they developed, of their contributions to the development of
religious, educational, and economic institutions, and of their degree
of political activity. The growing body of information that we have
suggests that these roles were more varied and more important than

have traditionally been recognized. For example, historians have only recently begun to uncover some of the patterns of women's community activity.

The oldest and most persistent form of community activity has been the development of and participation in women's support networks, networks that women have created for giving assistance and understanding to other women. This culture of women, whose major theme is *support,* has persisted, even when damaged by the cleavages of race and class. It has been the basis for a type of feminism on the farm whose role in allowing women to survive, and at times flourish, under severe pressure has not been given adequate attention by scholars. One reason, of course, is that it is difficult for scholars to document, although it is a thread that can be traced through oral histories, family histories, letters, and diaries. This fabric of support was important both to the women it helped and to the society they served.[2]

The role that women have played in the more formal community organizations is easier to document. For example, their involvement in religious and educational institutions played a major role in the development of these institutions at the rural level, as women used or created them to extend the range and effectiveness of their support network.

From the late eighteenth century in the United States, women have been moving more firmly into their established religions. The ministry of women began with the Quaker farm women who crisscrossed the forests of the early colonies, often travelling thousands of miles to bring spiritual comfort. Although women have moved into almost every denomination as ministers today, during most of the nineteenth and twentieth centuries women played a less obvious leadership role, even though in the nineteenth century they became the majority in church membership. It is clear that they handled most of the welfare functions of the church and were instrumental in moving the churches in the direction of a greater concern for the welfare of their communities. They often managed the maintenance of churches as well. Although there is no doubt about the physical and spiritual importance of the rural church for women, and of the degree to which this institution was used by women to support each other, we still know far too little about these institutions themselves.[3]

Women also moved into and began to create rural educational

institutions in the early nineteenth century. They took over an increasing amount of the educational functions of the rural church and stood at the foundation of the rural school. At exactly the period in American history when rural women needed these institutions the most, men were losing interest in both religion and education.

As family farms moved more toward commercial production, increasing the work each family member performed, education moved out of the home. Daughters could perform this educational work more competently and efficiently outside the farm house, and evidence suggests that they were only too happy to leave. Quaker women were among the first to go. Deep into the twentieth century women spread public education with their commitment to its importance and their willingness to work for low wages. Our knowledge of this poorly paid community work is entirely inadequate, but we know that women struggled to establish a good school system in many parts of the country. Although these schools, like other rural institutions, were scarred and weakened by racial and economic conflicts, they nonetheless formed the backbone of American public education. We know, in fact, that quality education could and did take place even in racially segregated rural schools, but we still have inadequate information about what went on in these one-room school houses, which formed the backbone of American public education.[4]

Historians are also finding that rural women took a more politically active role than traditional history has indicated. Quaker farm women, for example, were active in calling the first public meeting of women in the United States to discuss their political needs. This 1848 Seneca Falls meeting was attended primarily by rural women. When Lucretia Mott went home to Philadelphia from Seneca Falls to urge urban women to call their own state conference, she got no response. When she talked to Chester County farm women, however, they immediately took up the idea and organized the first statewide conference in West Chester, appropriately in the new Horticultural Hall. Women also formed anti-slavery and temperance associations, and later in the nineteenth century, farm women flooded into the Grange, one of the first national organizations to admit women. Farm women lobbied hard for oleomargarine laws in the 1880s, and joined the Farmer's Alliances and the Populist Party, moving it to become the first political party to support women's suffrage.

After Congress created the Cooperative Extension Service in 1914, rural women also rallied to form farm organizations. In New Mexico, for example, women were eager organizers of the earliest Farm Bureaus. Others formed separate rural women's clubs and extension clubs. By the 1930s rural women were far better organized in New Mexico than were urban women, and I expect that the same conditions existed in many other states. Farm Bureau women in Las Cruces, for example, organized a room where rural women could rest when they came to town to shop. When federal programs reached New Mexico in the 1930s, much needed and welcomed in the rural areas, farm women worked together to raise matching funds for paving farm roads and to organize community canneries to help feed their families and the poorer members of their communities. Fabiola Cabeza de Baca, who had moved from teaching in rural schools prior to World War I to agricultural extension work, helped organize Hispanic women in northern New Mexico. They responded enthusiastically. "If we have an excuse to leave work for one day a month, we ought to take advantage of it even if it is only to get away from work," urged one woman. For these women, organizing was a rest "from the daily routine of house and outdoor work." As another extension homemaker later recalled, "I just picked up my baby and went."[5]

I suspect that hard work was one of the reasons that farm women organized so much and so well. They were accustomed to organizing their own complex families and work and used many of these same skills, which they had been developing from childhood, in organizing publicly. Although it is commonly known that "women's work is never done," the true dimensions of women's work have not been adequately realized. Historians, for example, are still debating the amount of outdoor farm work women have done in the course of American history. While some historians have maintained that white women did not do outdoor work, anyone who has been on a farm, even today, knows that only a few farm women do not work outdoors as well as in. Ranch women in New Mexico have traditionally ridden in roundups, branded, and "pulled" (birthed) calves. Hispanic women have harvested chile. Homesteaders worked in the fields alongside their husbands. Who gathered all of those potatoes Americans have found to be their staff of life? In the San Luis Valley, women drive potato trucks in the harvest. Before there were harvesters, they loaded potatoes in sacks from the fields. Before sacks, into

West Texas Farm Tenant Woman, 1937. Dorothea Lange, Farm Security Administration Photograph. Source: Library of Congress.

bushel baskets. Women picked hops in New York and the state of Washington, gathered canteloupes in the Mesilla Valley of New Mexico and lettuce in the Imperial Valley of California. Black and white women both picked cotton in the valleys of the South. Without the outdoor labor of women at harvest time, few harvests could take place. While it is true that men—and women—have often said that women do not do certain types of farm work, in fact, women do and did almost every type of work whenever necessary. Not all women did all kinds of work, but the variety is impressive.[6]

Women on tractors and plows are part of a long history of work. Thomas Jefferson advocated a family farm and praised the male as yeoman, as the farmer upon whom the economy and politics of the new nation would be based. Yet on his farm, according to his farm diary of 1795, farm workers were black women who worked as plowers, sicklers, gatherers, binders, and cooks in his Virginia grain fields. When he gave the work cycle of the female workers on his farm, he said girls until ten should serve as nurses, from ten to sixteen spin, and at sixteen "go into the ground or learn trades." It was this kind of work that Sojourner Truth was referring to when she later objected at the Akron women's rights conference to a man who said that women should not have political rights because they were so helpless. He said men even had to help women over mud puddles. No one ever helped her over a mud puddle, Sojourner Truth retorted, "And ar'n't I a woman?" She made the point for all farm women.[7]

The work was hard for all women, and they could perform typically men's work when necessary even though men seldom reciprocated. Women still had to bear and care for dependent children, elders, and the ill, process most of the food used in the household for family and hired help, and care for smaller barnyard animals, especially poultry. Poultry was not a small item. In Delaware County, Pennsylvania, as early as 1848, for example, farm families raised eighty thousand hens, produced twenty-four thousand chicks and over six million eggs a year. Women usually milked cows and processed massive quantities of butter in most areas of the country before 1860. The Middle-Atlantic states alone produced almost 180 million pounds of butter in 1860. In addition, women processed textiles until factories took over this job in the early nineteenth century, sewed massive amounts of clothing and linens down through much of the twentieth century, managed and maintained household space, including large and growing amounts of all types of farm and household equipment. For most of history, rural women also had to carry much of the household water and wood for the fires. I am reminded of the comment of the grateful New Mexico farm woman who finally got running water in her farm house in the 1930s. She estimated that it saved at least 260 miles of walking done yearly to bring water from the well to her kitchen. Of nearly thirty thousand New Mexico farms in 1945, only 28 percent had running water.[8]

Even fewer had electricity. The major technology of New Mexico farm women in the 1930s was not one of the electric irons, washing machines, or vacuum cleaners that we hear so much about in urban areas, or even a treadle sewing machine. It was the pressure cooker, the symbol of farm women's technology in the 1920s and 1930s. The gardens and canning of thousands of rural women brought poor farm families through the worst depression in American history with relatively little starvation. Some rural Americans did die—a ranch woman from Hatch, New Mexico, remembered living in Oklahoma during the depression where a neighbor's baby died because she had only oatmeal to feed it. She was so busy, this woman remembered sadly, that she did not walk the mile over to see how her neighbor was doing. "Most any of us could have helped somewhat," she said, "so when you live through an experience and you know that a little baby starved to death, then you're for welfare." She saw the government doing women's work, something they needed help with. There was not time to do it all. Like education, welfare had to be done by specialists, because farm people could not take care of everybody.[9]

The family remained the social institution within which women performed both their service and production work. If women went to work for wages, as increasing numbers of farm daughters did after 1800, it was often on another family farm. If farm women were in bondage, as the majority of black women were before the 1860s, it was within the family. And earlier, the thousands of women indentured to work for others to pay their passage to the New World, worked within families. Women's labor took form within the family and remained there longest.

And yet women had only limited control of that family. For most of American history, males legally owned the land and any wages women earned working on the land. In the western community-property states, men still had management and control of women's half of the property during their lives, and, in some states, remained in control even in death. In New Mexico, for example, women could not dispose of their half of the community property by will until 1973 when the state Equal Rights Amendment was passed.[10]

Farm women are likely to make increasing policy demands in the next decades. For young women these will take the form of recognition of their desire to participate as full partners and as sole practitioners in agricultural ventures. Although women make up a third of many colleges of agriculture today, they are still not always taken seriously by the predominantly male faculties and administration of those colleges. Agricultural women will continue to demand an equal place in education that will include more women faculty and administrators, support for research interests, and consideration of their ideas about local and national agricultural policy.

Women already engaged in agriculture, most as members of a family farm, will want legal protection and recognition of their contributions to the productivity of the farm. They will want credit for themselves for partnerships as well as for full ventures. They will want greater assistance in obtaining off-farm job training and jobs; help with child care; more flexibility by cooperative extension personnel in planning family transitions to new crops and structures. Corporate structures are now being used to deny some farm women a role in decision making. Women want protection for their investment of time and resources. Widows and older women will want changes in laws so that they will not have to pay inheritance tax on farm businesses in which they have invested their life's work. Some states have already changed their laws to protect their interest; many have not. Most of these policy demands relate to the desire of women to enter or remain in agriculture, but women as a whole will ask for a larger part in determining the overall agricultural policy of the government.

Scholars have an obligation to assist in this reformulating of policy. They need to work with farm women to help them articulate their needs, to provide historical information to assist in developing viable policies, and generally to use the wisdom of their disciplines in aiding the transition to a new agricultural system. Mainly, scholars will be called upon to document the essential role that women have played in the agricultural development of the United States in the past and to point out the critical role they will play in the development of future agricultural policy.

Notes

Journal Abbreviations for Notes

AH   — *Agricultural History*
AS   — *American Studies*
BHSP   — *Buffalo Historical Society Publications*
JEH   — *Journal of Economic History*
JER   — *Journal of the Early Republic*
LH   — *Labor History*
MHM   — *Maryland Historical Magazine*
NMHR — *New Mexico Historical Review*
PMHB   — *Pennsylvania Magazine of History and Biography*
WMQ   — *William & Mary Quarterly*

Introduction

1. Laura Lane, "O Promise Me . . . But Put It in Writing" (Paper presented at the American Farm Women in Historical Perspective Conference, New Mexico State University, Las Cruces, New Mexico, February 2–4, 1984).

2. Carole Shammas, Marylynn Salmon, and Michel Dahlin, eds., *Inheritance in America: From Colonial Times to the Present* (New Brunswick and London: Rutgers University Press, 1987), pp. 21–79.

3. Eleanor Leacock, "Women as Farmers in Native North America"

(Paper presented at the American Farm Women in Historical Perspective Conference, New Mexico State University, Las Cruces, New Mexico, February 2–4, 1984). See also the chapter on the Seneca in this volume; and Victoria Brady, Sarah Crome, and Lyn Reese, "Resist! Survival Tactics of Indian Women," *California History* 63 (Spring 1984):141–51.

4. A description of western community property law is in Joan M. Jensen and Darlis A. Miller, eds., *New Mexico Women: Intercultural Perspectives* (Albuquerque: University of New Mexico Press, 1986), pp. 185–86, 230–31.

5. For French sugar plantation owners see U.S. Commissioner of Patents, *Report 1845* (Washington, 1845), Appendix 13, 876–913. For California see Joan M. Jensen and Gloria Ricci Lothrop, *California Women: A History* (San Francisco: Boyd and Fraser, 1987), pp. 10–16.

6. Shammas, Salmon, and Dahlin, *Inheritance in America*, pp. 103–22. I have also drawn on an unpublished paper by Sarah Deutsch, "Regionalism in U.S. Women's History: The West, 1870–1980."

7. Sonya Salamon and Anna Mackey Keim, "Land Ownership and Women's Power in a Midwestern Farming Community," *Journal of Marriage and Family* 41 (1979):109–19.

8. Lee Virginia Chambers-Schiller, *Liberty a Better Husband: Single Women in America; The Generations of 1780–1840* (New Haven: Yale University Press, 1984). See also the chapter in this volume "Farm Women in New Mexico, 1900–1940"; and Sheryll Patterson-Black, "Women Homesteaders on the Great Plains Frontier," *Frontiers I* (Spring 1976):67–88.

9. Carole Shammas, "Black Women's Work and the Evolution of Plantation Society in Virginia," *LH* 26 (Winter 1985):5–28.

10. Deborah G. White, *Ar'n't I A Woman? Female Slaves in the Plantation South* (New York: Norton, 1985).

11. Jacquelyn Jones, *Labor of Love, Labor of Sorrow: Black Women, Work, and the Family from Slavery to the Present* (New York: Basic Books, 1985), pp. 44–78.

12. Ibid., pp. 79–109.

13. Shammas, "Black Women's Work," 5–28.

14. David Galenson, *White Servitude in Colonial America: An Economic Analysis* (Cambridge: Cambridge University Press, 1981) and Sharon V. Salinger, "'Send No More Women': Female Servants in Eighteenth-Century Philadelphia," *PMHB* CVII (1983):29–48, and her "Colonial Labor in Transition: The Decline of Indentured Servitude in Late Eighteenth-Century Philadelphia," *LH* 22 (1981):165–91.

15. Joan M. Jensen, *Loosening the Bonds: Mid-Atlantic Farm Women, 1750–1850* (New Haven: Yale University Press, 1986), pp. 42–43.

16. Ibid., pp. 114–28. See also Sarah Deutsch, *No Separate Refuge:*

Culture, Class, and Gender on an Anglo-Hispanic Frontier in the American Southwest, 1880–1940 (New York: Oxford University Press, 1987), pp. 11–62.

17. John Mack Faragher, *Women and Men on the Overland Trail* (New Haven: Yale University Press, 1979) and Lillian Schlissel, "Frontier Families: Crisis in Ideology," in Sam B. Girgus, ed., *The American Self: Myth, Ideology, and Popular Culture* (Albuquerque: University of New Mexico Press, 1981), pp. 155–65.

18. Joan Iversen, "Feminist Implications of Mormon Polygamy," and Julie Dunfey, "Living the Principle of Plural Marriage: Mormon Women, Utopia, and Female Sexuality in the Nineteenth Century," in *Feminist Studies* 10 (Fall 1984):505–22, 523–36; J. Embry, "Mormon Women" (Paper presented at the American Farm Women in Historical Perspective Conference, New Mexico State University, Las Cruces, New Mexico, February 2–4, 1984); Justina W. Bernstein, "Her hands Are Labor Stained: Women's 'Inwork' and 'Outwork' in Ogden, Utah, 1850–1900" (MA thesis, New Mexico State University, 1989).

19. Sally McMurry, *Families & Farmhouses in 19th Century America: Vernacular Design and Social Change* (New York: Oxford University Press, 1988) and George W. McDaniel, *Hearth & Home: Preserving a People's Culture* (Philadelphia: Temple University Press, 1982), are the most detailed studies of vernacular rural architecture in the nineteenth century.

20. Cynthia Sturgis, "'How're You Gonna Keep 'Em Down on the Farm?': Rural Women and the Urban Model in Utah," *AH* 60 (Spring 1986):182–99; Dorothy Schwieder, "Education and Change in the Lives of Iowa Farm Women, 1900–1940," *AH* 60 (Spring 1986):200–15; Christine Kleinegger, "Out of the Barns and Into the Kitchens: Transformations in Farm Women's Work in the First Half of the Twentieth Century," in Barbara Drygulski Wright, ed., *Women, Work, and Technology: Transformations* (Ann Arbor: University of Michigan Press, 1987), pp. 162–81; and Nancy Grey Osterud, "The Valuation of Women's Work: Gender and the Market in a Dairying Farming Community During the Late Nineteenth Century," *Frontiers* 10, no. 2 (1988):18–24.

21. Corlann Bush and Sue Armitage, "Pacific Northwest Farmwomen and the Frontier Tradition" (Paper presented at the American Farm Women in Historical Perspective Conference, New Mexico State University, Las Cruces, New Mexico, February 2–4, 1984).

22. Margo McBane, "Tillie the Toiler: The World War I California Woman's Land Army" (Paper presented at the American Farm Women in Historical Perspective Conference, New Mexico State University, Las Cruces, New Mexico, February 2–4, 1984). Deborah Fink, "Sidelines and Moral Capital: Women on Nebraska Farms in the 1930s," Wava G. Haney

and Jane B. Knowles, eds., *Women and Farming: Changing Roles, Changing Structures* (Boulder and London: Westview Press, 1988), pp. 55–69 argues that the same pattern existed in Nebraska in the 1930s.

23. Deborah Fink and Dorothy Schwieder, "Iowa Farm Women in the 1930s—A Reassessment," *Annals of Iowa* 49, no. 7 (Winter 1989):570.

24. Adela de la Torre, "Agricultural Technological Change and the Employment of Seasonal Farm Labor Women: The Case of the Tomato Harvester" (Paper presented at the American Farm Women in Historical Perspective Conference, New Mexico State University, Las Cruces, New Mexico, February 2–4, 1984).

25. Donald B. Marti, "Sisters of the Grange: Rural Feminism in the Late Nineteenth Century," *AH* 58 (July 1984):247–346; Mary Jo Wagner, "The 'Money Question': Populist Women and Economics" (Paper presented at the American Farm Women in Historical Perspective Conference, New Mexico State University, Las Cruces, New Mexico, February 2–4, 1984).

26. Lu Ann Jones, "'The Task That Is Ours,' White North Carolina Farm Women and Agrarian Reform, 1886–1914" (Paper presented at the American Farm Women in Historical Perspective Conference, New Mexico State University, Las Cruces, New Mexico, February 2–4, 1984).

27. Ibid.

28. Ibid.

29. For research emphasizing ethnic differences see Joel Schor, "The Black Presence in the U.S. Cooperative Extension Service Since 1945: An American Quest for Service and Equity," *AH* 60 (Spring 1986):137–53.

30. Jane B. Knowles, "The United States Cooperative Extension Service: The Origin of the Gender Gap" (Paper presented at the American Farm Women in Historical Perspective Conference, New Mexico State University, Las Cruces, New Mexico, February 2–4, 1984).

31. Chester Wilbert Wright, "A History of the Black Land-Grant Colleges 1890–1916" (Ph.D. diss., American University, 1981). Also see Schor, "The Black Presence."

32. *The Southern Letter,* 23, no. 6 (June 1907) for Notasulga school, 23, no. 9 (September 1907) for school farms.

33. Fourth Annual Session of the Alabama State Teacher's Association, Marion, Alabama, April 8–9, 1885, *Minutes* (Hampton, Va.: Normal School Press, 1886), pp. 12–13; and Seventh Annual Session of the Alabama State Teachers' Association held at Montgomery, Alabama, April 11–13, 1888, *Minutes* (Tuskegee: Normal School Press, 1888), p. 37. For Margaret Washington see Cynthia Neverdon-Morton, *Afro-American Women of the South and the Advancement of the Race, 1895–1925* (Knoxville: University of Tennessee Press, 1989), pp. 122–39.

34. Max Bennett Thrasher, *Tuskegee: Its Story and Its Work* (Boston: Small Maynard, 1901), pp. 97–99, 100–103, 109–10.

35. Ibid., pp. 163–83. For one woman growing up in Tuskegee who attended the school, probably about 1914 to 1916, see Frances Mary Albrier, "Determined Advocate for Racial Equality" (Oral history conducted in 1977–78, Regional Oral History Office, University of California, Berkeley, 1979), 1–47. For black land ownership see Loren Schweringer, "A Vanishing Breed: Black Farm Owners in the South, 1651–1982," *AH* 63, no. 3 (Summer 1989):60. The percentage of owners crawled up to 18 percent (17,201 families in 1920) and then receded until post–World War II. Most of the nineteen thousand farm families that owned land in 1950 lost it during the next twenty-five years and the amount has continued to decline since 1982.

36. Neverdon-Morton, *Afro-American Women of the South*, pp. 126–32.

37. Karen Starr, "Fighting for a Future: Farm Women of the Nonpartisan League" (Paper presented at the American Farm Women in Historical Perspective Conference, New Mexico State University, Las Cruces, New Mexico, February 2–4, 1984).

38. Shiela Goldring Manes, "Depression Pioneers: The Conclusions of an American Odyssey, Oklahoma to California, 1930–1950" (Ph.D. diss., University of California, Los Angeles, 1982) and Jacqueline Gordon Sherman, "The Oklahomans in California During the Depression Decade 1931–1941," (Ph.D. diss., University of California, Los Angeles, 1940). See also Jensen and Lothrop, *California Women,* pp. 91–100.

39. Rachel Amy Rosenfeld, *Farm Women: Work, Farm, and Family in the United States* (Chapel Hill and London: University of North Carolina Press, 1985), pp. 3–5.

40. Rosenfeld, *Farm Women,* pp. 270–71; Patricia Garrett, Michael D. Schulman, and Damayanthi Herath, "Division of Labor and Decision-Making in a Poor Tobacco-Growing Area of North Carolina: A Male/Female Comparison"; and Judith Z. Kalbacher, "Today's American Farm Women" (Papers presented at New Mexico State University, Las Cruces, New Mexico, February 2–4, 1984). See also the interviews conducted by Carolyn E. Sachs, *The Invisible Farmers: Women in Agricultural Production* (Totowa, New Jersey: Rowman & Allanheld, 1983), pp. 75–117; and Gould Colman and Sarah Elbert, "Farming Families: 'The Farm Needs Everyone,'" *Research in Rural Sociology and Development,* ed. Harry K. Scharztweller, vol. 1, 61–78 (Greenwich, Conn.: JAI Press, 1984).

41. Ibid. See chapter in this volume "Keeping Down on the Farm."

42. Mark Friedberger, "Farm Families & Change in Twentieth Century America (Lexington: University Press of Kentucky, 1988), pp. 83, 98, 130.

43. Ibid., pp. 13, 73, 88, 91.

44. Ibid., pp. 246–48.
45. Lorna Clancy Miller and Mary Neth, "Farm Women in the Political Arena," in Haney and Knowles, eds., *Women and Farming,* pp. 357–80.
46. For the entry of women into traditional male fields see the special issue of *Rangelands,* 6 (Feb. 1984).

2 "Tillie": German Farm Woman

1. Most of this essay is based on family history, on my own memories, and on census and county records.
2. Czechoslovakian registries gave birth dates and Matilda's mother's name. Peter was born in Křišťanov but Cresencia was born in Zbytiny.
3. Joseph Jantsch, "The Jantsch Saga" (mimeograph, 1948).

3 Rozalija: Lithuanian Farm Woman

1. These interviews were conducted over a period of nine years, the first in 1980, the last after Rozalija had died in 1983. Rose's son, John Gustinis, translated the tapes and my questions and shared his recollections as well.
2. World War II and the Russian occupation is described in Joseph Pajanjis-Javis, *Soviet Genocide in Lithuania* (New York: Maryland Books, 1980) and in Milda Danys, *DP: Lithuanian Immigration to Canada After the Second World War* (Toronto: Multicultural History Society of Ontario, 1980), pp. 3–20.
3. Danys, *DP,* pp. 20–66, describes the experiences of other refugees. See also Mark Wyman, *DP: Europe's Displaced Persons, 1945–1951* (Philadelphia: The Balch Institute Press, 1989).

4 Recovering Her Story: Learning the History of Farm Women

1. The talk was given at the National Homemakers Conference, Laramie, Wyoming, August 3, 1983. The material is drawn mainly from family history, New Mexico Homemaker oral histories, and from my own research on farm women. Those wishing to read about the history of farm women will find my book *With These Hands: Women Working the Land* (Westbury: Feminist Press, 1981) and Sachs, *The Invisible Farmers,* good introductions. For doing women's oral history, look at the two special issues of *Frontiers* 2 (Summer 1977) and 7 (Fall 1983) and *The Oral History Review* (Spring 1989) on rural women.

2. Extension Homemaker oral histories for New Mexico are in National Extension Homemaker Council, Oral Histories, MS 248 3/5, New Mexico Women's History Archives, Rio Grande Historical Collections, New Mexico State University Library, Las Cruces, New Mexico. They are cited as Extension Homemaker Oral History, NMWHA, NMSU.

3. Ima Fairly, Extension Homemaker Oral History, NMWHA, NMSU, Beatrice Stagl, Interviewer, November 23, 1981.

4. Florence McDonald, Extension Homemaker Oral History, NMWHA, NMSU, Beatrice Stagl, Interviewer, November 17, 1981.

5. Frances Mathews, Extension Homemaker Oral History, NMWHA, NMSU, Mary Catherine Popejoy, Interviewer, December 14, 1981.

6. Mary Moore, Extension Homemaker Oral History, NMWHA, NMSU, Mary Catherine Popejoy, Interviewer, August 30, 1981.

7. Nona Berry, Extension Homemaker Oral History, NMWHA, NMSU, Mary Catherine Popejoy, Interviewer, December 8, 1981.

8. Nona Berry, Frances Mathews, Florence McDonald, and Ruth James, Extension Homemaker Oral History, NMWHA, NMSU, Mary Catherine Popejoy, Interviewer, January 7, 1982.

9. Frances Mathews, Nona Berry, Ruth James, Extension Homemaker Oral History, NMWHA, NMSU.

10. Nona Berry, Extension Homemaker Oral History, NMWHA, NMSU.

11. See "Butter-Making in the Mid-Atlantic, 1750–1850," this volume.

12. There are a few classic historical accounts that will be most helpful for the colonial American period of agriculture. See especially Laurel Thatcher Ulrich, *Good Wives: Image and Reality in the Lives of Women in Northern New England, 1650–1750* (New York: Knopf, 1982) and *A Midwife's Tale: The Life of Martha Ballard, Based on Her Diary, 1785–1812* (New York: Knopf, 1990); Mary Beth Norton, *Liberty's Daughters: The Revolutionary Experience of American Women, 1750–1800* (Boston: Little, Brown, 1980); and Nancy F. Cott, *The Bonds of Womanhood: 'Women's Sphere' in New England, 1790–1835* (New Haven and London: Yale University Press, 1977). For the nineteenth century, the best introductions are Julie Roy Jeffrey, *Frontier Women: The Trans-Mississippi, 1840–1880* (New York: Hill and Wang, 1979); Glenda Riley, *Frontierswomen: The Iowa Experience* (Ames: Iowa State University Press, 1981); and Deborah White, *Ar'n't I A Woman?* Jensen and Miller, *New Mexico Women,* has several chapters dealing with rural women.

13. Jensen, *Loosening the Bonds.*

14. Jensen, *With These Hands,* describes these women. There are also many fine novels that depict farm women, such as Willa Cather, *My Àntonia,* Tillie Olson, *Yonnondio,* Harriet Arnow, *The Dollmaker,* and Donna Smyth, *Quilt* (Toronto: Women's Educational Press, 1982).

5 New Mexico Farm Women, 1900–1940

Originally published as "Farm Women in New Mexico, 1900–1940," in Robert Kern, ed., *Labor in New Mexico: Strikes, Unions, and Social History Since 1881* (Albuquerque: University of New Mexico Press, 1983), 61–81.

1. This essay has greatly benefitted from the contributions of various people, and I gratefully acknowledge their assistance. Terri Flickinger collected and Molly Smith transcribed most of these interviews, and the New Mexico State University Research Center funded "The Working Lives of New Mexico Women" project under a minigrant. I would also like to thank the many students, some of whom wished to remain anonymous, for sharing their family histories with me. Demographic material that follows is compiled from U.S. Department of Commerce and Labor, Bureau of the Census, *Thirteenth Census of the United States, 1910: Abstract of the Census with Supplement for New Mexico* (Washington, 1913); U.S. Department of Commerce, Bureau of the Census, *Fourteenth Census of the United States, 1920, volume 4, part 3, Agriculture* (Washington, 1922); U.S. Department of Commerce, Bureau of the Census, *Farm Population of the United States, 1925, Census Monographs VI* (Washington, 1926); U.S. Department of Commerce, Bureau of the Census, United States Agriculture, 1925 (Washington, 1927); U.S. Department of Commerce, Bureau of the Census, *Fifteenth Census of the United States, 1930, Agriculture, Volume III* (Washington, 1932); and Sigurd Johansen, *The People of New Mexico* (Las Cruces: Agricultural Experiment Station Bulletin 606, n.d.). See also Joan M. Jensen, "Canning Comes to New Mexico: Women and the Agricultural Extension Service, 1914–1919," *NMHR* 57 (October 1982).

2. Robert Coles, *The Old Ones of New Mexico* (Albuquerque: University of New Mexico Press, 1973), pp. 16–36.

3. Glen Grisham to Ralph R. Will, September 25, 1940. Farm Security Administration, National Archives, Record Group 96. Hereafter referred to as FSA, NA, RG 96.

4. Victor Westphall, *The Public Domain in New Mexico, 1854–1891* (Albuquerque: University of New Mexico Press, 1965), p. 49.

5. Alvin R. Sunseri, "Agricultural Techniques in New Mexico at the Time of the Anglo-American Conquest," *AH* 47 (1973):334–37; *Report of the Governor of New Mexico to the Secretary of the Interior, 1903* (Washington, 1903), pp. 311–12.

6. R. Hall Williams, "George W. Julian and Land Reform in New Mexico, 1885–1889," *AH* 41 (1967):72–84. Julian eventually attempted to regain ten million acres he believed had been fraudulently obtained in the first forty years after occupation of New Mexico.

7. Jesse de la Cruz, "Rejection Because of Race: Albert J. Beveridge and

Nuevo Mexico's Struggle for Statehood, 1902–1903," *Aztlan* 7 (Spring 1976):79–88.

8. E. Louise Peffer, *The Closing of the Public Domain: Disposal and Reservation Policies, 1900–1950* (Stanford: Stanford University Press, 1951), p. 53; Santa Fe *New Mexican,* June 12, 1909; Benjamin Horace Hibbard, *History of the Public Land Policies* (New York: Peter Smith, 1939), p. 401; Sanford A. Mosk, "Land Policy and Stock Raising in the Western United States," in Vernon Carstensen, ed., *The Public Lands: Studies in the History of Public Domain* (Madison: University of Wisconsin Press, 1963), pp. 418–19. According to Mosk, a 1917 report indicated that 59 percent of the land in the public domain that was sold also went to the 3 percent who bought over five thousand acres.

9. William J. Parish, *The Charles Ilfeld Company: A Study in the Rise and Decline of Mercantile Capitalism in New Mexico* (Cambridge: Harvard University Press, 1961), pp. 153–74.

10. Olen Leonard and C.P. Loomis, *Culture of a Contemporary Rural Community: El Cerrito, New Mexico,* United States Department of Agriculture, Bureau of Agricultural Economics, Rural Life Studies, 1 (Washington, November 1941), 1–6; Olen E. Leonard, *The Role of Land Grant in the Social Organization and Social Process of a Spanish-American Village in New Mexico* (Albuquerque: Calvin Horn, 1970), p. 150; Nan Elsasser, Kyle MacKenzie, and Yvonne Tixier y Vigil, *Las Mujeres: Conversations with Hispanic Women of the Southwest* (Old Westbury: Feminist Press, 1980).

11. D. W. Meining, *Southwest: Three Peoples in Geographical Change, 1600–1790* (New York: Oxford University Press, 1971), pp. 66–71.

12. Emma Marble Muir, "Pioneer Ranch," *New Mexico Magazine* 36 (June 1958):63.

13. Agnes Morley Cleveland, *No Life for a Lady* (Lincoln: University of Nebraska Press, 1977 reprint of 1941 edition), p. 335.

14. Interviews with Florence Compary Hill, Stella Hatch, and Edna Gholson, February 1977, NMWHA, NMSU. Lillie Gerhardt Anderson, "A New Mexico Pioneer of the 1880s," *NMHR* 29 (October 1954):245–58, confirmed that 1908–9 homesteads were run primarily by women while the men went out to wage work.

15. Interview with Ellen Grubbs Reaves, February 1977, NMWHA, NMSU.

16. M. S. Kistin, *Preliminary Report on Migratory Workers in the Cotton Areas of New Mexico,* U.S. Department of Agriculture, Farm Security Administration (Washington, May 1941), p. 5, FSA, NA, RG 96.

17. Kistin, *Preliminary Report,* 35.

18. Margaret Reeves, Director, Bureau of Child Welfare to C.E. Baker, Chairman, Delinquency Section, Texas Conference of Social Work, Septem-

ber 15, 1931, and State Bureau of Child Welfare, Report for June 1931. Governors' Papers, Arthur Seligman, 1931–33, State Records Center and Archives, Santa Fe, New Mexico. Hereafter cited as Seligman Papers, SRCA. See also Sandra Kay Schackel, "Private and Public Spheres: Women and Social Welfare in New Mexico 1920–1940" (Ph.D. diss., University of New Mexico, 1988).

19. Undated reports on relief work, Seligman Papers, SRCA.

20. Undated report on relief work, by L. L. BonDurant, Field Representative, Seligman Papers, SRCA; Glen Grisham to Ralph R. Will, September 25, 1940, FSA, NA, RG 96; and anonymous family histories.

21. See various letters and reports in the Seligman Papers, SRCA.

22. R. W. O'Hara, Memorandum to Wilson Cowen, July 26, 1940, Clay L. Cochran to C. E. Hazard, February 13, 1942, and Claude R. Wickard Memorandum for Dr. H. R. Tolley, May 9, 1941, FSA, NG, RG 96, all explain policies in New Mexico.

23. Kistin, *Preliminary Report,* p. 35; interview with Nina Griffin, Mesilla, New Mexico, February 1977, NMWHA, NMSU.

24. U.S. Department of Commerce, Bureau of the Census, *United States Census of Agriculture, 1945, Volume I, New Mexico and Arizona* (Washington, 1946).

25. See note 1.

26. Interview with Lucille Tatreault, Mesilla, New Mexico, February 1977, NMWHA, NMSU.

27. Coles, *The Old Ones,* pp. 30–31. Interview with Nina Griffin, Mesilla, New Mexico, February 1977, NMWHA, NMSU.

28. District Intelligence Officer to Department Intelligence Officer, Southern Department, Fort Sam Houston, Texas, January 19, 1920, MID File 10095–584, NA, RG 165. For Southern Tenant Farmers Union activity in Las Cruces, see correspondence of J. E. Clayton and G. W. Holsome Reels 24–28, STFU Papers on Microfilm.

29. Patricia Cooper and Norma Bradley Buferd, *The Quilters: Women and the Domestic Art* (Garden City, New York: Doubleday, 1977), preface.

6 Women in the Hop Harvest from New York to Washington

Copyright 1986 by *Journal of the West,* Inc., 1531 Yuma, Manhattan, KS 66502, and reprinted with permission.

1. E. Meeker, *Hop Culture in the United States: Being a Practical Treatise on Hop Growing in Washington Territory* (Puyallup, WA, 1883; Seattle: Shorey Books, 1972), 62–65, 110.

2. Sharon Good, "The Hop Culture" (MA thesis, State University of New York College at Oneanta, 1968), 90a.

3. Ibid., 22, 64.

4. Ibid., 33–37.

5. Ibid., 19.

6. Ibid., 32.

7. Ibid., 40–55.

8. Ibid., 61, 68–69, 76.

9. Meeker, *Hop Culture,* 91.

10. Ibid., 91–92, 108.

11. Ibid., 18, 20.

12. *Atlas of Washington Agriculture* (Olympia: Washington State Department of Agriculture, 1963), 64.

13. G. Thomas Edwards, "The Early Morning at Yakima's Day of Greatness," *Pacific Northwest Quarterly* 73 (1982):82.

14. Maurice Helland, *They Knew Our Valley* (Yakima, WA, 1975), 118.

15. Meeker, *Hop Culture,* 20.

16. Interview with Florence Martin, courtesy of Yakima Valley Museum, author's possession.

17. L. V. McWhorter, *Yellow Wolf: His Own Story* (Caldwell, ID: Caxton, 1940), 13.

18. Interview with Louisa George, 1890. Washington Women's Heritage Project, Bellingham, WA.

19. Interview with Margaret Keys, courtesy of Yakima Valley Museum, author's possession.

20. George interview.

21. Keys interview.

22. Ibid.

23. Ibid.

24. *Yakima Golding Hop Farms* (Yakima,WA, n.p., n.d. [ca 1940], 42 (Photo Collection, Manuscripts Archives and Special Collections, Washington State University Libraries, Pullman, WA).

25. Ibid.

26. Meeker, *Hop Culture,* 20.

7 *Southwest Monuments of the Salinas*

1. I would like to thank Darlis Miller, Steadman Upham, and Jack Wilson for their criticism of this article. For other women builders see Doris Cole, *From Tipi to Skyscraper: A History of Women in Architecture* (Boston: i Press, 1973), pp. 14–22; Labelle Prussin, "Tents: Lady of the Builders," *Mimar Houses* (Singapore: Concept Media, 1987), pp. 115–20. Bernard

Rudofsky, *Architecture Without Architects: A Short Introduction to Non-Pedigreed Architecture* (Garden City: Doubleday, 1964; reprint, University of New Mexico, 1987). Heather Huyck, "Beyond John Wayne: Using Historic Sites to Interpret Western Women's History," in Lillian Schlissel, Vicki L. Ruiz, and Janice Monk, eds., *Western Women: Their Land, Their Lives* (Albuquerque: University of New Mexico Press, 1988), pp. 303–29, has called for analysis of these women's monuments. A national survey is now underway to identify and describe such historical sites.

2. Richard W. Lang, "Early Prehistory in the Estancia Basin," *Exploration: Annual Bulletin of the School of American Research* (1982):2–5.

3. Victor Mindeleff, *A Study of Pueblo Architecture in Tusayan and Cibola*, 2 vols., (Washington and London: Smithsonian Institution Press, 1989; reprint of 1891 edition) identified men and women who worked at masonry 1:101–2. The men were stonecutters, the women laid the stone, plastered, roofed, and laid floors. Elsasser, MacKenzie, and Tixier y Vigil, *Las Mujeres,* pp. 14, 122; and Marianne L. Stoller, "The Hispanic Women Artists of New Mexico: Present and Past," *El Palacio* 92, no. 1 (Summer/Fall 1986):21.

4. Mrs. Edward E. Ayer, trans., and Frederick Webb Hodge and Charles Fletcher Lummis, annotators, *The Memorial of Fray Alonso de Benavides, 1630* (Albuquerque: Horn and Wallace, 1965), p. 33; George Hammond and Agapito Ray, *Narratives of the Coronado Expedition, 1540–1542* (Albuquerque: University of New Mexico Press, 1940), p. 254.

5. Thomas J. Caperton, "An Archeological Reconaissance," in Alden C. Hayes, *Contributions to Gran Quivira Archeology: Gran Quivira National Monument/New Mexico,* Publications in Archeology 16 (Washington, D.C.: National Park Service, 1981), pp. 3–7.

6. Alden C. Hayes, "The Humanos Pueblos," and Dan Murphy, "Salinas: A View Through Time," in *Exploration* (1982):10, 14.

7. Ibid., 201–2. Minimum numbers are from John P. Wilson, "Before the Pueblo Revolt: Population Trends, Apache Relations and Pueblo Abandonments in Seventeenth-Century New Mexico," in *Prehistory and the History of the Southwest* (Albuquerque: Papers of the Archaeological Society of New Mexico, 11, 1985). Much larger numbers are in Thomas D. Hall, *Social Change in the Southwest, 1350–1880* (Lawrence: University Press of Kansas, 1989), pp. 40, 76. The total numbers for Indian villages and populations are still being hotly debated by historians and archeologists. For a detailed discussion see Russell Thornton, *American Indian Holocaust and Survival* (Norman and London: University of Oklahoma Press, 1987).

8. Steadman Upham, *Polities and Power: An Economic and Political History of the Western Pueblo* (New York: Academic Press, 1982), pp. 181–83.

9. Alden C. Hayes, Jon Nathan Young, and A. H. Warren, *Excavation of*

Mound 7: Gran Quivira National Monument/New Mexico, Publications in Archeology 16 (Washington, D.C.: National Park Service, 1981), p. 36 for storerooms.

10. Gordon Vivian, *Excavations,* p. 2; Hayes, Young, and Warren, *Excavation,* p. 176; Hayes, "The Jumanos," 15; and Steadman Upham, "The Tyranny of Ethnographic Analogy in Southwestern Archeology," in Sylvia Gaines, ed., *Coasts, Plains, and Deserts: Essays in Honor of Reynold J. Ruppe* (Tempe: Arizona State University Anthropological Research Papers, No. 38, 1987), pp. 265–79 discuss populations and disease.

11. Hayes, Young, and Warren, *Excavation,* p. 46; Vivian, *Excavations,* p. 105.

12. Hayes, *Contributions,* p. 67.

13. Katharine Bartlett, *Pueblo Milling Stones of the Flagstaff Region and Their Relation to Others in the Southwest: A Study in Progressive Efficiency* (Flagstaff: Museum of Northern Arizona, 1933), p. 3; David H. Snow, "A Note on Encomienda Economics in Seventeenth-Century New Mexico," in Marta Weigle, ed., *Hispanic Arts and Ethnology in the Southwest* (Sante Fe: Ancient City Press, 1983), pp. 349–50.

14. George Hammond and Agapito Rey, *Don Juan de Oñate, Colonizer of New Mexico, 1595–1628,* 2 vols., (Albuquerque: University of New Mexico Press, 1953), 1:219, 255. Jensen, *With These Hands,* pp. 17–19 reprints one of the Pueblo grinding songs recorded early in the twentieth century.

15. Hayes, *Contributions,* p. 58; Hayes, Young, and Warren, *Excavation,* pp. 141, 177; Vivian, *Excavations,* p. 133.

16. Hayes, *Contributions,* pp. 91, 106.

17. Alfonso Ortiz, *The Tewa World: Space, Time, Being, and Becoming in a Pueblo Society* (Chicago and London: University of Chicago Press, 1969), p. 58.

18. Charles Wilson Hackett, ed., *Historical Documents Relating to New Mexico, Nueva Vizcaya, and the Approaches Thereto, to 1773,* 3 vols., (Washington, D.C.: Carnegie Institution of Washington, 1937), 2:110, 296–99; Petition of Fray Juan de Prada, September 26, 1638, and Petition of Fray Francisco de Ayeta, May 10, 1679. James E. Ivey, "Another Look at Dating the Scholes Manuscript: A Research Note," *NMHR* (July 1989):341–47.

19. Upham, *Polities,* p. 110. *Memorial of Benavides,* pp. 16, 30–32.

20. Ortiz, *Tewa World,* pp. 36, 64, 90.

21. Hackett, *Historical Documents,* 2:133, 134, 137, 152.

22. Byron Harvey, III, "An Overview of Pueblo Religion," and Don L. Roberts, "The Ethnomusicology of the Eastern Pueblos," in Alfonso Ortiz, ed., *New Perspectives on the Pueblos* (Albuquerque: University of New Mexico Press, 1972), pp. 197–217 and 243–55.

23. Hackett, *Historical Documents,* 3:495 for 1674 appearance.

24. Christine Ward Gailey, "Evolutionary Perspectives on Gender Hierarchy," in Beth B. Hess and Myra Marx Ferree, *Analyzing Gender: A Handbook of Social Science Research* (Newbury Park, Ca.: Sage 1987), pp. 32–67 has the best overview of prehistorical societies on this issue.

25. Ezra B. W. Zubrow, *Population, Contact, and Climate in the New Mexican Pueblos* (Tucson: Anthropological Papers of the University of Arizona, No. 24, 1974), p. 10.

26. Vivian, *Excavations*, p. 12.

27. Ibid., p. 13.

28. Ibid., p. 14; John P. Wilson, "Quarai: A Turbulent History," *Exploration: Annual Bulletin of the School of American Research* (1982), 21.

29. Hall, *Social Change in the Southwest*, pp. 18–21.

30. See John Leddy Phelan, *The Hispanization of the Philippines: Spanish Aims and Philipino Responses, 1565–1700* (Madison: University of Wisconsin Press, 1959), for an analysis of the Spanish empire during the late fifteenth and sixteenth centuries.

31. Hall, *Social Change*, pp. 18–19.

32. Hackett, *Historical Documents*, 2:108.

33. Ibid., 2:111, 113.

34. Ibid., 2:109, 143, 146.

35. Ibid., 2:108.

36. Wilson, "Quarai," 24; France V. Scholes, "Troublous Times in New Mexico, 1659–1670," *NMHR* 12, no. 2 (1937):396. Charles Wilson Hackett, *Revolt of the Pueblo Indians of New Mexico and Otermin's Attempted Reconquest, 1680–1682*, 2 vols., (Albuquerque: University of New Mexico Press, 1942), 2:299–300, 302.

37. France V. Scholes, "Some Aspects of the Jumano Problem," in *Contributions to American Anthropology and History*, no. 34 (Washington, D.C.: Carnegie Institutions of Washington Publication 523, 1940).

38. Hackett, *Historical Documents*, 2:133–34, 137, 152; Hayes, Young, and Warren, *Excavation*, p. 761.

39. Donovan Senter, "The Work on the Old Quarai Mission, 1934," *El Palacio* 37, nos. 21–23 (1934):169–74; Albert Grim Ely, "The Excavation and Repair of Quarai Mission," *El Palacio* 39, nos. 25–26 (1935):133–44.

40. James E. Ivey, "'In the Midst of Loneliness': The Architectural History of the Salinas Missions." Santa Fe: Southwest Cultural Resources Center Professional Papers no. 15, 1988, pp. 55–110.

41. Vivian, *Excavations*, pp. 89–91.

42. Ivey, "In the Midst of a Loneliness," pp. 157–200.

43. France V. Scholes and Eleanor B. Adams, "Inventories of Church Furnishings in Some of the New Mexico Missions," in *Dargan Historical Essays* (Albuquerque: University of New Mexico Publications in History, no. 4, 1952), pp. 29–31.

44. Hackett, *Historical Documents,* 2:144, 192.
45. Ibid., pp. 191, 112–113.
46. Scholes, "Troublous Times," 394.
47. Snow, "A Note on Encomienda Economics in Seventeenth-Century New Mexico," pp. 347–57.
48. This account is from San Juan Pueblo in 1601. Vivian, *Excavations,* p. 16.
49. Hackett, *Historical Documents,* 2:271.
50. Ibid.
51. Ibid., 2:398.
52. For pottery see Hayes, *Contributions,* p. 73; David H. Snow, "Spanish American Pottery Manufacture in New Mexico: A Critical Review," *Ethnography* 31, no. 2 (1984):93–113; and Barbara D. Staley, "Production of Rio Grande Glaze-Paint Wares: Refining the Concepts of Standardization and Specialization" (MA thesis, New Mexico State University, 1988).

8 Native American Women and Agriculture: A Seneca Case Study

Originally published as "Native American Women and Agriculture: A Seneca Case Study," *Sex Roles: A Journal of Research* 3 (1977):423–41 and reprinted by permission.

1. Criticism by many women helped the development of this article at different stages. Anthropologists Bea Medicine and Peggy Sanday, women historians at Arizona State University, and community women in Phoenix all made valuable contributions to its evolution.
2. I use the term agriculture rather than horticulture because horticulture, along with "hoe culture," has so often been used negatively. Fritz L. Kramer, "Eduard Hahn and the End of the 'Three Stages of Man,'" *Geographical Review* 57 (1967):73–89.
3. General discussions are in Lyman Carrier, *The Beginnings of Agriculture in America* (New York: McGraw-Hill, 1923); Preston Holder, *The Hoe and the Horse on the Plains: A Study of Cultural Development Among North American Indians* (Lincoln: University of Nebraska Press, 1970); John Terrell and Donna M. Terrell, *Indian Women of the Western Morning: Their Life in Early America* (New York: Dial, 1974); Anthony F. C. Wallace, *The Death and Rebirth of the Seneca* (New York: Knopf, 1970); and George F. Will and George E. Hyde, *Corn Among the Indians of the Upper Missouri* (Lincoln: University of Nebraska Press, 1917). Since the publication of this article, R. Douglas Hurt, *Indian Agriculture in America: Prehistory to the Present* (Lawrence: University of Kansas Press, 1987) has provided an overview. See also Diane Rothenberg, "The Mothers of the Nation: Seneca

Resistance to Quaker Intervention," in Mona Etienne and Eleanor Leacock, eds., *Women and Colonization: Anthropological Perspectives* (New York: Praeger, 1980), pp. 63–87.

4. Peggy R. Sanday, "Toward a Theory of the Status of Women," *American Anthropologist* 75 (1973):1682–1700; Peggy R. Sanday, "Female Status in the Public Domain," in Michelle Zimbalist Rosaldo and Louise Lamphere, eds., *Woman, Culture and Society* (Stanford: Stanford University Press, 1974), pp. 189–206; Judith K. Brown, "Economic Organization and the Position of Women Among the Iroquois," *Ethnohistory* 17 (1970):151–67; Judith K. Brown, "A Note on the Division of Labor by Sex," *American Anthropologist* 72 (1970):1073–78.

5. Gilbert L. Wilson, *Agriculture of the Hidatsa Indians: An Indian Interpretation*, University of Minnesota Studies in the Social Sciences no. 9 (Minneapolis: University of Minnesota Press, 1917).

6. Carrier, *The Beginnings of Agriculture.*

7. Quoted in Wilcomb Washburn, *Red Man's Land/White Man's Law* (New York: Scribner's, 1959).

8. J. N. B. Hewitt, ed., "Seneca Fiction, Legends and Myths," U.S. Bureau of American Ethnology, *Annual Report 1910–1911* (Washington, D.C., 1918), pp. 636–42, 643–45; Arthur C. Parker, *Seneca Myths and Folk Tales* (Buffalo, New York: Buffalo Historical Society, 1923), pp. 60–64; and *Idem.* "Analytical History of the Seneca Indians," *New York State Archeological Association Researches and Transactions* 7 (1927):1–162.

9. Charles Hawley, *Early Chapters of Seneca History: Jesuit Missions in Sonnontouan, 1656–1684* (Auburn, New York: Cayuga County Historical Society Collection, 1884); and Lewis H. Morgan, *Houses and House-Life of the American Aborigines* (Chicago and London: University of Chicago Press, 1965), pp. 64–66.

10. Hawley, *Early Chapters*; and Joseph François Lafitau, *Moeure des Sauvages Ameriquains: Comparées aux Moeurs des Premier Temps*, 2 vols., (Paris: Hochereau, 1724), 1:555. It is not clear from early accounts whether the Seneca couple always joined the household of the woman. Arthur C. Parker, *Red Jacket: Last of the Seneca* (New York: McGraw-Hill, 1952), p. 4 says the couple lived with her women for the first year, then with his women. Other accounts say the Seneca couples joined the husband's household. The Seneca may have changed from living with the wife's clan to living with the husband's clan because of the increasing military demands of the tribe. M. Kay Martin and Barbara Voorhies, *Female of the Species* (New York and London: Columbia University Press, 1975), pp. 222–23.

11. Arthur C. Parker, "Iroquois Uses of Maize and Other Food Plants," in William N. Fenton, ed., *Parker on the Iroquois* (Syracuse: Syracuse University Press, 1968); and James Everett Seaver, *Life of Mary Jemison: White Woman of the Genessee* (Canadaigua, N.Y.: Beamis, 1824), p. 47.

12. Parker, *Red Jacket,* p. 133; and Wallace, *Death and Rebirth,* p. 28.

13. William N. Fenton, "Toward the Gradual Civilization of the Indian Natives: the Missionary and Linguistic Work of Asher Wright (1803–1875) Among the Senecas of Western New York," *American Philosophical Society Proceedings* 100 (1965):567–81; George H. Harris, "Life of Horatio Jones," *BHSP* 6 (1903):383–514; and Frederick Houghton, "The History of the Buffalo Creek Reservation," *BHSP* 24 (1920):3–181.

14. Quoted in William L. Stone, *The Life and Times of Red-Jacket, or Sa-Go-Ye-Wat-Ha* (New York and London: Wiley & Putnam, 1841), p. 56.

15. Quoted in Parker, *Red Jacket,* p. 130.

16. Quoted in Parker, *Red Jacket,* p. 133.

17. Houghton, "The History."

18. Arthur C. Parker, "Notes on the Ancestry of Cornplanter," *New York State Archeological Association Researches and Transactions* 6 (1927):4–22. Cornplanter's mother was a hereditary matron of the Wolf clan who passed over him to nominate her younger full-blooded son as sachim. Cornplanter had no official title but became an elder and was given the right to sign treaties because of his military role. His mother later lived in his village. Merle H. Deardorff and George S. Snyderman, "A Nineteenth-century Journal of a Visit to the Indians of New York," *American Philosophical Society Proceedings* 100 (1956):582–612.

19. Elkanah Holmes, "Letters from Fort Niagara in 1800," *BHSP* 6 (1903):187–204.

20. Deardorff and Snyderman, "A Nineteenth Century Journal"; "Visit of Gerard T. Hopkins," *BHSP* 6 (1903):217–22; and Wallace, *Death and Rebirth,* p. 311.

21. Yolanda Murphy and Robert F. Murphy, *Women of the Forest* (New York and London: Columbia University Press, 1974), p. 182; and Arthur C. Parker, "The Code of Handsome Lake, the Seneca Prophet," in Fenton, *Parker on the Iroquois,* p. 32.

22. Mary Douglas, ed., *Witchcraft: Confessions and Accusations* (London: Tavistock, 1970), pp. xxv, xxvii; Houghton, "History of Buffalo Creek Reservation"; De Cost Smith, "Witches and Demonism of the Modern Iroquois," *Journal of American Folk-Lore* 1 (1888):184–93; Wallace, *Death and Rebirth,* pp. 236, 292, 301.

23. Fenton, "Toward the Gradual Civilization of the Indian Natives": 567–81; and Wallace, *Death and Rebirth,* pp. 283, 313.

24. J. B. Hyde, "Teacher Among the Senecas," *BHSP* 6 (1903):245–70.

25. Thompson Harris, "Journals," *BHSP* 6 (1903):313–79.

26. Ibid.

27. Grant Foreman, *Indian Removal: The Emigration of the Five Civilized Tribes of Indians* (Norman: University of Oklahoma Press, 1953); and Henry

Thompson Malone, *Cherokees of the Old South: A People in Transition* (Athens: University of Georgia Press, 1956).

28. *Case of the Seneca Indians in the State of New York* (Philadelphia: Merrihew & Thompson, 1840); and Fenton, "Toward the Gradual Civilization."

29. Harriet S. Casewell, *Our Life Among the Iroquois Indians* (Boston: Congregational Sunday School, 1892), p. 76; and Fenton, "Toward the Gradual Civilization."

30. Henry A. S. Dearborn, "Journals," *BHSP* 7 (1904):60–137.

31. Ibid.

32. Ibid.

33. Ibid.

34. Rayner Wickersham Kelsey, *Friends and the Indians, 1655–1917* (Philadelphia: Friends on Indian Affairs, 1917), pp. 125–28.

35. The Seneca replaced this new government with the older "government by chiefs" in 1854, but people of both sexes over the age of twenty-one had to consent to the sale or lease of reservation land under this second constitution. *Constitution of the "Government by Chiefs" of the Seneca Nation of Indians* (Buffalo, N.Y.: Thomas & Lathrop, 1854), p. 5; Casewell, *Our Life Among the Iroquois,* p. 79.

36. Orlando Allen, "Personal Recollections of Captain Jones and Parrish and the Payment of Indian Annuities in Buffalo," *BHSP* 6 (1903):539–42; Lewis H. Morgan, *League of the Ho-De-No-Sau-Nee or Iroquois* (New York: Dodd, Mead, 1904), p. 32; Robert A. Trennert, "William Medill's War with the Indian Traders, 1847," *Ohio History* 82 (1973):46–62; U.S. Congress, Joint Special Committee on the Conditions of the Indian Tribes, *Report* (Washington, D.C., 1867), pp. 11–14; and E. E. White, *Experiences of a Special Agent* (Norman: University of Oklahoma Press, 1965), p. 244.

37. Casewell, *Our Life Among the Iroquois,* p. 204.

38. Ibid., p. 206.

39. Elizabeth Fee, "The Sexual Politics of Victorian Social Anthropology," in Mary Hartman and Lois W. Banner, eds., *Clio's Consciousness Raised: New Perspectives on the History of Women,* (New York: Harper & Row, 1974), p. 96; Morgan, *Houses and Houselife,* p. 32; Leslie A. White, ed., *Lewis Henry Morgan: The Indian Journals, 1859–1862* (Ann Arbor: University of Michigan Press, 1959), p. 136. The reason for Morgan's reluctance to discuss women's production seems to have been his desire to protect Native Americans from criticism by whites. Since Morgan believed that male industry replacing female industry was a sign of progress, he seldom commented on the widespread women's work, but praised men's labor when he found it. Many white women sewed at home during the Civil War and into the twentieth century, and later Puerto Rican women stitched nightgowns for

wealthy New Yorkers in their island slums, but women resorted to sewing in their homes only when desperate.

40. Frederick Engels, *The Origin of the Family, Private Property and the State* (New York: International, 1972), p. 137; Fee, "The Sexual Politics of Victorian Social Anthropology"; Morgan, *League of the Ho-De-No-Sau-Nee*, p. 315; Karen Sacks, "Engels Revisited: Women, the Organization of Production, and Private Property," in Rosaldo and Lamphere, eds., *Women, Culture and Society*, pp. 207–22.

41. Hampton Institute, *Ten Years' Work for Indians at the Hampton Normal and Agricultural Institute, 1879–1888* (1888), pp. 5, 29, 65.

42. Quoted in Francis Paul Prucha, ed., *Americanizing the American Indians: Writings by the "Friends of the Indian" 1880–1900* (Cambridge: Harvard University Press, 1973), p. 20.

43. Ibid., p. 226.

44. Casewell, *Our Life Among the Iroquois*, p. 294.

45. Thomas Indian Schools, *Annual Report for 1906* (Albany: New York State, 1906), p. 32; Thomas Indian Schools, *Annual Report for 1910* (Albany: New York State, 1911), pp. 13–14; and Thomas Indian Schools, *Annual Report for 1913* (Albany: State of New York, 1914), p. 42.

46. U.S. Department of Commerce, Bureau of the Census, *Indian Population of the United States and Alaska, 1910* (Washington, D.C., 1915); U.S. Department of Commerce, Bureau of the Census, *Indian Population of the United States and Alaska* (Washington, D.C., 1937).

47. U.S. Department of Commerce, Bureau of the Census, *Indian Population of the United States and Alaska, 1910* (Washington, D.C., 1915).

48. Carl O. Sauer, *Seeds, Spades, Hearths and Herds: The Domestication of Animals and Foodstuffs*, 2d. ed. (Cambridge: Massachusetts Institute of Technology, 1969), pp. 93–94.

49. Nancy Oestreich Lurie, "Indian Women: A Legacy of Freedom," in R. L. Iacopi, ed., *Look to the Mountain Top* (San Jose: Gousha, 1972), pp. 29–36; Martha Champion Randle, "Iroquois Women, Then and Now," in W. N. Fenton, ed., *Symposium on Local Diversity in Iroquois Culture*, Bureau of American Ethnology Bulletin no. 149 (Washington, D.C., 1951), pp. 177–79; U.S. Commissioner of Indian Affairs, *Report 1910* (Washington, D.C., 1910), p. 28; and U.S. Commissioner of Indian Affairs, *Report 1915* (Washington, D.C., 1915).

9 Rise Up Like Wheat: Plantation Women in Maryland

A National Endowment for the Humanities Travel to Collections Grant and a grant from the New Mexico State University College of Arts and Sciences Research Center partially supported research for this article.

1. W. Emerson Wilson, ed., *Plantation Life at Rose Hill: The Diaries of Martha Ogle Forman, 1814–1845* (Wilmington, Delaware: Historical Society of Delaware, 1976), 9–12 May 1841, pp. 421–22. Tammy Jebb assisted me in tabulating material from the manuscript Martha Forman Diaries, Forman Papers Ms. 403, Manuscripts Division Maryland Library and Museum of History. Hereafter cited as MLMH.

2. Forman Diaries, 11 February 1842, Ms. 403, MLMH.

3. Wilson, *Plantation Life*, pp. 350–51.

4. Forman Diaries and Plantation Lists, Ms. 403, MLMH; and U.S., Manuscript Federal Census, Maryland, 1800, 1830, 1850.

5. I have used both the published Forman Diaries and the manuscript Diaries, Ms. 403, MLMH.

6. Forman Diaries, 11 February 1842, Ms. 403, MLMH.

7. Thomas Marsh Forman to Martha Callender, 4–7 April 1814, Ms. 1277, MLMH.

8. Ibid.

9. Thomas Marsh Forman to Martha Forman, 16 October 1814, Ms. 1277, MLMH.

10. Wilson, *Plantation Life*, 5 January 1815, p. 7.

11. Forman Diaries and Plantation Lists, Ms. 403, MLMH.

12. Forman Diaries, Ms. 403, MLMH.

13. Aubrey C. Land, "Economic Base and Social Structure: The Northern Chesapeake in the Eighteenth Century," *JEH* 25 (1965):639–55; Paul G. E. Clemens, "From Tobacco to Grain: Economic Development on Maryland's Eastern Shore, 1660–1750," *JEH* 35 (1975):256–59; Lois Green Carr, "Diversification in the Colonial Chesapeake: Somerset County, Maryland, in Comparative Perspective," in Louis Green Carr, Philip D. Morgan, and Jean B. Russo, eds., *Colonial Chesapeake Society* (Chapel Hill and London: University of North Carolina Press, 1988), pp. 342–88; *Cecil County Whig*, August 1966, MLMH, Clipping File.

14. Gary L. Browne, "The Evolution of Baltimore's Marketing Controls Over Agriculture," *The Maryland Historian* 11, no. 1 (1980):1–11; G. Terry Sharrer, "The Merchant Millers: Baltimore's Flour Milling Industry," *AH* 56, no. 1 (1982): 138–50 and "Flour Milling in the Growth of Baltimore, 1750–1830," *MHM* 71, no. 3 (Fall 1976):322–33.

15. William E. Burkhardt, "Cecil County," in Charles B. Clark, *Eastern Shore of Maryland and Virginia* (New York: Lewis Historical Publishers, 1950), 2:1033–52.

16. John Wesley Lord, "Cecil County, Maryland in the Civil War," (MA thesis, University of Delaware, 1950), pp. 71–73.

17. Barbara Jeanne Fields, *Slavery and Freedom on the Middle Ground: Maryland During the Nineteenth Century* (New Haven and London: Yale University Press, 1978), pp. 11–13.

18. Shepard Krech, III, "Black Family Organization in the Nineteenth Century: An Ethnological Perspective," *Journal of Interdisciplinary History* 12, no. 3 (Winter 1982):429–52.

19. Darold D. Wax, "Black Immigrants: The Slave Trade in Colonial Maryland," *MHM* 73, no. 1 (March 1978): 32, 35, 43; Allan Kulikoff, "The Beginnings of the Afro-American Family in Maryland," in Aubrey Land, Lois Green Carr, and Edward Papenfuse, eds., *Law, Society, and Politics in Early Maryland* (Baltimore and London: Johns Hopkins University Press, 1977), p. 191. See also Shammas, "Black Women's Work."

20. Fields, *Slavery and Freedom*, pp. 17, 24; and William Calderhead, "The Role of the Professional Slave Trader in a Slave Economy: Austin Woolfolk, A Case Study," *Civil War History* 23 (1977):195–211.

21. Plantation Lists, Forman Diaries, Ms. 403, MLMH.

22. Forman Diaries, Ms. 403, MLMH.

23. Forman Diaries, Ms. 403, MLMH.

24. Reconstituted Family Histories, Forman Diaries, Ms. 403, MLMH.

25. Wilson, *Plantation Life*, 2 July 1826, p. 220.

26. Ibid., 18 February 1824, p. 175.

27. Forman Diaries, Ms. 403, MLMH.

28. Field notes for cemetery plots. Eating arrangements described in Thomas Marsh Forman to Martha Callender, 4–7 April 1814, Forman Papers, Ms. 1277, MLMH.

29. Demitri B. Shimkin, Gloria Jean Louis, and Dennis A. Frate, "The Black Extended Family: A Basic Rural Institution and a Mechanism of Urban Adaptation," in Demitri D. Shimkin and Dennis A. Frate, eds., *The Extended Family in Black Society* (The Hague: Mouton, 1978), pp. 25–147.

30. U.S., Manuscript Federal Census, Maryland, 1850.

31. Ibid.

32. Indentures, lists, summons and 16 June 1848 permit of Hazard are in Free Negroes, Ms. 1281, MLMH.

33. W. Emerson Wilson, ed., *Mount Harmon Diaries of Sidney George Fisher, 1837–1850* (Wilmington, Delaware: Historical Society of Delaware, 1976), p. 253.

34. Wilson, *Mount Harmon*, 1 April 1850, p. 285; 8 May 1850, p. 295; and 28 May 1850, p. 306.

35. U.S., Manuscript Federal Census, Maryland, 1850.

36. Wilson, *Mount Harmon*, 5 May 1841, p. 103.

37. Wilson, *Mount Harmon*, 13 December 1845, p. 166; 15 December 1845, p. 167.

38. Reconstituted Family History from Forman Diaries and Plantation Lists, Ms. 403, MLMH.
39. Wilson, *Mount Harmon*, 13 May 1846, pp. 172–73.
40. Wilson, *Mount Harmon*, 20 May 1846, p. 177.
41. Wilson, *Mount Harmon*, 25 May 1846, p. 187.
42. Forman Diaries, 27 March 1847, Ms. 403, MLMH.
43. U.S., Manuscript Federal Census, Maryland, 1850.
44. U.S., Manuscript Federal Census, Georgia, 1860, shows Forman living in Savannah. I am indebted to Eileen Lelmini of the Georgia Historical Society for helping me locate information on Thomas Marsh Forman Bryan.

10 Butter Making and Economic Development in Mid-Atlantic America, 1750–1850

Originally published as "Butter-Making in Mid-Atlantic America from 1750–1850," *Signs* 13, no. 4 (Summer 1988):813–29 and reprinted by permission. © 1988 by the University of Chicago. All rights reserved.

Research for this chapter was made possible in part by a Senior Fellowship from the Regional Economic History Research Center, Eleutherian Mills-Hagley Foundation. It was delivered in slightly different form at the Women and Industrialization Conference in Bellagio, Italy, August 1983.

1. Sachs, *The Invisible Farmers* and Jensen, *With These Hands* are the best overviews of farm women.
2. The longer study of this region is Jensen, *Loosening the Bonds*. Cheese making, a woman's task, in many ways similar to that of butter making and also important in parts of the Philadelphia hinterland, is not discussed here.
3. U.S., Manuscript Agricultural Census, Pennsylvania, 1850.
4. Billy G. Smith, "The Material Lives of Laboring Philadelphians, 1750 to 1800," *WMQ* 33, no. 2 (April 1981):163–202. For an example of the wealthy, see Frederick B. Tolles, "Town House and Country House: Inventories from the Estate of William Logan, 1776," *PMHB* 82 (1958): 397–410. For the Revolution, see Nicholas Wainwright, ed., "A Diary of Trifling Occurrences: Philadelphia, 1776–1778," *PMHB* 82 (1958):411–65; Henry Drinker Biddle, *Extracts from the Journal of Elizabeth Drinker from 1759 and 1807 A.D.* (Philadelphia: Lippincott, 1889), pp. 62–64, 106; Gary B. Nash and Billy Smith, "The Population of Eighteenth-Century Philadelphia," *PMHB* 99 (July 1975):362–68.
5. Samuel Taylor, Journal, 1798–99, Chester County Historical Society, West Chester, Pennsylvania.
6. Elinor F. Oakes, "A Ticklish Business: Dairying in New England and Pennsylvania, 1750–1812," *Pennsylvania History* 47, no. 3 (July 1980): 195–212; Annie Bezanson, Robert D. Gray, and Miriam Hussey, *Wholesale*

Prices in Philadelphia, 1784–1861 (Philadelphia: University of Pennsylvania Press, 1937), pp. 25, 62, 99, 405. Retail prices are in the Taylor diary; Benjamin Hawley, diary, Chester County Historical Society, West Chester, Pennsylvania; Rev. Patrick Kenney Papers, microfilm, and Special Accounts, 1803–22, series C, box 14, group 3, Eleuthère Irénée du Pont, Longwood Manuscripts, Hagley Museum and Library, Greenville, Delaware; and Eli W. Strawn Collection, Butter and Egg Book, Fonthill Library, Mercer Museum, Doylestown, Pennsylvania.

7. See "Cloth, Butter, and Boarders" in this volume.

8. David M. Gordon, Richard Edwards, and Michael Reich, *Segmented Work, Divided Workers: The Historical Transformation of Labor in the United States* (Cambridge: Cambridge University Press, 1982), pp. 54–77; Diane Lindstrom, "American Economic Growth before 1840: New Evidence and New Directions," *Journal of Economic History* 39, no. 1 (March 1979):289–301; and *Idem.*, "The Industrialization of the East, 1810–1860," *Working Papers from the Regional Economic History Research Center* 2, no. 3, Hagley Museum and Library (Greenville, Del.: Hagley Museum and Library, 1979):19–37; Edward Pessen, "How Different from Each Other Were the Antebellum North and South?" *American Historical Review* 85, no. 5 (1980):1119–49; Julia A. Matthaei, *Economic History of Women in America: Women's Work, the Sexual Division of Labor and the Development of Capitalism* (New York: Schocken, 1982), pp. 143–46; Barbara Epstein, "Industrialization and Femininity: A Case Study of Nineteenth-Century New England," in *Women and Work: Problems and Perspectives,* ed. Rachel Kahn-Hut, Arlene Kaplan Daniels, and Richard Colvard (New York: Oxford University Press, 1982), p. 93; and Tom Dublin, *Women at Work: The Transformation of Work and Community in Lowell, Massachusetts, 1826–1860* (New York: Columbia University Press, 1979). For black farm women, Jacqueline Jones, *Labor of Love, Labor of Sorrow,* pp. 44–78; White, *Ar'n't I a Woman?* and Shammas, "Black Women's Work," 5–28.

9. Earl W. Hayter, *The Troublesome Farmer, 1850–1900: Rural Adjustment to Industrialism* (DeKalb: Northern Illinois University Press, 1968).

10. Cuthbert William Johnson, *The Farmer's Encyclopedia and Dictionary of Rural Affairs* (Philadelphia: Carey & Hart, 1844), p. 394; and *American Agriculturalist* 4, no. 8 (August 1845):336.

11. Samuel Buckley Ruggles, *Tabular Statements from 1840 to 1870 of the Agricultural Products of the States and Territories of the United States of America* (New York: Chamber of Commerce, 1874), pp. 11, 38; Diane Lindstrom, *Economic Development in the Philadelphia Region, 1810–1850* (New York: Columbia University, 1978), p. 142.

12. U.S., Manuscript Agricultural Census, Pennsylvania, 1850. See also Fred Bateman, "Labor Inputs and Productivity in American Dairy Agriculture, 1850–1910," *Journal of Economic History* 29, no. 2 (June 1969):206–

29, and the "'The Marketable Surplus' in Northern Dairy Farming: New Evidence by Size of Farms in 1860," *AH* 52, no. 3 (July 1978):345–63.

13. Jensen, *Loosening the Bonds*, pp. 92–113, discusses these changes in greater detail.

14. Ibid.

15. Ibid., 100–108.

16. Ibid., 98.

17. *American Agriculturalist* 4, no. 8 (August 1845):320.

18. Jensen, *Loosening the Bonds*, pp. 97–98.

19. Ibid., pp. 104–106.

20. Ibid., pp. 87–91.

21. Tenche Cox, *A Statement of the Arts and Manufactures of the United States of America for the Year 1810* (Philadelphia: Cornman, 1814), pp. 44–45.

22. Duane E. Wall and Gary M. Walton, "Agricultural Productivity Change in Eighteenth-Century Pennsylvania," *JEH* 36, no. 1 (March 1976): 102–17, esp. 109, n.b. There are virtually no studies of the labor of children for this period. School attendance is one way to track time spent away from farm work, but only studies of skills needed in various tasks can explain the hours spent on farm work.

23. U.S., Manuscript Population Census, Kennett Township, Chester County, Pennsylvania, 1850.

24. Esther Lewis to Rebecca Fussell Trimble, April 18, 1833, and Esther Lewis to Edwin and Rebecca Fussell, April 10, 1839, RG5, series 2, Esther Lewis Papers, Friends Historical Library, Swarthmore College, Swarthmore, Pennsylvania.

25. Wilson, *Plantation Life at Rose Hill*, pp. 421–22.

26. U.S. Department of the Interior, Census Office, *Report of the Productions of Agriculture* (Washington, 1883), vol. 3, 146, 167–68, 260, 306–7. For rural labor in later periods and in other areas, see Nancy Grey Osterud, *Bonds of Community: The Lives of Farm Families in Nineteenth Century New York* (Ithaca: Cornell University Press, 1991) and John Mack Faragher, *Sugar Creek: Life on the Illinois Prairie* (New Haven: Yale University Press, 1987). Rural women also performed new manufacturing tasks at home and sold their labor outside the farm. For proto-industrialization, see Tom Dublin, "Women and Outwork in a Nineteenth-Century New England Town: Fitzwilliam, New Hampshire, 1830–1850," in *The Countryside in the Age of Capitalist Transformation*, ed., Steven Hahn and Jonathan Prude (Chapel Hill: University of North Carolina Press, 1984), pp. 51–70; and Jaclyn Greenberg, "Industry in the Garden: A Social History of the Canning Industry and Cannery Workers in the Santa Clara Valley, California, 1870–1920" (Ph.D. diss., University of California, Los Angeles, 1986). For rural

harvest work, see Joan Jensen and Susan Armitage, "Women in the Hop Harvest" in this volume.

27. "Philadelphia Butter," U.S. Commissioner of Agriculture, *Report, 1867* (Washington, 1867), p. 294, mentioned one West Chester farmer as being his own "dairymaid." See also "Butter and Cheese," *Harper's Monthly Magazine* 51 (November 1875):813–27; Henry Elijah Alvord, "Dairy Development in the United States," *Yearbook of the Department of Agriculture* (Washington, 1899), pp. 382–83. Alvord was chief of the dairy division of the Federal Bureau of Animal Industry.

28. Ester Boserup, *Women's Role in Economic Development* (New York: St. Martin's Press, 1970); Preface to special issue on "Women and National Development: The Complexities of Change," *Signs: Journal of Women in Culture and Society* 3, no. 1 (Autumn 1977):xi–xiv; Wava Gillespie Haney, "Farm Family and the Role of Women," in *Technology and Social Change in Rural Areas,* ed. Gene F. Summers (Boulder, Colo.: Westview, 1983), pp. 179–93; Harriet Friedman, "Family Enterprises in Agriculture: Structural Limits and Political Possibilities," in *Agriculture: People and Policies,* ed. Graham Cox, Philip Lowe, and Michael Winter (London: Allen and Unwin, 1986), pp. 41–60; Harriet Friedman, "World Market, State and Family Farm: Social Bases of Household Production in the Era of Wage Labour," *Comparative Studies in Society and History* 20, no. 4 (1978):545–86, "Patriarchy and Property: A Reply to Goodman and Redclift," *Sociologia Ruralis* 26, no. 2 (1986):186–93, and "The Transformation of Wheat Production in the Era of the World Market, 1873–1935" (Ph.D. diss., Harvard University, 1976). For an analysis of change in one English region, see Mary Bouquet, "Production and Reproduction of Family Farms in Southwest England," *Sociologia Ruralis* 22 (1982):227–44.

29. Marylynn Salmon, "The Property Rights of Women in Early America: A Comparative Study" (Ph.D. diss., Bryn Mawr College, 1980), 184, and *Women and the Law of Property in Early America* (Chapel Hill: University of North Carolina Press, 1986). Lisa Wilson Waciega, "A 'Man of Business': The Widow of Means in Southeastern Pennsylvania, 1750–1850," *WMQ* 44, no. 1 (January 1987):40–64, argues conditions for widows became better with urbanization.

30. Charles W. Dahlinger, "The Dawn of the Woman's Movement: An Account of the Origin and History of the Pennsylvania Married Women's Property Law of 1848," *Western Pennsylvania Historical Magazine* 1 (1918): 73–78.

31. Annette Kolodny, *The Land Before Her: Fantasy and Experience of the American Frontiers, 1630–1860* (Chapel Hill: University of North Carolina Press, 1984), pp. 161–77; Jeremy Atack and Fred Bateman, *To Their Own Soil: Agriculture in the Antebellum North* (Ames: Iowa State University

Press, 1987), pp. 79–81; Donald R. Adams, Jr., "The Standard of Living during American Industrialization: Evidence from the Brandywine Region, 1800–1860," *Journal of Economic History* 42, no. 4 (December 1982):903–17, indicates that wages were not high enough in the industrializing areas to lure women away from farm work. For women's rights activity, see Jensen, *Loosening the Bonds,* pp. 184–204; and Nancy A. Hewitt, "Feminist Friends: Agrarian Quakers and the Emergence of Women's Rights in America," *Feminist Studies* 12, no. 1 (Spring 1986):27–50.

    32. Atack and Bateman, *To Their Own Soil,* pp. 151–52, 161.

    33. "Butter and Cheese"; and Alvord, "Dairy Development."

11   Cloth, Butter and Boarders: Women's Household Production for the Market

    Originally published as "Cloth, Butter and Boarders: Women's Household Production for the Market," *The Review of Radical Political Economics* 12 (Summer 1980):14–24 and reprinted by permission.

    1. Renate Bridenthal, "The Dialectics of Production and Reproduction in History," *Radical America* 10 (March-April 1976):3–14 and "Loom, Broom and Womb: Producers, Maintainers and Reproducers," *Frontiers* 1 (Fall 1975):1–41 both use the dual model. Patricia Branca, "A New Perspective on Women's Work: A Comparative Typology," *Journal of Social History* 9 (Winter 1975):129–53, makes the point that in some countries domestic manufacturing remained important into the late nineteenth century and constructs models that emphasize nonfactory wage work and what I have here defined as household production for the market. Michael Merrill, "Cash Is Good to Eat: Self-Sufficiency and Exchange in the Rural Economy of the United States," *Radical History Review* 4 (Winter 1977): 42–71, has three main divisions of production: household, simple commodity production, and capitalist. He includes barter and some cash income in household production. No attempt is made here to review the extensive literature on the political economy of women's work. Some of the most important works are: Mary Inman, *In Woman's Defense* (Los Angeles: Mercury, 1940), *The Two Forms of Production Under Capitalism* (Los Angeles: Mary Inman, 1964), and Robert Shaffer, "Women and the Communist Party, USA, 1930–1940," *Socialist Review* 9 (May–June 1979):83–87, who reviews her early argument that women participated in two modes of production under capitalism—wage labor and production of labor-power—and should form separate labor organizations; Al Szymanski, "The Socialization of Women's Oppression: A Marxist Theory of the Changing Position of Women in Advanced Capitalist Society," *The Insurgent Sociologist* 6 (Winter 1976):31–60; Margaret Benston, "The Political Economy of Women's Liberation," *Monthly Review* (1970), all assume a single mode of production

as essential for political activity. Wally Seccome, "The Housewife and Her Labour Under Capitalism," *New Left Review* 83 (Jan–Feb 1973):3–24; Jean Gardiner, "The Role of Domestic Labour"; and Margaret Coulson, Branka Magas, and Hilary Wainwright, "Women and the Class Struggle," *New Left Review* 89 (Jan–Feb 1975):47–58, 59–71; Ann R. Markusen, "The Economics of the Women's Movement," *Frontiers* 1 (Fall 1975):42–52; Margaret H. Simeral, "Women and the Reserve Army of Labor," *Insurgent Sociologist* 8 (Fall 1978), 164–79; and the past special RRPE issues on women all discuss various aspects of women's work.

2. The work by women under slavery and share cropping may have to be considered as part of a separate plantation mode of production. See Jay R. Mandle, *The Roots of Black Poverty: The Southern Plantation Economy After the Civil War* (Durham, North Carolina: Duke University Press, 1978). For farm women's work for male farm laborers see D. Schob, *Hired Hands and Plowboys: Farm Labor in the Midwest, 1815–60* (Urbana: University of Illinois Press, 1975), p. 228.

3. Hazel Kyrk, *Economic Problems of the Family* (New York: Harper, 1933), p. 132.

4. Schob, *Hired Hands and Plowboys,* pp. 145, 196. U.S. Bureau of the Census, *Thirteenth Census, 1910* (Washington, 1914) 4:27, explained an increase in women farm laborers when women's non-wage outdoor farm work was included.

5. Instructions to Enumerators, January 1920, quoted in Bertha M. Nienburg, *The Woman Home-Maker in the City: A Study of Statistics Relating to Married Women in the City of Rochester, N.Y. at the Census of 1920* (Washington, 1923), pp. 23–24, and A. J. Jaffe, "Trends in the Participation of Women in the Working Force," *Monthly Labor Review* 79 (May 1956):559–65.

6. Stevenson Whitcomb Fletcher, *Pennsylvania Agriculture and Country Life, 1640–1840* (Harrisburg, Pennsylvania Historical and Museum Commission, 1950), pp. 324–25, 389, 399, 413–14. Through a study of 159 wills from the most affluent agricultural areas in southeastern Pennsylvania during the period 1740 to 1790, James T. Lemon concluded that an average of 40 percent of produce was sold and that perhaps 80 percent of the farmers had some surplus to sell. See Lemon, "Household Consumption in Eighteenth-Century America and Its Relationship to Production and Trade: The Situation Among Farmers in Southeastern Pennsylvania," *AH* 41 (1967): 59–70.

7. For Native American women selling hand ground flour, see Benjamin Hayes, *Pioneer Notes From the Diaries of Judge Benjamin Hayes, 1849–1875* (Los Angeles, P.P., 1929), p. 122.

8. Lois Green Carr, "The Planter's Wife: The Experience of White Women in Seventeenth-Century Maryland," *WMQ* 34 (1977):542–71 and

"Changing Life Styles in Colonial St. Mary's County," *Working Papers from the Regional Economic History Research Center* 1 (1978):73–118. See Nancy Folbre, "Patriarchy in Colonial New England," *The Review of Radical Political Economics* 12 (Summer 1980), for an argument that surplus was not sold in eighteenth-century New England.

9. Mary Alice Feldblum, "The Formation of the First Factory Labor Force in the New England Cotton Textile Industry, 1800–1848" (Ph.D. diss., New School for Social Research, 1977). Dublin, in *Women at Work,* argues that in some farm communities young women did not go to the mills to pay off mortgages but to earn money for themselves. D'Ann Campbell, "Women's Life in Utopia: The Shaker Experiment in Sexual Equality Reappraised—1810 to 1860," *The New England Quarterly* 51 (March 1978): 36, gives one example of Massachusetts women weavers who were thrown out of work in 1811 by factory textiles and then joined the Shakers.

10. Rolla M. Tyron, *Household Manufactures in the United States, 1640–1860* (New York, 1966 reprint of 1917 edition). Calico sold for fifteen to twenty-five cents a yard in Nebraska in the late 1860s. By 1885 cloth sold for as little as ten cents a yard in parts of Nebraska. A few Nebraska women still wove in the 1880s, however. See Nellie T. Mages Papers, Mary Margaret Harpster Papers, and Autobiography of Ella Newell Likes, all at the Nebraska Historical Society, Lincoln, Nebraska.

11. For Mormon women, see Kate B. Carter, *Our Pioneer Heritage,* 17 vols. (Salt Lake City: Daughters of Utah Pioneers, 1963), 15:476, 480. They also wove sheets, ticking, material for men's suits, and some dress material. For Navajo weaving, see U.S. Department of Interior, *Report of the Governor of New Mexico* (Washington, 1904), p. 173.

12. Richard Easterlin, "Farm Production and Income in Old and New Areas at Mid-Century," in David C. Klingaman and Richard K. Vedder, eds., *Essays in Nineteenth Century Economic History: The Old Northwest* (Athens: Ohio University Press, 1975), p. 106; Rita Moore Krouse, "The Germantown Store," *North Louisiana Historical Association Journal* 8 (1977): 53–64; and Fred Bateman, "The 'Marketable Surplus' in Northern Dairy Farming: New Evidence by Size of Farm in 1860," *AH* 52 (1978):345–63. Material on Delaware is from the agricultural census of 1850 and 1860 for the Brandywine Hundred in New Castle County.

13. Theodore C. Blegen, "Immigrant Women and the American Frontier," Norwegian-American Historical Association," *Norwegian American Studies and Records* 5 (1930):26–29; U.S. Department of the Interior, Census Office, *Report on Indians Taxed and Indians Not Taxed* (Washington, 1894), pp. 120, 126; Elinore Pruitt Stewart, *Letters of a Woman Homesteader* (Lincoln: University of Nebraska Press, 1961), pp. 279–82.

14. Dennis Sven Nordin, *Rich Harvest: A History of the Grange, 1867–1900* (Jackson: University Press of Mississippi, 1974), and Earl W. Hayter,

The Troubled Farmer 1850–1900: Rural Adjustment to Industrialism (De-Kalb: Northern Illinois University Press, 1968), pp. 60–84.

15. Allen Walder Read, "The Comment of British Travelers on Early American Terms Relating to Agriculture," *AH* 7 (1933):99–109.

16. Minnie Miller Brown, "Black Women in American Agriculture," *AH* 50 (1976):202–12.

17. Almost any account of Native American women includes references to these sales. See Conservation Society of York County, *Seneca Home Life and Culture* (York, Pa.: Conservation Society of York County, 1944), pp. 41–43, and U.S. Department of the Interior, Census Office, *Report on Indians Taxed and Not Taxed,* pp. 132, 158, 114. Accounts of the large amounts of handcrafts sold in the late nineteenth and early twentieth centuries are in various reports of the governor of New Mexico.

18. Leonard J. Arrington, "Latter-Day Saint Women on the Arizona Frontier," (Address for the Eyring Lectures, LDS Institute of Religion, Tucson, Arizona, 1973); Hilda Faunce, *Desert Wife* (Boston: Little, Brown, 1934), p. 36; Mary Margaret Harpster Papers, *Pioneer Stories of Furness County, Nebraska* (Beaver-City *Times-Tribune,* 1914), p. 90; and "Auto-biography of Ella Newell Likes," Nebraska Historical Society.

19. Ruth Alice Allen, *The Labor of Women in the Production of Cotton* (New York: Arno, 1975 reprint of 1931 edition), pp. 86–94, 150.

20. Ellen M. Troop Papers, Family Account Book, and Julia Baptist Letters, Nebraska Historical Society. In Nebraska in 1885 a windmill cost $150 and a well $76. Viola I. Paradise, *Maternity Care and Welfare of Young Children in a Homesteading County in Montana,* Children's Bureau Bulletin no. 32 (Washington, D.C., 1919); and Mary Meek Atkeson, "Women in Farm Life and Rural Economy," American Academy of Political and Social Science, *Annals* 143 (May 1929):188–94.

21. William L. Bowers, *The Country Life Movement in America, 1900–1920* (Port Washington, N.Y.: Kennikat, 1974).

22. John L. Shrover, *First Majority—Last Minority: The Transforming of Rural Life in America* (DeKalb: Northern Illinois University Press, 1976), gives the best overview of the demographic transition. For women see Ruth Crawford Freeman and Lita Bane, "Savings and Spending Patterns of the Same Rural Families Over a 10 Year Period, 1933–1943," *American Economic Review* 34 (June 1944):344–50, who show that the value of noncash items and services produced by a group of Illinois farms dropped from 42 percent in 1933 to 28 percent in 1942 of total farm output; Wallace E. Huffman, "The Value of Productive Time of Farm Wives: Iowa, North Carolina, and Oklahoma," *American Journal of Agricultural Economics* 28 (1976):836–41; and Cornelia Butler Flora, "Rural Women," *Associates NAL Today* 2 (Sept 1977), 16–21.

23. The history of home sewing has not yet been systematically studied

but farm women sewed at home for factories throughout the nineteenth century, and as late as the 1920s Maine women knitted baby clothes for New York shops. During much of the nineteenth century, women also produced extra items of clothing, like shirts and overalls, for sale to neighbors and to barter at stores. Lucy Johnson, "An Investigation of the Methods by Which Farm Women in Maine are Adding or May Add to the Cash Income of the Family" (MA thesis, University of Maine, 1927), 31. Women made from $.50 for a dozen pair of socks to $1.50 for a baby jacket and cap. Working constantly they could make $5 a week. "Pioneer Days," Ellen M. Troop Papers, 4, Nebraska Historical Society, mentions making shirts and overalls for her brother's store. Many Nebraska accounts talk of selling shirts to neighbors. For the elimination of home sewing in one city see Joan M. Jensen, "The Great Uprising in Rochester," in Joan M. Jensen and Sue Davidson, eds., *A Needle, A Bobbin, A Strike: Women Needleworkers in America* (Philadelphia: Temple University Press, 1984), pp. 94–113. Miriam Cohen, "Changing Educational Strategies Among Immigrant Generations: New York Italians in Comparative Perspective," *Journal of Social History* 15 (Spring 1982):443–46, argued that home sewing among New York Italian women did not die out until the 1930s.

24. John Modell and Tamara K. Haraven, "Urbanization and the Malleable Family: An Examination of Boarding and Lodging in American Families," *Journal of Marriage and Family* 35 (1973):470–71, note that in Boston's South End in 1880, 30 percent of all families took in boarders. See also Nienburg, *The Woman Home-Maker*, p. 23, and Kyrk, *Economic Problems of the Family*, p. 15.

25. U.S. Bureau of Labor, *Seventh Annual Report of the Commissioner of Labor*, 2 vols. (Washington, 1892), 2, Pt. 3; U.S. Bureau of Labor, *Eighteenth Annual Report of the Commissioner of Labor* (Washington, 1904), pp. 50, 260.

26. Ibid., 46–50, 236–60.

27. Ibid., 100–101. Modell and Haraven, "Urbanization and the Malleable Family," 471, found that in 1880 Boston more native born than Irish took in boarders. Their study linked age with taking in boarders.

28. Margaret Byington, *Homestead: Households of a Mill Town* (Pittsburgh: University of Pittsburgh Press, 1974 reprint of 1910 edition), pp. 42, 142, 144.

29. Ibid.; Kyrk, *Economic Problems of the Family*, p. 136.

30. Modell and Haraven, "Urbanization and the Malleable Family," 468; Ray Lubove, *The Progressives and the Slums: Tenement House Reform in New York City, 1890–1917* (Pittsburgh: University of Pittsburgh Press, 1962), p. 98; and Edith Abbott, *The Tenements of Chicago, 1908–1935* (Chicago: University of Chicago Press, 1936), p. 345.

31. Herbert G. Gutman, "Work, Culture, and Society in Industrializing

America, 1815–1919," *American Historical Review* 78 (June 1973):531–88 provides a perceptive model for the way this question might be handled.

32. Some parallels are in a British study of farm women, Jennie Kitteringham, "Country Work Girls in Nineteenth-Century England," in Raphael Samuel, ed., *Village Life and Labour* (London: Routledge and K. Paul, 1975), pp. 73–138.

33. For graphic proof of the continued lack of involvement of women in privately owned businesses see U.S. Department of Commerce, Bureau of the Census, Office of Minority Business Enterprise, *Women-Owned Businesses, 1972* (Washington, D.C., 1976), p. 1. Women owned 4.6 percent of all industries and made .3 of all receipts. Not surprisingly, almost three-fourths of the businesses were in retail trade (restaurants and food stores) and services. Most were single proprietorships.

34. Ester Boserup, *Women's Role in Economic Development* (New York: St. Martin's, 1970); Robert I. Rodes, *Imperialism and Underdevelopment: A Reader* (New York: Monthly Review, 1971); Tamás Szentes, *The Political Economy of Underdevelopment* (Budapest: Akadémiai Kiadó, 1971); and Rodolfo Stavenhagen, *Social Classes in Agrarian Societies* (Garden City: Anchor, 1975); and Carmen Diana Deere, "Rural Women's Subsistence Production in the Capitalist Periphery," *The Review of Radical Political Economics* 8, no. 1 (Spring 1976):9–17 all have stimulating ideas on development but none contains any overall theory about the role of women in development. Scott Burns, *The Household Economy: Its Shape, Origins, and Future* (Boston: Beacon, 1977 reprint of 1975 edition) suggests the household economy receded from 1840 to 1960 and then advanced and attempts to relate the household to the overall economy, but his conclusions are questionable. Unfortunately, studies like Nadia Haggag Youssef, *Women and Work in Developing Societies* (Westport, Conn.: Greenwood, 1976 reprint of 1974 edition), pp. 33, 123, neglect household labor. She does note that during the early phases of industrialization local trade is an important source of women's income. Elyce J. Rotella, "Women's Labor Force Participation and the Decline of the Family Economy in the United States" (Paper presented at the Newberry Library Conference on Women's History and Quantitative Methods, July 5–7, 1979), argued that by 1930 single women in the wage labor force were no longer responsive to the household economy but married women were more responsive.

12 On Their Own: Women on the Wisconsin Frontier

1. I have borrowed this title from Arlene Scadron, ed., *On Their Own: Widows and Widowhood in the American Southwest 1849–1939* (Urbana and Chicago: University of Illinois Press, 1988), especially the Introduction.

2. There is only scattered information available on the county poorhouses. I have been unable to find any county records. Some information can be found in records such as County Clerk, Proceedings of the County Board, 1874–1887, Lincoln Series 1, vol. 1, Historical Society of Wisconsin, Madison. Hereafter cited as HSW.

3. U.S. Department of Labor, Census Bureau, Emma O. Lundberg, "Dependent Wards of the State of Wisconsin: A Study of Children Indentured into Family Homes by the State Public School" (Washington, 1924). Typescript draft is in series 1401, Box 7, HSW.

4. "Public and Private Child Welfare Agencies in 1934," Series 1401, Box 5, HSW, gives history.

5. Rebecca Edith Rabinoff, "Problems of Children Born Out of Wedlock Based on a Study of Wisconsin Board of Control," (BA thesis, University of Wisconsin, 1925). Copy in Series 1401, Box 6, State Department of Public Welfare, HSW.

6. "The Children's Code in Wisconsin, 1929–1934: Child Placement, Adoptions, and Illegitimacy in 1934," Series 1401, Box 5, HSW, discusses history.

7. Ibid.

8. Series 1401, Box 2, State Department of Public Welfare, Division for Children and Youth, Director's Subject File, 1913–, HSW.

9. This information is from family history and from various census and death records.

10. Publicity committee, Newsletters and News Releases are in Box 21, Series 1649, HSW.

11. Descriptions of weighing in County Reports, Series 1649, Box 6, HSW.

12. See various reports, such as "Report from Nellie Evjue on Child Welfare Work in Lincoln County," in Series 1649, Box 9, HSW.

13. Minutes of Meeting, Woman's Advisory Committee of the State Council of Defense, Madison, December 13, 1918, and Minutes of the State-Wide Conference of the Woman's Committee, State Council of Defense, February 4–5, 1919, Box 3, Series 1649, HSW.

14. Child Welfare Report, Final Report of Department Chairmen, Woman's Committee, State Council of Defense, Series 1649, Box 3, HSW.

15. Questionnaire on Demobilization, Box 2, Series 1649, HSW.

16. See "Crossing Ethnic Barriers" in this volume.

13 Crossing Ethnic Barriers in the Southwest: Women's Agricultural Extension Education, 1914–1940

Originally published in *Agricultural History* 60 (Spring 1986):168–80 and reprinted by permission.

Notes

1. For a more detailed study of the demographic changes between 1900 and 1940 see "New Mexico Farm Women, 1900–1940," in this volume.

2. Ibid.

3. These generalizations are drawn specifically from the annual reports of Fabiola Cabeza De Baca for 1930 to 1940 for Rio Arriba and Santa Fe counties, New Mexico College of Agriculture and Mechanical Arts, State College, Agricultural Extension Service, Annual Reports, New Mexico, National Archives, Microcopy, Reels 12–18, 20–22, 25 (NMCAAES, Annual Reports). Hispanic families in southern New Mexico probably differed in some respects but there are no similarly detailed reports for them.

4. For the early period see Joan M. Jensen, "Canning Comes to New Mexico: Women and Agricultural Extension, 1914–1919," *NMHR* 57 (October 1982):351–86.

5. Ibid.

6. Information from NMCAAES, Annual Reports, NA T876, Reels 4–19, 21–22, 24.

7. Annual Report for 1924, NMCAAES, Annual Reports, NA T876, Reel 6.

8. U.S. Manuscript Census for 1910. Based on a systematic random sample of the farms in the country. For a more detailed account of the effect of the Elephant Butte Dam project on loss of land by Hispanics see Joan M. Jensen, "Farm Families Organize Their Work: New Mexico: 1900–1940" (Paper presented at the New Mexico Family and Community History Conference, Albuquerque, New Mexico, July 14–16, 1983).

9. Meeting with a "Mexican who could not even speak English," and with blacks at Vado noted in Annual Report for 1927 and "Colored girls" mentioned in Annual Report for 1937, NMCAAES, Annual Reports NA T876, Reels 9 and 19. The only known Farm Bureau records are in the Freudenthal Family Papers, Box 10, Folders 2, 3, Rio Grande Historical Collections, New Mexico State University Library.

10. Annual report for 1922 and 1923, NMCAAES, Annual Reports, NA Y876, Reels 5 and 6.

11. Annual report for 1940, NMCAAES, Annual Reports, NA Y876, Reel 24.

12. Annual report for 1922, NMCAAES, Annual Reports, NA T876, Reel 5.

13. Agricultural Agent's Annual Report for Doña Ana for 1935, NMCAAES, Annual Reports, NA T876, Reel 17. See also Jensen, "New Mexico Farm Women, 1900–1940," this volume.

14. Agricultural Agent's Annual Report for Rio Arriba for 1931, NMCAAES, Annual Reports, NA T876, Reel 13.

15. For more details on De Baca see Joan M. Jensen, "I've Worked, I'm Not Afraid of Work: Farm Women in New Mexico, 1920–1940," in Jensen and Miller, *New Mexico Women*, pp. 227–55.

16. Ibid., and Annual Reports for Santa Fe for 1930–1940 in NMCAAES, Annual Reports, NA T876, Reels 12–18, 20–22, 25.

17. Percentages given in Annual Reports for Santa Fe for 1936 and 1938, NMCAAES, Annual Reports, NA T876, Reels 18–21.

18. Annual Report for Santa Fe for 1983, NMCAAES, Annual Reports, NA T876, Reel 21.

19. Annual Report for Rio Arriba and Santa Fe for 1932, NMCAAES, Annual Reports, NA T876, Reel 14.

14 Keeping Down on the Farm: Farm Women in Farm Crisis

1. Talk presented at University of Illinois, Champaign-Urbana and Eastern Illinois University, March 5, 1987. A selection of papers from that conference are in Wava G. Haney and Jane B. Knowles, eds., *Women and Farming: Changing Roles, Changing Structures* (Boulder & London: Westview Press, 1988).

2. Unfortunately, none of the comments of women farmers were included in the Haney and Knowles collection cited above.

3. By 1989 the protests had spread to the public when officials announced that BGH was being tested in milk being sold to the public but not identified as such. W. P. Norton and Kevin J. Kelley, "Just Say Moo: Now They Want to Drug the Cow," *Progressive* 53 (Nov. 1989):26.

4. Deborah MacKenzie, "Science Milked for All Its Worth," *New Scientist* 117 (March 24, 1988):28.

5. This has been confirmed by numerous people working in rural welfare agencies.

6. Jensen, *Loosening the Bonds*. The crises are well documented; their effect on women are not.

7. See "American Indian Population Recovery: 1900 to Today," in Thornton, *American Indian Holocaust and Survival*, pp. 159–85. Between 1900 and 1980 the Indian population increased from 250,000 to almost one and one-half million.

8. Alice Walker, *In Search of Our Mothers' Gardens* (New York: Harcourt Brace Jovanovich, 1983).

9. Paula Gunn Allen, *Shadow Country* (Los Angeles: University of California Native American Center, 1982) and *The Sacred Hoop: Recovering the Feminine in American Indian Traditions* (Boston: Beacon Press, 1986).

10. See Joan M. Jensen, "Pioneers in Politics," *El Palacio* 92, no. 1 (Summer/Fall 1986):12–19.

11. Jensen, *Loosening the Bonds*, pp. 18–35.

12. Sonya Salamon and Karen Davis-Brown, "Farm Continuity and Female Land Inheritance: A Family Dilemma," in Haney and Knowles, *Women and Farming,* pp. 171–94.

13. See "Tillie" and "On Their Own" in this volume.

14. Lorna Clancy Miller and Mary Neth, "Farm Women in the Political Arena," in Haney and Knowles, *Women and Farming,* pp. 357–80.

15. Sarah Elbert, "Women and Farming: Changing Structures, Changing Roles," in Haney and Knowles, *Women and Farming,* pp. 245–64. This is not to say women did not often resent their sacrifices, but they were expected by family and community to hide that resentment. See, for example, Ann Marie Low, *Dust Bowl Diary* (Lincoln and London: University of Nebraska Press, 1984), p. 68.

16. See Alison Macewen Scott, ed., "Rethinking Petty Commodity Production," *Social Analysis* (Special Issue Series no. 20, December 1986).

17. For the end of this type of crop in one state see Fink, "Sidelines and Moral Capital," 55–69.

18. The area of High Rolls near Cloudcroft in Southern New Mexico.

19. See Haney and Knowles, *Women and Farming.*

15 "*You May Depend She Does Not Eat Much Idle Bread*": Mid-Atlantic Farm Women and Their Historians

Originally published as "'You May Depend She Does Not Each Much Idle Bread': Mid-Atlantic Farm Women and Their Historians," *Agricultural History* 61 (Winter 1987):29–46 and reprinted by permission.

1. Robert Gough, "The Myth of the Middle Colonies," *PMHB* 107 (1983):393–419.

2. Douglas Greenberg, "The Middle Colonies in Recent American Historiography," *WMQ* 36 (1979):396–427. Trina Vaux, *Guide to Women's Resources in the Delaware Valley Area* (Philadelphia: University of Pennsylvania Press, 1983); and Elizabeth Steiner-Scott and Elizabeth Pearce Wagle, *New Jersey Women, 1770–1970: A Bibliography* (Rutherford: Fairleigh Dickinson University Press, 1978). Older guides like Robert V. Remini and Edwin A. Miles, *The Era of Goodfeelings and the Age of Jackson, 1916–1841* (Arlington Heights, IL: AHM Publishing, 1979) provide some references to useful published sources. Cynthia Horsburgh Requardt, "Women's Deeds in Women's Words: Manuscripts in the Maryland Historical Society," *MHM* 73 (1978):196–204 has a listing of one collection. The best general bibliography is Susan Bentley and Carolyn Sachs, *Farm Women in the United States: An Updated Literature Review and Annotated Bibliography* (A.E. &

R.S.I., Department of Agricultural Economics and Rural Sociology, Pennsylvania State University, College Park, PA., May 1984).

3. Kathleen Neils Conzen, "Historical Approaches to the Study of Rural Ethnic Communities," in Frederick Luebke, ed., *Ethnicity on the Great Plains* (Lincoln: University of Nebraska Press, 1981), pp. 1–18.

4. Bruce C. Trigger, "American Archaeology as Native History: A Review Essay," *WMQ* 40 (1983):413–52 is an excellent model. See also Anthony F. C. Wallace, "Women, Land, and Society: Three Aspects of Aboriginal Delaware Life," *Pennsylvania Archaeologist* 17 (Spring 1947):1–35 and *The Death and Rebirth of the Seneca* (New York: Knopf, 1969); Jensen, "Native American Women and Agriculture: A Seneca Case Study" in this volume.

5. Susan Klepp, "Five Early Pennsylvania Censuses," *PMHB* 106 (1982):483–514.

6. Berry Levy, "The Light in the Valley: the Chester and Welsh Tract of Quaker Communities and the Delaware Valley, 1681–1750," (Ph.D. diss., University of Pennsylvania, 1976) contains some important material on the disappearing Welsh. Older studies of the Welsh, such as Charles H. Browning, *Welsh Settlement of Pennsylvania* (Philadelphia: Campbell, 1912), and Alan Conway, *Welsh in America: Letters from Immigrants* (Minneapolis: University of Minnesota Press, 1961), contain almost nothing on women. Anne Catherine Bieri Herbert, "The Pennsylvania French in the 1790s: The Story of Their Survival," (Ph.D. diss., University of Texas, Austin, 1981), documents the French presence though it says little about French women.

7. Jean R. Soderlund, "Black Women in Colonial Pennsylvania," *PMHB* 107 (1983):5; Carl D. Oblinger, "Alms for Oblivion: the Making of a Black Underclass in Southeastern Pennsylvania, 1780–1860," in John E. Bodnar, ed., *The Ethnic Experience in Pennsylvania* (Lewisburg: Bucknell University Press, 1973), 94–119 and "Freedom Foundations: Black Communities in Southeastern Pennsylvania Towns: 1780–1860," *Northwestern Missouri State University Studies* 33 (November 1972): 3–23; Lewis V. Baldwin, "'Invisible' Strands in African Methodism: A History of African Union Methodist Protestant and Union American Methodist Episcopal Churches, 1805–1980," (Ph.D. diss., Northwestern University, 1980); Charles L. Coleman, "The Emergence of Black Religion in Pennsylvania, 1776–1850," *Pennsylvania Heritage* 4 (1977):24–28; Merle Gerald Brouwer, "The Negro as Slave and as a Free Black in Colonial Pennsylvania," (Ph.D. diss., Wayne State University, 1973) and "Marriage and Family Life Among Blacks in Colonial Pennsylvania," *PMBH* 99 (1975):368–72. For Maryland see Russell R. Menard, "The Maryland Slave Population, 1658 to 1730: A Demographic Profile of Blacks in Four Counties," *WMQ* 32 (1975):29–54; Allan Kulikoff, "The Beginnings of the Afro-American Family in Maryland," in

Michael Gordon, ed., *The American Family in Social-Historical Perspective* (New York: St. Martin's Press, 1978); and Jean Butenhoff Lee, "The Problem of Slave Community in the Eighteenth Century Chesapeake," *WMQ* 43 (1986):333–61.

8. Susan M. Forbes, "'As Many Candles Lighted': The New Garden Monthly Meeting, 1718–1774," (Ph.D. diss., University of Pennsylvania, 1972); Jean R. Soderlund, "Conscience, Interest and Power: the Development of Quaker Opposition to Slavery in the Delaware Valley, 1688–1780," (Ph.D. diss., Temple University, 1981) and *Quakers and Slavery: A Divided Spirit* (Princeton: Princeton University Press, 1985); and Jensen, *Loosening the Bonds*. See also Levy, "The Light in the Valley."

9. Forrest McDonald and Ellen Shapiro McDonald, "The Ethnic Origins of the American People, 1790," *WMQ* 37 (1980):180, document the numbers of Germans but not by gender. Among older studies, F. J. F. Schantz, *The Domestic Life and Character of the Pennsylvania German Frontier* (Lancaster: Pennsylvania German Society, 1900) and Amos Long, Jr., *The Pennsylvania German Farm Family: A Regional Architectural and Folk Cultural Study of an American Agricultural Community* (Breinigsville, Pa: Pennsylvania German Society, 1972) are examples of works on the household that say almost nothing about women. For newer, more carefully documented studies that, unfortunately, add nothing about German, Elizabeth Augusta Kessel, "Germans on the Maryland Frontier: A Social History of Frederick County, Maryland, 1730–1800," (Ph.D. diss., Rice University, 1981) and "'A Mighty Fortress is Our God': Germans on the Maryland Frontier, 1734–1800," *MHM* 77 (1982):370–87; and Marianne Wokeck, "A Tide of Alien Tongues: the Flow and Ebb of the German Immigration to Pennsylvania, 1683–1776 (Ph.D. diss., Temple University, 1983) and "The Flow and the Composition of German Immigration to Philadelphia, 1727–1775," *PMHB* 105 (1981):249–78.

10. Frank Trommler and Joseph McVeigh, ed., *America and the Germans: An Assessment of a Three-Hundred-Year History*, 2 vols., (Philadelphia: University of Pennsylvania Press, 1985), 1:41–130. Milton Drake, *Almanacs of the United States* (New York: Scarecrow, 1962), lists each of the German almanacs by title and date. The number is just about one-fourth of the English almanacs. Less than a dozen were in French. For "Mountain Mary," see Frank Brown, "New Light on 'Mountain Mary,'" *Pennsylvania Folk Life* 15 (Spring 1966):10–15. The *Weiber-Buchlein* (Euphrata, 1806) is in the Pennsylvania Farm Museum Library, Lancaster, Pennsylvania. The Goschenhopper Museum in Green Lane, Pennsylvania, contains a wealth of German store accounts that document household purchases.

11. Charlotte Erickson, *Invisible Immigrants: The Adaptation of English and Scottish Immigrants in Nineteenth-Century America* (Coral Gables: Uni-

versity of Miami Press, 1972), on p. 160 does mention one woman taking in boarders in 1835 and contains general background on how immigrants coped with economic problems. Karie Diethorn, "Nineteenth-Century Immigration and the Family: The Irish of Christiana Hundred, Delaware," (Unpublished paper, 1983) made a preliminary study that indicated large numbers of Irish there.

12. Robert V. Wells, "Quaker Marriage Patterns in a Colonial Perspective," *WMQ* 29 (1972):415–42; and "Demographic Change and the Life Cycle of American Families," *Journal of Interdisciplinary History* 2 (1971): 272–82; Daniel Snydacker, "Kinship and Community in Rural Pennsylvania," *Journal of Interdisciplinary History* 13 (Summer 1982):41–61; and Gary L. Laidia, Wayne A. Schutijer, and C. Shannon Stokes, "Agricultural Variation and Human Fertility in Antebellum Pennsylvania," *Journal of Family History* 6 (Summer 1982):198–205.

13. Mark J. Stern, "The Demography of Capitalism: Industry, Class, and Fertility in Erie County, New York, 1855–1915," (Ph.D. diss., York University, 1979) and "Differential Fertility in Rural Erie County, New York 1855," *Journal of Social History* 16 (Summer 1983):49–61. See also Rodger Craiger Henderson, "Community Development and Revolutionary Transition in Eighteenth Century Lancaster County, Pennsylvania (Ph.D. diss., State University of New York at Binghamton, 1983).

14. Claire Elizabeth Fox, "Pregnancy, Childbirth and Early Infancy in Anglo-American Culture, 1675–1830" (Ph.D. diss., University of Pennsylvania, 1966); Janet McClintock Robinson, "Country Doctors in the Changing World of the Nineteenth Century: An Historical Ethnolography of Medical Practice in Chester County, Pennsylvania 1790–1861," (Ph.D. diss., University of Pennsylvania, 1975); Jane Bauer Donegan, "Midwifery in America, 1760–1860: A Study in Medicine and Morality," (Ph.D. diss., Syracuse University, 1972); and Catherine M. Scholten, "Changing Customs of Childbirth in America, 1760 to 1825," *WMQ* 34 (1977):426–45. For seasonality of conception in England see Ann Kussmaul, "Time and Space, Hoofs and Grain: The Seasonality of Marriage in England," *Journal of Interdisciplinary History* 15 (1985):755–99 and "Agrarian Change in Seventeenth-Century England: The Economic Historian as Paleontologist," *JEH* 45 (1985):1–31.

15. Peggy A. Rabkin, *Fathers to Daughters: the Legal Foundations of Female Emancipation* (Westport, Ct.: Greenwood, 1980); Norma Basch, *In the Eyes of the Law: Women, Marriage, and Property in Nineteenth-Century New York* (Ithaca: Cornell University Press, 1982); Marylynn Salmon, "The Property Rights of Women in Early America: A Comparative Study," (Ph.D. diss., Bryn Mawr College, 1980) and *Women and the Law of Property in Early America* (Chapel Hill: University of North Carolina Press, 1986). Suzanne

Dee Lebstock, "Women and Economics in Virginia: Petersburg, 1784–1820," (Ph.D. diss., University of Virginia, 1977) and *The Free Women of Petersburg: Status and Culture in a Southern Town, 1784–1860* (New York: Norton, 1984); Linda E. Speth, "More Than Her 'Thirds': Wives and Widows in Colonial Virginia," *Women and History* 4 (1982):5–42; Toby L. Ditz, *Property and Kinship: Inheritance in Early Connecticut, 1750–1820* (Princeton: Princeton University Press, 1986) and Susan Dwyer Amussen, "Governors and Governed: Class and Gender Relations in English Villages, 1590–1725," (Ph.D. diss., Brown University, 1982). Gail S. Terry, "Wives and Widows, Sons and Daughters: Testation Patterns in Baltimore County, Maryland, 1660–1759"; Jean B. Lee, "Land and Featherbeds: Parents Bequest Practices in Charles County, Maryland, 1733–1783," in *The Colonial Experience: The Eighteenth Century Chesapeake* (University of North Carolina, in press). Lois Carr, "Inheritance in the Colonial Chesapeake," David E. Narrett, "Patterns of Inheritance, the Status of Women, and Family Life in Colonial New York," Carole Shammas, "Early American Women and Control Over Capital," and Marylynn Salmon, "Republican Sentiment, Economic Change, and the Property Rights of Women in American Law," in Ronald Hoffman and Peter J. Albert, eds., *Women in the Age of the American Revolution* (Charlottesville: University Press of Virginia, 1989). Lisa Wilson Waciega, "A 'Man of Business': The Widow of Means in Southeastern Pennsylvania, 1750–1850," *WMQ* 44 (1987):40–64 and "Widowhood and Womanhood in Early America: The Experience of Women in Philadelphia and Chester County, 1750–1850," (Ph.D. diss., Temple University, 1986). Lois Green Carr and Lorena S. Walsh, "The Planter's Wife: The Experience of White Women in Seventeenth-Century Maryland," *WMQ* 34 (1977):542–71, raises many issues about fertility and marriage patterns in the Chesapeake.

16. Mary Ryan, *Cradle of the Middle Class: The Family in Oneida County, New York, 1790–1865* (Cambridge: Cambridge University Press, 1981).

17. For slavery see Soderlund, "Conscience, Interest, and Power" and *Quakers and Slavery*. For labor see Farley Grubb, "Immigrant Servant Labor: Their Occupational and Geographic Distribution in the Late Eighteenth-Century Mid-Atlantic Economy," *Social Science History* 9 (Summer 1985):249–75; Sharon V. Salinger, "'Send No More Women': Female Servants in Eighteenth-Century Philadelphia," *PMHB* 57 (1983):29–48, "Colonial Labor in Transition: The Decline of Indentured Servitude in Late Eighteenth-Century Philadelphia," *LH* 22 (1981):165–91 and "Labor and Indentured Servants in Colonial Pennsylvania," (Ph.D. diss., University of California, Los Angeles, 1980). On property, see Lucy Simler, "The Township: The Community of the Rural Pennsylvanian," *PMHB* 106 (1982): 41–68; and Stern, "Differential Fertility in Rural Erie County."

18. For Britain see Ann Kussmaul, *Servants in Husbandry in Early Modern England* (Cambridge: Cambridge University Press, 1982); K. D. M. Snell, "Agricultural Seasonal Unemployment, the Standard of Living, and Women's Work in the South and East, 1690–1860," *Economic History Review* 34 (August 1981):407–33; J. A. Perkins, "Harvest Technology and Labour Supply in Lincolnshire and the East Riding of Yorkshire 1750–1850," *Tools and Tillage* 3:1 (1976):47–58 and 3:2 (1977):125–35; and M. Roberts, "Sickles and Scythes: Women's Work and Men's Work at Harvest Time," *History Workshop* 7 (1979):3–28. The best description of American women's field work is Alexander Marshall, "The Days of Auld Lang Syne: Recollections of How Chester County Countians Farmed and Lived Three-Score Years Ago," Don Yoder, ed., *Pennsylvania Folklore* 13 (July 1964):13–19. For dairy tools see Joan Jensen, "Churns and Butter Making in the Mid-Atlantic Farm Economy, 1750–1850," *Working Papers from the Regional Economic History Research Center* 5, nos. 2 & 3 (1982):60–100 and *Loosening the Bonds*, 92–113. See also Lois Carr and Lorena Walsh, "The Transformation of Household Production in the Chesapeake, 1650–1850." An excellent model for the account book that focuses on late nineteenth-century New York is Nancy Grey Osterud, *Bonds of Community*.

19. Jack Michel, " 'In a Manner and Fashion Suitable to Their Degree': A Preliminary Investigation of the Material Culture of Early Rural Pennsylvania," *Working Papers from the Regional Economic History Research Center* 5, no. 1 (1981):1–83; Lorena S. Walsh, "Urban Amenities and Rural Sufficiency: Living Standards and Consumer Behavior in the Colonial Chesapeake, 1643–1777," *JEH* 43 (1983):109–17; and Jensen, *Loosening the Bonds*, 35–56. Mary Douglas and Baron Usherwood, *The World of Goods: Towards an Anthropology of Consumption* (New York: Basic Books, 1982).

20. Glenn C. Altschuler and Jan. M. Saltzgaber, "Clearinghouse for Paupers: The Poorfarm of Seneca County, New York, 1830–1860," *Journal of Social History* 17 (1984):573–600. Joan Underhill Hannon, "The Generosity of Antebellum Poor Relief," *JEH* 44 (September 1984):810–21, her "Poverty in the Antebellum Northeast: The View from New York State's Poor Relief Rolls," *JEH* 44 (1984):1014; and Jensen, *Loosening the Bonds*, 57–78.

21. Michael MacDonald, *Mystical Bedlam: Madness, Anxiety, and Healing in Seventeenth Century England* (Cambridge: Cambridge University Press, 1981) discusses England. For America see Nancy Tomes, "The Domesticated Madman: Changing Concepts of Insanity at the Pennsylvania Hospital, 1780–1830," *PMHB* 106 (1982):271–82; Ellen Dwyer, "Sex Roles and Psychopathology: A Historical Perspective," in Cathy S. Widom, ed., *Sex Roles and Psychopathology* (New York: Plenum, 1984) and "The Weaker Vessel: Legal Versus Social Reality in Mental Commitments in Nine-

teenth-Century New York," in Kelly Weisburg, ed., *Women and the Law: Social Historial Perspectives* (Cambridge, MA: Schenkman, 1983). Sharon Ann Burston, "Babies in the Well: An Underground Insight into Deviant Behavior in Eighteenth-Century Philadelphia," *PMHB* 106 (1982): 151–86, points out how anthropology might be used to trace infanticide. In Pennsylvania, women were hanged for infanticide in public executions well into the nineteenth century, before public outrage put an end to them.

22. Leonore Davidoff, "The Role of Gender in the 'First Industrial Nation': The Case of East Anglican Agriculture, 1780–1850" (Paper presented at the Women and Industrialization Conference, Bellagio, Italy, August 8–12, 1983). Donald McPherson, "The Fight Against Free Schools in Pennsylvania: Popular Opposition to the Common School System, 1834–1874," (Ph.D. diss., University of Pittsburgh, 1977).

23. Ellinor Oakes, "A Ticklish Business: Dairying in New England and Pennsylvania, 1750–1812," *Pennsylvania History* 47 (July 1980):195–211; Fred Bateman, "The 'Marketable Surplus' in Northern Dairy Farming: New Evidence by Size of Farm in 1860," *AH* 52 (July 1978):345–63; and Jensen and Armitage, "Women in the Hop Harvest" in this volume.

24. Elsie M. Lewis, "Mary Ann Shadd Cary," in Edward T. James, ed., *Notable American Women, 1607–1950: A Biographical Dictionary* (Cambridge: Harvard University Press, 1971):3, 300–301. For methodology see Burton W. Folsom II, "The Collective Biography as a Research Tool," *Mid-America: An Historical Review* 54 (April 1972):108–22; Richard Jensen, "Family, Career, and Reform: Women Leaders of the Progressive Era," in *The American Family in Social-Historical Perspective*, Michael Gordon, ed., (New York: St. Martin's Press, 1973):267–80; and Barbara Campbell, *The "Liberated" Women of 1914: Prominent Women of the Progressive Era*, Studies in American History and Culture, No. 6 (Ann Arbor: University Microfilms, 1979).

25. Mary Maples Dunn, "Saints and Sisters: Congregational and Quaker Women in the Early Colonial Period," *American Quarterly* 30 (Winter 1978):582–601 and "Women of Light," in Carol Ruth Berkin and Mary Beth Norton, eds., *Women of America: A Study* (Boston: Houghton Mifflin, 1979):114–36; Janis Calvo, "Quaker Women Ministers in Nineteenth-Century America," *Quaker History* 63 (1974):75–93, and Jensen, *Loosening the Bonds*, 146–66.

26. Richard A. Meckel, "Educating a Ministry of Mothers: Evangelical Maternal Associations, 1815–1860," *JER* 2 (Winter 1982):403–23; and Mary P. Ryan, "A Women's Awakening: Evangelical Religion and the Families of Utica, New York 1800–1840," *American Quarterly* 30 (1978):602–23.

27. Joanna Bowen Gillespie, " 'The Clear Leadings of Providence':

Pious Memoirs and the Problems of Self-Realization for Women in the Early Nineteenth Century," *JER* 5 (Summer 1985):197–221.

28. Anne M. Boylan, "The Role of Conversion in Nineteenth-Century Sunday Schools," *AS* 20 (1979):35–48; and Ruth C. Linton, "The Brandywine Manufacturers' Sunday School: An Adventure in Education in the Early Nineteenth Century," *Delaware History* 20 (1983):168–84.

29. Anne Firor Scott, "The Ever Widening Circle: the Diffusion of Feminist Values from the Troy Female Seminary, 1822–1872," *History of Education Quarterly* 19 (1979):3–23; Jensen, *Loosening the Bonds,* 167–83; Keith Melder, "Woman's High Calling: the Teaching Profession in America, 1830–1860," *AS* 13 (1972):19–32 and "Masks of Oppression: The Female Seminary Movement in the United States," *New York History* 55 (1974): 261–79. The best study of rural literacy is Alan Tully, "Literacy Levels and Educational Development in Rural Pennsylvania, 1729–1775," *Pennsylvania History* 39 (1972):301–12.

30. The role of blacks in the Mid-Atlantic early abolitionist movement remains relatively unstudied. Larry Gara, *The Liberty Line: The Legend of the Underground Railroad* (Lexington: University of Kentucky, 1961) rightly emphasizes the influence of the blacks but probably underemphasizes the role of Quaker Hicksites.

31. Gerda Lerner, *The Majority Finds Its Past: Placing Women in History* (New York: Oxford University Press, 1979), pp. 112–201; Judith Welman, "Women and Radical Reform in Antebellum Upstate New York: A Profile of Grassroots Female Abolitionists," in Mabel E. Deutrich and Virginia C. Purdy, eds., *Clio Was a Woman: Studies in the History of American Women* (Washington: Howard University Press, 1980): pp. 113–27; Nancy A. Hewitt, *Women's Activism and Social Change: Rochester, New York, 1822–1872* (Ithaca and London: Cornell University Press, 1984): pp. 97–138; Jensen, *Loosening the Bonds,* pp. 184–204; and Ellen DuBois, "Women's Rights and Abolition: the Nature of the Connection," in Lewis Perry and Michael Fellman, eds., *Anti-Slavery Reconsidered: New Perspectives on the Abolitionists* (Baton Rouge and London: Louisiana State University Press, 1979): pp. 239–51. For temperance see Jed Dannenbaum, "The Origins of Temperance Activism and Militancy Among American Women," *Journal of Social History* 15 (1981):235–52; and Ian R. Tyrrell, "Women and Temperance in Antebellum America, 1830–1860," *Civil War History* 28 (1982): 128–52.

32. Norma Basch, "Equity vs. Equality: Emerging Concepts of Women's Political Status in the Age of Jackson," *JER* 3 (Fall 1985):297–318.

33. Hewett, *Women's Activisim and Social Change,* pp. 130–132; and Jensen, *Loosening the Bonds,* pp. 199–204.

16   The Role of Farm Women in American History: Areas for Additional Research

Originally published in *Agriculture and Human Values* 2 (Winter 1985): 13–18 and reprinted by permission.

1. This paper is a revised version of the Keynote address delivered at the American Farm Women in Historical Perspective Conference, New Mexico State University, Las Cruces, New Mexico, February 3, 1984.

2. Jessie Bernard, *The Female Word* (New York: The Free Press, 1981), pp. 322–42. For fictionalized accounts of this support structure see Susan Keating Glaspell, "A Jury of Her Peers," in Lee Edwards and Arlyn Diamonds, eds., *American Voices, American Women* (New York: Avon, 1973) and Smyth, *Quilt.*

3. For Quaker women see Jensen, *Loosening the Bonds.*

4. New Mexican Fabiola Cabeza de Baca, for example, remembered being paid in eggs for her rural school teaching in New Mexico before World War I, *We Fed Them Cactus* (Albuquerque: University of New Mexico Press, 1979), while Agnes Smedley, who wrote *Daughter of the Earth* (Old Westbury: Feminist Press, 1973), remembered teaching for little more. See also Jensen, *Loosening the Bonds*; and "Women Teachers, Class, and Ethnicity: New Mexico, 1900–1950," *Southwest Economy and Society* 4 (Winter 1978/79). For one rural black school see Maya Angelou, *I Know Why the Caged Bird Sings* (New York: Bantam Books, 1971).

5. Jensen, *Loosening the Bonds*; and *With These Hands.*

6. The literature is growing steadily. The best recent guide to the literature is Bentley and Sachs, "Farm Women in the United States."

7. Sojourner Truth, "The Narrative of Sojourner Truth, 1978," in Wendy Martin, *The American Sisterhood: Writings of the Feminist Movement from Colonial Times to the Present* (New York: Harper and Row, 1972), p. 103.

8. Jensen, "Women and Industrialization: The Case of Buttermaking in Nineteenth-Century Mid-Atlantic America," in this volume; and Jensen, "'I've Worked, I'm Not Afraid of Work': Farm Women in New Mexico, 1921–1940," in Jensen and Miller, *New Mexico Women.*

9. Jensen, "Canning Comes to New Mexico"; and "Farm Women in New Mexico, 1900–1940," in this volume; "I've Worked, I'm Not Afraid of Work"; and Jensen, "Recovering Her Story: Learning the History of Farm Women," in this volume.

10. Jensen, "The Campaign for Women's Community Property Rights in New Mexico, 1940–1960," in Jensen and Miller, *New Mexico Women.*

Index

Abo Pueblo, 110, 111–12, 113, 115, 120, 123–24, 125, 128
Agrada, Maria, 117
agricultural colleges: and gender division of labor, 17–18; and gender neutrality, 36; and women as faculty and administrators, 265; and women as students, 18, 21, 26
Agricultural Extension Service, 14, 21; and bilingualism, 223–25, 231; of New Mexico, 208, 221–31
Alabama State Teachers' Association, 19
Alcott, Louisa May, 81
Allen, Paula Gunn, 236
Alvord, Henry, 185
American Farm Women in Historical Perspective conferences, 231, 232
American Revolution, 80, 138, 172, 173, 177, 179
Anthony, Susan B., 28, 81, 253
Apache Indians: and hostility to Spanish colonialism, 121, 127–28; and trade with Salinas Valley pueblos, 113
Austro-Hungarian Empire, 39, 41, 73, 211
Ayeta, Francisco de, 118

Bayard, Leonora, 167–68
Benavides, Alonso de, 111, 117

Bernal, Juan, 127
Berry, Nona, 76–77, 78
black rural women, 264; and education, 18, 19, 20, 21–22; and free white women, 81; and kinship groups, 8; and slave plantations, 7, 131, 132, 153–69, 174, 180; in New Mexico, 84; in Pennsylvania, 245–46. *See also* slavery
Blue Corn Woman, 116, 117
bridal pregnancy: as German tradition, 40; in Lithuania, 60
Bryan, Thomas, 166, 167, 168. *See* Thomas Marsh Forman
Buffalo Woman, 134
Bureau of Child Welfare: in New Mexico, 91, 93; in Wisconsin, 208, 213, 216–17
Burk, Rachel, 154–57, 161, 162, 167. *See also* Rachel Teger
Byington, Margaret, 201

Cabeza de Baca, Fabiola, 227–30, 261
Carlisle Indian School, 149
Chautauqua: and rural women's education, 208
Cherokee Indian women: and opposition to Removal, 143
Chililí Pueblo, 115, 122, 124
Civilian Conservation Corps, New Mexico, 93
Cleaveland, Agnes Morley, 87–88